GENTLEMEN ON THE PRAIRIE

OTHER BOOKS BY CURTIS HARNACK

The Work of an Ancient Hand (1960)
Love and Be Silent (1962)
Persian Lions, Persian Lambs (1965, 1981)
We Have All Gone Away (1973, 1981)
Under My Wings Everything Prospers (1977)
Limits of the Land (1979)

GENTLEMEN on the PRAIRIE

CURTIS HARNACK

The Iowa State University Press • A M E S

FOR NAONA AND BEECHER MOORE

Composed and printed by the Iowa State University Press, Ames, Iowa 50010

Library of Congress Cataloging in Publication Data

Harnack, Curtis, 1927–
    Gentlemen on the prairie.

    Bibliography: p.
    Includes index.
    1. Close Colony (Iowa)—History. 2. Cowan, Walter. 3. Cowan, James. 4. British—Big Sioux River Valley (S.D. and Iowa)—History—19th century. 5. Big Sioux River Valley (S.D. and Iowa)—History. 6. Agricultural colonies—Big Sioux River Valley (S.D. and Iowa)—History—19th century. I. Title.
F629.C65H37   1985   978.3'3   85–14212
ISBN 0–8138–0791–3

CONTENTS

PREFACE

THIS SOCIAL HISTORY makes extensive use of unpublished letters, diaries, journals, and information gathered in interviews by the author over the last thirty years. Particular biographical attention is paid to William B. Close and his brothers, since their ingenuity and enterprise created the colony of gentlemen on the prairie, and to a great extent their personal lives affected its destiny.

To portray a sense of what homesteading in Iowa was actually like for these upper-class immigrants, a substantial portion of the book also concerns the lives of Walter and James Cowan, who established a stock farm on the banks of the Big Sioux River on the border between Iowa and South Dakota. These bright, well-educated young men wrote letters home that are wonderfully witty, telling in detail, and full of the pathos of self-knowledge regarding their difficult situation.

William Van Der Zee's early account of the colony for the State Historical Society of Iowa *The British in Iowa* (1922), has been an invaluable research source because he corresponded with William B. Close just before his death and consulted other colonists still living in the area. Since the subject was recent history then, frontier newspapers with stories on colony activities were still available; many of these, unless transcribed to microfilm, have been lost. Van Der Zee viewed the British immigration in terms of its impact on Iowa, but the perspective of time and the uncovering of many new sources of information have greatly enlarged the picture. Increasing public interest in genealogy and cultural backgrounds has not only heightened curiosity about this colorful immigration venture but also resulted in new information from family sources.

My researches began in 1953 for "The Amazing English Colony of Northwest Iowa," published the following year in the *Iowan* magazine. Having been born in Le Mars and raised on a farm nearby, I had long known about the colony. My paternal grandfather (of German ancestry), a pioneer during this period, had been acquainted with some of these immigrant gentlemen in the course of his harvest work. I interviewed a few colony survivors who remembered the days of the British, including T. J. Maxwell (Frederic Close's groom) whom I found in Kingsley, just down the road from the old Close farms. I made pilgrimages to each of the colony farms I could identify from early plat records and local hearsay. Since I recorded this research, material from it comes into this account when the story of the tracking down of information seems appropriate to the narrative.

With publication of a second article, "An English Colony on the Prairie," in the London periodical, *Country Life Annual* (1957), descendants of colonists wrote me from all over the world. Some twenty years later while living in England I successfully located relatives of the Closes and learned that William B. Close had kept a journal during the early years of his American stay. "The Prairie Journal," as he entitled it, had been transcribed to typescript by his niece, Anne Eaden, although upon her death in the early 1950s the original manuscript was lost. Close's journal, dispatched in sections to friends and family, conveys a sense of what a sharp, amusing Cambridge graduate noted about Americans and their ways. With such a wealth of new information on how the colony came into being, followed by discovery of a cache of Close Brothers, Limited, business letters, I decided to write a history of the Close Colony, also referred to as the Le Mars Colony or the English Colony.

Another important research source was James P. Reed's 1974 thesis manuscript, "The Role of an English Land Company in the Settlement of Northwestern Iowa and Southwestern Minnesota," in the library of the University of Nebraska at Omaha. He had scrutinized courthouse records throughout the area, resulting in a detailed assessment of the Closes' land-buying and selling operations. I am also indebted to Professor Bernard Crick of the London School of Economics for his advice and for his compendium, *A Guide to Manuscripts Relating to Americans in Great Britain and Ireland,* which put me onto the Cowan brothers letters. And to J. O. C. Willson, my appreciation for permission to quote from these letters of his grandfather and great-uncle.

I particularly wish to thank Susanne Knowles, granddaughter of James Close, for her aid on the Close family history; Jonathan Close-Brooks, great-grandson of John Close, for his extensive help; also, James Close, grandson of the James Close in this account, for permission to use extensive portions of William B. Close's "The Prairie Journal" and Close Brothers letters.

Thanks, also, to Gordon and Malcolm Brodie for allowing me to use their grandfather's diary and to the late Roger Close-Brooks for crucial information, including the material in the Close family Bible and various letters. I am also grateful to Eleanor Jackson Piel for her legal services providing access to papers in the archives of the Superior Court of the State of New York, and to Gordon Boyd for initiating action which brought about a change in the law of New York State regarding closed files on matrimonial cases; to Carter Pitts, Glada and Dick Koerselman of the *Le Mars Sentinel* for their Plymouth County help; Robert Maxtone Graham for information regarding his ancestors; and James Paullin for genealogical aid; also, Cynthia Brants, Mrs. C. W. Sloan, Robert Van Der Zee, E. V. Heacock, Beverly Brodie, Bettie Brodie, Lois and Rex Allen, Mrs. W. H. McHenry, James McCowan of the University of Iowa library, Maureen Duffy, Professor Leland L. Sage for his editorial suggestions; and most especially, Naona and Beecher Moore, whose London home was my headquarters during the years of research.

GENTLEMEN ON THE PRAIRIE

Introduction

EUROPEANS have emigrated to the United States for a wide variety of reasons, but rarely has it been "the thing to do" to preserve social status. After all, America is supposedly without class structure or social hierarchies. All the more remarkable, then, that a sizable colony of British gentry should have flourished on the frontier in western Iowa and southeastern Minnesota in the 1880s, "a colony of 500 wealthy Englishmen, many of them of noble blood, who live like veritable lords and spend from $500 and $600 a month for their common living expenses," according to a contemporary issue of *Macmillan's* magazine.[1] For these privileged young men who sailed into New York harbor past the newly erected Statue of Liberty, Emma Lazarus's famous lines, "Give me your tired, your poor/ Your huddled masses yearning to breathe free," did not pertain. They had crossed the Atlantic in saloon or cabin class, and their conversation had been the delight of the captain's table. The American West with its cowboys and gunslingers lured them as romantically as the Hindu Kush, the Transvaal, the Sudan, or any other exotic setting where young Englishmen "of the better class" sought adventure — or were sent to be gotten rid of.[2]

They came to Iowa (many of them imagining it was part of the fabled West) from England's public schools, especially Cheltenham, Wellington, Eton, and Harrow, or had just finished studies at Oxford or Cambridge — or possibly been "sent down." They were the sort Thomas Hardy in *Tess of the D'Urbervilles* portrays in Angel Clare, a clergyman's son, who tries to learn about agriculture on an English dairy farm in preparation for his removal to "the colonies or America."[3] In Great Britain a limited choice of careers lay before them, given the strictures of the Victorian class code: a commission in the army or navy, ordination as a clergyman, government civil service — and for the eldest son, farming the ancestral lands. Beyond that, a few of the professions were socially acceptable, among them medicine and law, and even high finance in the city of London, provided a good deal of money was made. But they should have nothing to do with commerce, trade, or industry. Little wonder, then, that an attractive alternative was to go overseas with a remittance of some sort, establish a ranch or plantation or farm, and pursue the life of the landed gentleman.

For parents, this solved the problem of "What to do with our Boys?" — the second, third, or other son.[4] The margin of money left for these extra boys was sometimes fairly scant, particularly since dowries had to be provided for daughters to make them marriageable. It did not much matter where in the world the young man might be sent, but a place where other British of his kind already were was an important consideration. It could be Iowa, Tennessee, British Columbia, New Zealand, Africa, or Ceylon, and the farther away the more likely his life accomplishments might be viewed as a fulfillment of Victorian ideals of manhood, with its emphasis on practical achievements and Christian piety. Just as the playing fields of the public schools were the scene of contests of larger implications, so a boy in a far land was engaged in proving to himself and his family that he was capable of carrying on and even advancing the Empire. True, neither Iowa nor Minnesota were part of the Union Jack's territories, but questions of citizenship and loyalty could be held in abeyance because the farm might turn out to be a temporary venture, depending on how financially successful it was and if emigration "took."

But why Iowa, with its brutal extremes of climate, lack of cosmopolitan centers, and without mountains, large lakes, or other appealing topography? Romantic travel literature, such as Sir William Drummond Stewart's *Altowan* and *Edward Warren,* the Earl of Dunraven's *The Great Divide,* and Isabella Lucy Bird's *A Lady's Life in the Rocky Mountains* depicted the glories of the Far West. Getting there, the British traveler hardly noticed the dull, flat plains, except as an enormous tract to be traversed as quickly as possible. By the 1880s Colorado, with its big game hunting and splendid fishing, had lured scattered English settlers, and Colorado Springs was commonly called "Li'l London." In the Rawlins area of Wyoming a British cattle-ranching community was thriving, but it required considerable capital and ranching skill for a man to get started there.

Iowa in the late 1870s happened to be the place where fertile land was newly coming on the market, after having been held for years by the railroads, which had received land grants from the government. It took an enterprising young Cambridge graduate, William B. Close, to envision the possibilities of creating a colony of "like-minded men and women" in northwestern Iowa, a group so self-contained and resourceful, so sure of native abilities and talents, that the unpromising prairie setting would make little difference.[5] Not only would Iowa become *the* place to be, but money could also be made there, doubling the attractiveness of the venture.

Close first visited the United States as captain of the British crew participating in the international Centennial Regatta at Philadelphia in the summer of 1876. One weekend while training for the race he met a wealthy Illinois landowner who suggested that a fortune could be made buying and selling western lands. In the fall, Close toured the middle western prairies and became convinced of this vocational direction for himself. The next year he and his brother began farming in Iowa, an enterprise that yielded a 54 percent return on their investment the very first year.[6] With this testimony and facts to back it up, Close quickly caught the attention of British squires who had sons needing to be set up properly on good land somewhere. It helped that Close was a famous oarsman, the only man who ever rowed three years in the University Boat Race (Cambridge vs. Oxford) and in every respect seemed a model for any young man to pattern himself after.

Frederick Jackson Turner in his classic treatise, *The Frontier in American History,* remarked: "The wilderness masters the colonist....It takes him from the railroad car and puts him in the birch canoe. It strips off the garments of civilization...."[7] But this was exactly what those who directed the Close Colony in Iowa would not allow to happen. Instead, the young British immigrant was placed as an apprentice in an agricultural "school," the farm of a retired Royal Navy captain — the brother of the Earl of Ducie — or on some other suitable gentleman's place, where he was tutored in the rudiments of Iowa farming. Once the farm pupil, or "pup" as he was called in the ragging way of public school locution, became acquainted with the basic techniques of American agriculture, Close Brothers helped him purchase land with funds from "the Guv" back home. In this way a young man from Great Britain presumably could become a country gentleman almost instantly, in a county in Iowa instead of Wiltshire or Bucks, but a landowning farmer just the same — a sort of aristocrat.

Poultney Bigelow, the American journalist, described the Close Colony in *Harper's:* "They have the very best ground for fox hunting in the world — a rolling prairie with a creek here and there. Every colonist makes it his chief care, after buying his farm, to breed a good hunter for the steeplechase. They have regular meets for fox or 'paper' hunts, as the case may be. They last year opened a racing track, and wound up the race with a grand ball."[8] These high-living frontier British were among the earliest polo players in America, if not the first. Their Prairie Club in Le Mars, Iowa, was patterned after a London club, with English and Scottish newspapers and magazines in plentiful supply, imported wines and spirits, billiard tables, and traditional British cooking. Some of the married colonists brought over their housekeepers, butlers, nannies, overseers, and maids, as well as bathtubs, favorite horses, and hunting dogs.

A newspaper reporter in Le Mars, population 2,500 at the time, described the arrival of one batch of these well-heeled immigrants: "They descend from the recesses of the Pullman palace cars dressed in the latest London and Paris styles, with Oxford hats, bright linen shining on their bosoms, a gold repeater ticking in the depths of their fashionably cut vest pockets....We recall last summer a single family that had eighty-two pieces of luggage."[9]

During the heyday of the Close Colony, 1879–1885, many of Great Britain's socially prominent families had some son or relative there, among them: Ronald Jervis, who became Viscount St. Vincent; Eric Rollo, son of the tenth

Lord Rollo; the son of Sir John Lubbock, M.P. for the city of London; the sons of Admiral Sir Arthur Farquhar, who established "Carlogie Ranch," named after their father's home in Aberdeenshire; and the son of Lord Alfred Paget, Almeric Paget, who later married the sister of Harry Payne Whitney and eventually became Lord Queenborough. Even the Duke of Sutherland, crony of the Prince of Wales and England's largest landowner, was shown around Iowa by William B. Close, who hoped to get him to invest.

By 1884 the pound-sterling purchasing of American soil had reached such huge proportions that a bill was introduced in Congress to stop the "Leviathan squatters" from buying more of America.[10] At that time the British owned tracts equal to about one-fourth the size of the British Isles. Close Brothers controlled a firm called the Iowa Land Company, believed to be the largest foreign company doing business in the United States.[11] Close Brothers, in the course of buying and selling acres in Iowa, Minnesota, Kansas, Texas, and other states, owned at various times about 400,000 acres of some of the choicest soil in the country.[12]

What happened to this glittering enterprise, and why didn't the Close Colony play an important historic role in the cultural and economic life of the Middle West? From immigration failures one can sometimes see more clearly the qualities of those who succeeded—as well as why history took one direction instead of another. The Close Colony actually had little to bind it together aside from the social code of the English class system, which colonists attempted to import to America intact. They expected the old rules would work in the new land, anticipated loyalties and friendships would hold because of it, and were determined to live in a style decreed by birth and cultural upbringing. For the German, Dutch, and Scandinavian immigrants to this area of Iowa during the period, the old country was left behind of necessity, along with most of its associations. Many of these immigrants held onto native languages and religious convictions but became assimilated in most ways, accepting America as their new home.

Few British immigrants in the Close Colony were so sure that a home had been chosen. In most cases these settlers had the options that are available when money is at hand or easily procurable. They could try something else if homesteading on the Iowa prairie did not ultimately suit them. To the all-or-nothing immigrants who had uprooted themselves from Europe, often consuming assets in the process of the transplantation while leaving family members and homeland, the British gentleman immigrant seemed dilettantish, an easy figure of fun. The incongruity of the rough life of the frontier and the presence of these drawing-room individuals struck many "real" Americans, even if they had only recently arrived, as ridiculous. What did polo playing or cricket have to do with farming? What was the point of a hunt, if not for killing game for the family table? Some of the Close Colonists relished the contrast between effete British social life and the middle western pigstyes and barnyards, since it seemed an appropriate antidote to overstuffed Victorian life. Lord Hobart, when he left his Iowa farm for visits to England, carried with him cards that read: "Lord Hobart, Dealer in Hogs," to leave on silver trays at friends' houses.[13]

One of the chief difficulties colonists encountered was who would do the farm labor? In the early years, almost any itinerant with a little cash could buy land and farm on his own, not work as a hired hand. Of necessity, the Close Colony apprentices, fresh from the public schools and universities, became the labor supply. As soon as these greenhorns learned a little, they persuaded their fathers to buy them farms and in turn engaged "pups" to work for them—a pyramid scheme of labor that evolved because there was no native population to exploit, unlike the situation of their friends in Africa or India. Many settlers in the colony kept trying to import a yeoman class from home, but when they arrived most of these workingmen were lured away by other opportunities, saw their chance and took it. Housemaids, cooks, and nannies were besieged by marriage offers in this woman-scarce region, making domestic help also a problem. Some English landowners with the bluest of blood in their veins ended up baking bread, scrubbing floors, and doing the washing, as well as all the field work and animal husbandry. A few such gentlemen found housekeepers by marrying local women; they dropped out of colony high life and disappeared into the ordinariness of American middle-class life.

But such a destiny was not what most of them had in mind. Instead, living within the atmosphere of the Close Colony, they could almost believe they were still part of the British Empire. They deliberately kept themselves from integrating into the local scene. When President Garfield was shot in 1881, the colony leaders sent a telegram to the widow: "As from representatives of the largest English Colony in America..." as if a sort of sovereignty held, and as leaders of a separate principality they were communicating a state message following proper protocol.[14]

In the Prairie Club their British identities could always be reaffirmed; the club was probably an institution even more important in this respect than St. George's Episcopal Church, in which prayers were offered each Sunday for the health and well-being of Queen Victoria. The young gentlemen-immigrants drank away loneliness in their favorite taverns, the House of Lords, the House of Commons, and Windsor Castle; their principal hotel was Albion House. Their June horse-racing meet was called "the Derby," with thoroughbred racers shipped from England to compete and gentlemen-owners in bright colored silks frequently serving as jockeys. The Race Ball with men in white tie and tails and bejeweled ladies was always a glittering affair. *This* was life on the frontier as they intended it could and must be, not the grinding, dispiriting experience it might have been had they no money and a different social attitude. It was an adventure that enlivened their sense of individual accomplishments—a triumph over circumstances—and in the end, faith in their birthright was bolstered. The enterprise would remain in memory, particularly if they left Iowa in time, as an interesting movement to have been part of.

The colony did not disappear overnight. It dwindled under the onslaught of several unfortunate turns of event, among them, the death of its leader, Frederic Close, in a polo accident in 1890; also that year marked the beginning of an economic depression that reached its worst in 1893, lowering land values and turning most agriculture unprofitable. In 1895 a fire destroyed the Prairie Club, and although the rebuilt club continued to exist well into the twentieth century, the new establishment began to admit Americans. The British packed and left; those who remained were forced to consider themselves American— certainly their children were of this new citizenry. The few British who stayed saw their colony wither and themselves becoming increasingly distant from who they once were, since nobody was left to view them as gentlemen or help shore up their fading image of themselves as part of "the better class."

The British had based their colony in Iowa upon the idea that the future should closely resemble the Victorian present. But it is seldom possible to impose upon tomorrow a set of circumstances and conditions that are fully developed today. What the colonists in Iowa and their parents who had sent them out could not have imagined was that the Empire had painted as much of the globe pink as it ever would, had reached its peak, and was already starting its great decline. "For each age is a dream that is dying, / Or one that is coming to birth."[15] The settlers in the Close Colony felt they could do anything because they were gentlemen and British. It was a faith that took them far.

CHAPTER ONE

Athlete into Immigrant

E W young men have arrived in America under such auspicious circumstances. In the summer of 1876 William B. Close of Trinity College, Cambridge, was twenty-three years old, a handsome, noted athlete of the day, president of the University Boat Club and captain of the British crew scheduled to row in the Centennial Regatta at Philadelphia. President Ulysses S. Grant was expected to watch the regatta. New York newspapers ran front-page articles about the English visitors; as the *Times* explained, the extensive coverage was called for "because the Centennial Regatta will raise amateur boating from a local to an international position." Even while the *Brittanic* was still on the high seas, the virtues of "the English stroke" were discussed in print and whether it was patriotic or merely foolish to stick to the "thoroughly American stroke." "Are not Oxford, Cambridge, and Dublin undergraduates formidable opponents? If so, is it not probable that their stroke is dangerous?"[1]

William B. Close had been around water all his life. He was the fifth of eight children who had grown up on board the sailing yacht *Sibilla*, which cruised the Mediterranean and Adriatic, with a home base at Antibes, France. His father, a banker and intimate business advisor of Ferdinand II of Naples, had accumulated enough money at the time of the king's death in 1859 to retire and devote himself to his family, yachting, and other hobbies. When he died of a heart attack six years later, the boys were placed in English schools and expected to pursue careers that would enable them to earn a proper living, although only the year before their mother's father, Samuel Brooks of the well-established firm of Brooks Bank, had died, leaving her £100,000. William's father hoped his sons would learn the habits of gentlemen, yet "acquire the impression that labour and industry are absolute requisites to their independence and happiness." Thus at an early age, William was exposed to the idea that being a gentleman and earning money were in no way incompatible. His father had done just that. The Closes even had connections with the British aristocracy. While William was still a schoolboy at Wellington, his cousin Amy Brooks married the Marquis of Huntly, a socially lustrous name since the seventeenth century, when the daughter of King James I of Scotland married the second Earl of Huntly. This family access to the upper levels of society later helped William in the development of his Iowa colony; proper blue-blood credentials enabled him to reach persons of means who could invest.[2]

"CHAMPAGNE corks fly about and they welcome us to America," wrote William in his journal as the Cambridge oarsmen arrived in New York on a hot July morning in 1876. Writing a journal was not only more economical in time than composing individual letters, but it was also a suitable way to relate his adventures and gain a perspective on them. He seldom postured or played false with his brothers, sisters, and other relatives reading the journal—they all knew him too well. He enjoyed the role of bright observer and seized upon aspects of his experiences that would throw light on the American character, in the manner of Tocqueville, Martineau, or Dickens. For instance, the bad streets and roads puzzled him; there was even grass growing on famous Fifth Avenue: "one could keep three cows comfortably." He reported discussing this situation with a fictional Jonathan.

> I said, "The American nation, instead of being the go-ahead people one had heard of so much were behind the age in patronising such bad streets."
> "Not a bit of it. It only proves we are far ahead of the time. What does it matter to us if our roads are rough? We build carriages to suit the roads, with such light springs that going over these rough stones only makes a pleasant rocking motion, and the Corporation save vast amounts of public money which ought to be spent on roads, but which the Corporation spend on themselves, and thus encourage trade."
> "But your carriages and horses cannot last you long. They must get worn out by this rough usage."
> "So they do, and that is just another proof that we are not behind time. In England your grandfather's coach will last until your Grandchildren. It cannot be worn out with your good roads. Here we keep up with the fashion—being obliged to—having to get a new carriage every six months, about. And after having had a horse for sometime we get tired of it, and want a change, so are very glad when it goes lame. We get rid of it and buy a new one."[3]

American boosterism was rampant during the height of the centennial celebrations, and William was wryly amused that this cause for joy—separation from England—did not seem incompatible with the requests of newspaper reporters for interviews to obtain intimate information about their persons. William was described in the *Times* as a five feet eleven inch blond with sandy whiskers, weighing 164 pounds, and measuring 42 inches around the chest. Their daily movements and "impressions" were recorded, often inaccurately. The English oarsmen were taken through Central Park to the Harlem River boat clubs and introduced one by one to each member of fifteen clubs, some of them in bathing suits, lounging about, drinking beer, and plunging into the river to cool off. William was outraged by the indignity of having to meet these louts, many of whom were quite indifferent to the British visitors, and yet the newspapers reported that they were "handsomely entertained."[4] What particularly affronted him was that these Americans were called "amateur oarsmen," but only two clubs aside from the Columbia College club were actually comprised of gentlemen. "Carpenters, tailors, shop-keepers, etc., abound and predominate in the others." In boating circles at home such riffraff would not be tolerated: the rules of Henley Regatta stated that any man was ineligible to participate who was "by trade or employment for wages a mechanic, artisan, or labourer."[5]

Later, in Philadelphia, the Cambridge crew was again treated in a rather cavalier manner because of American ignorance of British regard for class distinctions. William's report to his family explained how he managed to prevail despite American egalitarian customs. The lodging house where they were driven upon arrival was barely completed. After they were shown a room with three beds, a washstand, and chair, their host remarked, "I guess this room will suit you all first style." Five members of the crew and their boatman were expected to sleep there, and while the whole American committee agreed they were fine accommodations, William quietly insisted that he did not concur, stating that "we were not accustomed to sleep two in a bed, nor to have our boatman sleeping with us." This astonished the Americans, who "seemed to consider this as only one more instance of the prejudices and effete customs of bloated England."

However, they were provided with two more rooms, and the oarsmen got down to work practicing on the Schuylkill, using their own boats, their seats moving on rollers—a major innovation first used in the Henley Regatta of 1872. One day the slide under William's seat became very stiff; he became quite bruised and unable to sit down without cushions. The crew went to Cape May, New Jersey, for the weekend, and although William accompanied them, he could not train. Thus he happened to find himself in conversation with a man from Quincy, Illinois—Daniel Paullin—whose son and daughter were staying with him at the resort hotel. Mary Paullin, a Bradford and Andover graduate, was an attractive girl of William's age and the first he had thus far met who displayed a refinement comparable to what he expected in English ladies of his class. William commented that on their first meeting Daniel Paullin "told me how he had made his fortune by buying lands in Illinois in the early 1860s, which had grown very much more valuable, and stated that he was going to start his sons in Iowa in the same way, as the same opportunity occurred. He invited me to go West to pay him a visit at Quincy, and volunteered to lead an expedition into Western Iowa."[6]

This fortuitous encounter, which so profoundly affected William Close's life, was in strong contrast to the ill luck he experienced in what seemed to be his crucial moment—the great contest of the international regatta. The Cambridge four did well in the trial heats, although in England the *Pall Mall Gazette* termed them "a miserably moderate crew" and hoped Americans wouldn't accept them as a specimen of ordinary college rowing, indicating that if Close hadn't been president of the boat club he would not even be participating. They might well have won, however, if William had not suddenly collapsed in his seat, too ill with diarrhea to continue. "These beastly Yankees are crowing over us," William wrote home, and yet all the foreign crews suffered from the bad water of Philadelphia.[7]

William recuperated at the British Commission, while his mates enjoyed a festive round of entertainments in Washington, D.C., at the invitation of the Washington boat club. General William T. Sherman presented them with flags, there were receptions, balls, "a perfect furore about them," but William missed it all. By mid-September he felt well enough to travel with a crewmate to West Virginia, where his younger brother Frederic had been farming the last two years. Frederic, like William, attended Wellington College but decided he was "no good at books" and didn't want to matriculate at Cambridge, as his three older brothers had done. He asked instead that his mother give him the money to buy a ranch in the United States. Since Frederic knew nothing about agriculture, he was placed through family connections on a farm in Scotland. This prudent course to gain experience before land ownership was to be developed later in the Close Colony, with an agricultural "school" as part of the scheme.[8]

The visit to West Virginia was William's first chance to study the American countryside, and now that Mr. Paullin had put ideas into his head regarding his future, he tried to learn as much as possible about the land. The South seemed slow, sleepy, and fatigued from the ordeal of the Civil War. Frederic was slated to be a possible witness in a shooting case, and so William observed a ludicrous scene of justice, with an inattentive jury, a tobacco-spitting lawyer, and a judge so bored that he read a newspaper while the defending attorney cross-examined a witness. William and his companion travelled by horseback with Frederic forty-two miles to his farm, staying overnight with a hospitable farmer along the way. The brick house where they put up, once a grand structure, was infested with rats and surrounded by unkempt gardens, all because "of their having slaves to do so for them, but now they have to work themselves and have no time to devote to ornamenting their farms." Three years later, when William was promoting Iowa as a place for settlement, he wrote that he found good land in the backwoods of the Alleghenies too expensive and most of the soil seemed played out. "Also, I formed a very bad opinion of the lower class of population. Everywhere I went I saw far too much loafing about at the saloon doors, and the blacks would only work just sufficiently to keep themselves from actual starvation."[9]

After leaving Virginia they stopped in Washington, toured the national monuments, and were entertained by American friends; "it was the ladies who especially looked after us, and made much of us. . . . They *were* fun, didn't care what they said, full of spirits, in fact regular American girls." Daisy Millers everywhere — a type that interested him because of their boldness, although he knew his sisters upon reading these remarks "would hold . . . hands up in horror at them." One evening the boat club hosted a barge party on the Potomac and outfitted the English visitors in uniforms, "exact imitations of sailors' clothes. We returned by moonlight, and the Capitol and its white marble dome rising above the city with the moon shining on it made an admirable effect, the town and the river being yet in darkness from the shadows of the adjacent hills; and the ladies' sweet voices rose in tuneful time to our oars, singing comic songs in which we joined."

Fred's nickname was "Ginger," probably because of the color of his hair and sharpness of his personality. He took quickly to the pleasures of society, after rusticating so long in the country. The American girls, eager to hear how English ladies were brought up, were amused and surprised to learn of the strict use of chaperones, that girls who had not yet "come out" were forbidden to attend parties unsupervised. They exchanged photographs, each man collecting about a dozen girls' pictures. "But the most remarkable thing is the fondness of the ladies for giving one a bit of ribbon, or a bow, or a necktie or scarf, and even one lady aged but seventeen gave me a small locket...I am buying a box on purpose to bring these trophies back...." The forwardness of an American girl was often preliminary to a display of her accomplishments or talent. One was very good at rowing and decided to compete in a race, but she got William to do a little coaching beforehand, and he observed that "her form was decidedly better than that of any American oar I have seen." These brash American girls fascinated him—as they did many other Europeans of the time—and William would have been deaf to Anthony Trollope's warning regarding American women: "They are sharp as nails, but then they are also as hard."[10]

Leaving Washington, the Englishmen toured the buildings of the Centennial Exhibition in Philadelphia; then, on 17 October they departed for Quincy, Illinois, and a reunion with landowner Daniel Paullin and "his pretty daughter." The train ride afforded them continuous views of America and further discomforts of travel. From St. Louis they boarded a Mississippi steamboat ("one can hardly call them boats—just as if a couple of funnels were placed on a row of cottages") to Quincy.

With the Paullins, they immediately felt at ease, for Daniel Paullin seemed the American counterpart of an English gentleman. The first Paullin to emigrate from England to America bought land from William Penn and settled in southern New Jersey in the latter part of the seventeenth century. Daniel Paullin's father was a tobacco merchant who lived in Philadelphia and Camden, until he bought a tract of land in Adams County, Illinois, and moved there in 1849, making his home in Quincy. He was a supporter of Abraham Lincoln's early efforts in politics, and he married the daughter of Jonathan B. Turner, pioneer educator and friend of Lincoln's. Turner framed the first congressional bill to set aside public lands for colleges of agriculture and mechanical arts, which finally passed as the Morrill land-grant act in 1862 during

Lincoln's presidency. This single piece of legislation profoundly affected the course and quality of American life.[11] In the Paullin's Quincy home the Closes found themselves among people they liked to regard as their own sort—leaders in society and public affairs. Among the Paullins, William wrote, "we felt as they wished us to—completely at home." With their mother dead, the five Paullin siblings were perhaps more united because of this loss, in much the way the Close children maintained strong ties following the death of their father when they were still quite young. Quincy society had "not a vestige of narrow-mindedness," William found. "Nearly everybody had been a year or two in Europe, and that improves Americans very much." The ladies were well-read and accomplished, but with the exception of Henry Paullin, "I did not come across any young man worth knowing." They were mostly interested in billiards, saloons, and trading.

Quincy, a long-established city on the Mississippi, was open to the world and served as a departure point for many settlers headed West. The pioneers' line of movement was no single demarcation, such as a general might draw to show the advance of troops. Certain areas, including most of northwest Iowa, were still largely open prairie. In 1862, when the Homestead Act was passed, Iowa had only 1,720,000 acres remaining to be claimed out of an original 36 million.[12] The act was intended to encourage small-claim settlers; title to 160-acre tracts could be had without payment, provided the pioneer occupied the land for five years and accomplished certain improvements, such as building house, barns, and clearing and cultivating part of the farm. But in practice the Homestead Act actually encouraged land monopoly instead of preventing it. False claims were entered on plat books and foreign and U.S. syndicates purchased huge tracts, sometimes 100,000 acres or more at a time. Land from the public domain was first bought by these speculators, who in turn sold it to actual settlers. Daniel Paullin had made a small fortune in just such intermediary investment speculation. By 1876, the best area for such money-making opportunities lay in western Iowa. The Illinois Central Railroad had pushed through a line connecting Sioux City with Chicago in 1870, and other routes were being built or planned in the area.

Why had some of the finest land in the world been left so long without settlement? Why had the frontier jumped over this region and moved farther west? For one thing, would-be settlers were still uneasy following Inkpaduta's Spirit Lake massacre of 1857. Problems with the Indians still threatened. The battle of the Little Big Horn and Custer's last stand happened only a few weeks before William Close's arrival for the centennial. Also, the grasshopper plagues in the upper Middle West had been reported in newspapers throughout the world; the epidemics were especially severe in 1874, 1875, and 1876. The sky would darken, limbs of trees would break off under the weight of the insects, and railroad trains were unable to get traction on the rails, the wheels slipping as if oiled or soaped by the crushed grasshoppers. They flew in clouds resembling storms, usually with the wind, and when they descended, devoured everything in a matter of minutes—sideboards of prairie schooners, shovel handles, curtains, sheets, and the clothes of homesteaders.[13]

Congress in 1856 had granted the railroads four million acres of public lands in Iowa as an incentive to build four east-west rail routes across the state. Some companies received six miles on both sides, others got nine miles if portions of the strip were already occupied. Occasionally, if a large quantity of land was already homesteaded, the railroad was awarded twenty miles on both sides. The Civil War stopped much of the railroad construction until the 1870s. This effectively retarded settlement; actually many of the railroad lands, particularly in northwest Iowa, did not come onto the market until the 1880s when Close Brothers, Limited, was in full operation.[14]

"To see what sort of land we should buy and to have some idea of their value we organized our party for a week or ten days cruise on wheels through the western and less settled parts of the State of Iowa," William wrote in his journal. They would stop first in Des Moines to interview land agents about available tracts. The party consisted of crewmate Jerry Mann, nicknamed "Ptolemy," because of his silence and wisdom; Henry Paullin, son of Daniel, called "Grin," because of his happy disposition; Fred or "Ginger," and William, now referred to as "Brag," no doubt because he did too much of it. In Des Moines, "like all western American towns, there is nothing worth looking at," and so they projected a swing through the western part of the state, making a circle that would cover about 250 miles by team from the railroad town of Stuart located 40 miles west of Des Moines. They set out with a buggy and hired team, arranged for by the hotel in Stuart.

Ordinary roads and civilization were left behind. William had his first encounter with the fabled mid-American prairie, about which Trollope had waxed eloquent: "The earth is rich with the vegetation of thousands of years, and the farmer's return is given to him without delay."[15] William wrote his family that there was nothing at all like it in Europe, "rolling prairie. . .none of the hills rising to much above 100 feet above the level of the larger creeks." No trees, only a very few "mean looking specimens" growing along the creeks, and hedges were rare. There were hardly any fences because the stock laws allowed open grange grazing, usually with a herd boy in attendance. This adjunct use of lands was a crucial resource of the stockman. When lands began to be fenced (by 1883 Glidden's produced 600 miles of barbed wire daily), a different kind of agriculture came into being: smaller farms, with grains raised primarily for the feeding of livestock, since the open pastures of wild prairie were gone.

They were touring in early November, after frost, and no green was visible; "all the grass had turned into a dry reddish brown and the only contrast to it was either the pale yellow of the dry stalks of the Indian corn or here and there the dark brown, almost black, of newly ploughed land." The roads were in a dreadful state, although usually straight, since the surveyors had created blocklike mile-square sections; one could never reach a destination on the diagonal but always had to zigzag, checkerboard fashion, "which is a nuisance." The land they inspected was selling for six to seven dollars an acre, higher than they wished to pay. On their return to Stuart they had a terrible time with the balky team. It took them three hours to cover five miles. Their buggy fell off a bridge the horses refused to cross. The travellers had to walk the last six miles in a cold rain, night having fallen. It was so dark they couldn't see one yard in front of them. "Now wading through a slough, then up to our knees in mud, then stumbling over a mud heap. I can tell you we were glad when at last the lights of Stuart showed themselves—and still more when we got to the inn—and still more when we got to supper and got some warm drink in us (only tea, Stuart is a temperance town), and *still more glad* when we got to bed and asleep."

Next day the drizzly weather had turned to sleet and snow as they boarded a train west another forty miles to the county seat town of Atlantic. They discovered the land there was too expensive and so they hired a team, pushed north, off the route of settlement. That night they turned in at a farm although only the third farm where they stopped agreed to take them, possibly because there were four of them and most frontier cabins were already crowded. The normal courtesy of pioneer life was to welcome a passerby if he needed a room or a meal, for a small charge, which provided the farmer with auxiliary cash. "The farmer's wife told us afterwards that she was nearly sending us on, but that she took Ginger, who was quite muffled up, for an old man, and thought of her own old man who was yet out, and took pity on him." Their shelter for the night was a two-storied wooden cabin occupied by the farmer, his wife, her pipe-smoking mother, and five strapping sons. They didn't mind the crowding, saying they once had as many as seventeen divided up for sleeping in the three rooms. In the middle of the night, however, William and Jerry Mann's bed gave way, and the farmer's wife shouted: "I guess you boys had better pull the mattress off and make yourselves happy on the floor."

The next day the touring Englishmen planned their strategy for meals and accommodations. Since the charges for lodging would be scaled down if they looked poor, Paullin in his dark flannel shirt and old trousers, and Fred in his Virginia hat and outfit were to step forward to engage rooms. Jerry Mann and William in their English-cut clothes "did duty when we wished to impress people with our importance." They moved on into wilder country, now and then encountering Germans for their noon meal at a farmhouse, "very unsociable, and what was worse, had just finished all edibles (they weren't sure we would pay)." Even in remote areas they found schoolhouses on the corner of alternate square miles, which suggested proper public aims and boded well for future settlers. Good land alone couldn't be the sole criterion for determining the best location.

On their latest excursion they found rich loam three to ten feet thick "and so fertile that no attempt is made to manure it." The weather turned fine — Indian summer — and in their exuberance to discuss the country with the driver of an immigrant wagon in the distance, they got off the trail and became deeply sloughed, "the horses up to their stomachs in mud." These notorious quagmires presented a serious obstacle to early farming, since the land could not be worked. In later years a network of tiling was constructed six feet down, below the frost level, neighbors cooperating to hook up with tiling systems of one another, creating a drainage route that emptied into a creek or river.

The inhabitants William met were a different sort from the Virginians he had encountered. "Everyone is busy, and attending to his business." Little towns were bustling with enthusiasm and energy, and there was a refreshing absence of provinciality. "The people in the remotest districts know what is going on in all corners of the world." He was even able to buy George Eliot's latest novel, *Daniel Deronda,* in the village of Stuart, as well as the current issue of *Punch.* And yet a few years before there was nothing to Stuart but a couple of cabins alongside the railroad tracks.

The national presidential election had just been held, but nobody knew whether Samuel Tilden or Rutherford B. Hayes had been elected. In the little town of Exira, where they spent the night, the Democrats were celebrating a Tilden victory, making speeches and gathering around a bonfire in the town square, bells ringing. The landlord of the hotel kept pulling his bell, "and it seemed likely as not that he would go on ringing this all night." Frederic noticed a trombone hanging on the wall, took it down, put it close to "our unsuspecting landlord. . .and blew such a blast that might easily have been mistaken for the report of an 81 tonner. . . .I suspect *that* landlord will never forget the sound of his own trombone."

The following day they left by rail for Quincy, where they relaxed in the Paullin home before continuing home to England. For William it had been the most important few months of his life. He had sailed from England as a well-known university athlete on a mission representing his country but was returning with life plans beginning to take a distinct shape — a career in the American West, once he arranged his financial affairs. His emotional involvement with the whole Paullin family was an important aspect of those plans.

Toward the end of his life, William mused over the twists of fate: "If the builder of our racing shell at Newcastle-on-Tyne had not happened to put this faulty screw into the bars supporting my slide, I should never have had the bruise; I should have gone out with the boys at Cape May on the training walk; I should never have met Mr. Daniel Paullin, who well advised me as to my business career; and I should never have married his daughter!"[16]

The Prairie Lords

HE following spring, before William emigrated to America with his brother Frederic, he had one last moment of glory as an oarsman. He rowed in the annual Oxford/Cambridge University Boat Race; and in 1877, for the only time in its history, the contest was a dead heat. There was a great to-do, and William enjoyed living at this fast pace. But a few days later their ship sailed, and a large family contingent saw them off at the dock. The Close boys were loaded down with serviceable all-weather gear, "easy-chairs for the voyage and for our future comfort in Iowa," and two fox terriers.

In New York and Philadelphia they looked up friends from the previous fall until they received word from Ed Paullin that his father and sister Mary, now in Boston, would soon embark by train for the 1,550-mile trip west. Would the Closes care to join the party? They left for Boston at once, staying with Ed in his Harvard rooms, and William was asked to guest-coach the college crew. Harvard students struck him as more like schoolboys than university men; although they studied a great number of courses, "only a superficial knowledge is required." William was amused by their secret societies, their attempts to dress like Englishmen, and was certain that fox terriers would soon supplant other dogs, "without which no swell swaggers."

At Andover a few days later they met Daniel Paullin and Mary—she had returned for a reunion at her old school—and they boarded a train for Quincy, passing the long hours by singing together. "In the Pullman's car from Chicago to Quincy there was a small harmonium, on which the conductor discoursed sweet music." After a brief rest, Daniel Paullin fulfilled his promise and escorted William and Fred to prairie country in Iowa. Now they were in the hands of an expert who believed that because 1876 had been a poor agricultural year, many speculators holding land, expecting a rising price, might be induced to sell and take what profit was still left to them.

They stopped again at Stuart, west of Des Moines, and while out walking before dinner, William noticed a field of clover nearly black with small grasshoppers. "It was a horrid sight, and I confess to having felt like packing up my baggage and at once beating a retreat out of Iowa." He heard that grasshoppers tended to fly toward the northwest and preferred wheat and other small-grain crops. They would settle on the edge of a field and work their way in, then for some reason fly to a fresh location. The grasshoppers were said to have "cleared out the country" further north, and indeed William had seen several prairie schooners coming from that direction, packed with belongings, "room still being left for the family." He wondered what this reappearance of the grasshopper scourge might mean for his homesteading plans, for at this stage he and Fred were aiming to become settlers.

Covering about forty miles a day, they hunted land designated as available by Des Moines agents only to discover that much of it had already been sold. They were often badly sunk in sloughs. On one occasion "the horses quietly lay down and the buggy sank in up to over the hubs," and only the immense efforts of the Close brothers got them out, with Daniel Paullin's face showing exactly how well they were progressing. "When we moved a little his face brightened up, and he grew cheerful, but when it seemed as if we were fast stuck, his countenance fell at the prospect of his wading out through the sea of mud. . . ."

They did locate possible farmland for themselves in Crawford County near the town of Denison, but Daniel Paullin counselled them to leave the deal unconsummated, open to further bargaining. While Fred stayed on at the Denison Hotel, Daniel Paullin and William returned to Quincy, where he learned to his surprise that his cousin Jack Eaden would soon arrive for a visit. This meant another family member in addition to "the infant" Fred would have a chance to meet Mary Paullin and appraise her charms. When William announced his betrothal later that year, Jack Eaden's good opinion of Mary was a comfort to anxious family members, most of whom were alarmed by William's action because he was too young and hadn't achieved financial security — and *she* was an American.

William went back to Denison, after depositing $4,500 with a Quincy banker — ready for their Iowa investment. He found Fred surrounded by fascinated admirers in the hotel. "I don't know whether it is the effects of the moon (for it is a lovely night) but he is treating them to a concert. 'Darling, I am growing bald,' 'There is a crew of Jolly Dogs,' 'The Darling of the Ladies is Frederic Brooks Close,' and other songs he is famous for." When Fred produced a waltz or a rhythmical song on the harmonium, his audiences were enchanted, for few played anything other than the hymn tunes of Ira David Sankey — even though Fred's performance involved mostly a slapdash run here, "a flourish there, bang-bang."

One evening at a farmhouse, after Fred had been entertaining the company on the harmonium, the proprietor announced with pride that his daughters "could tune a bit." Fred urged them to play, but through shyness or realization of their own limitations, they giggled and refused. "What can I do to persuade you ladies?" Ginger asked. "Why, I'd stand on my head if that would make you play." Thinking he was joking, one girl replied that on these conditions she would, "and without more ado Ginger springs onto his hands and walks about head downwards, and then leads the blushing maiden fairly captured to the harmonium."

The presence of the young British gentlemen quite dazzled the local population. Soon after the Closes arrived they received an invitation addressed to "the Lords the brothers Closes." They accepted in the same style, assuming the title was in jest, only to learn that the citizens of Denison "concluded we must be lords," since British immigrants thus far had been lowly farmers, and the Closes seemed on a grander level. Many of them had heard tales, however, about the son of a Scottish laird who had earned a bad reputation in a town twenty miles away. The youth and a servant dispatched to look after him had been shipped off to Iowa on a remittance, to work for one of the rich Scot's former tenant farmers. "When he arrived," William wrote, "he was dressed in knickerbockers," and with the servant standing in attendance, it was "too much for the minds of the people, and they straightaway pronounced him a *lord*. He was called Lord White after that." But the servant, instead of watching over him, turned out to be a ne'er-do-well himself, "and their quarters were the rendezvous of all the *mauvais-sujets* of the country." But as soon as "Lord White's" father died, the emancipated son immediately returned home to enjoy his inheritance. There would be a number of these "lords" in the Close Colony a few years later.

During their first weeks in Denison, William and Fred became acquainted with the countryside, entertained their cousin, went on excursions to a nearby lake for fishing and swimming, and watched crude sulky racing at a trotting track. All the while they were also "looking after the main chances" and trying to decide what land to buy. On 7 August the Closes purchased 2,593⅓ acres from the American Emigrant Company in Des Moines, paying approximately $3.25 per acre. The land lay in the vicinity of Denison, where they resided at the Denison Hotel.

The county-seat town then had 900 inhabitants, five churches, two banks, a number of stores, residences, and two schools. Although the size of the place might suggest *village,* the term was never used, William noted. Every settlement was either a town or a city, and even a small burg like Denison had stores stocked with a general line of merchandise, whereas an equivalent English village had nothing for sale but a few jars of lollipops and the most ordinary household articles. "Here it would be difficult to find anything they have not got in their stores." A proprietor wouldn't try to sell you things out of fashion in the city but sent down to the small towns to be in fashion again, as was done in England. "Here everything moves up to the age, and everyone lives up to it. . . . The system of advertising is so perfect (far too much so) that if a new thing comes out everyone knows of it, and if it is a good thing everyone will have it. Farmers especially waste the greater part of their earnings in buying new machinery." He noticed perfectly good farm equipment lying about in the weeds, exposed to the weather, merely because of a farmer's neglect. "I almost think the farmer is glad when he has spoilt a good machine, for then he has the pleasure of buying some wonderful new machine with the latest improvements. Now no one thinks of walking behind his plough or harrow.... All their machines have seats and require the driver to ride, and comfortably, too; many of them have large umbrellas so that our farmer works in the shade and rides along at his ease, his seat being supplied with a good spring." William does not foresee that bigger and fancier machinery will necessitate larger and larger areas of land to farm; the American farmer's obsession with turning agriculture into a complicated mechanical operation will eventually result in the small farmer himself becoming obsolete.

It was too late to count 1877 as a farming year for the Closes so far as crops were concerned. They decided to embark on stock raising, which could be carried on throughout the fall and winter, if shelters were built in time. With so much open prairie grasslands available, during good weather a herd might be fattened at virtually no cost. New railroad networks made it possible to ship live cattle to the Chicago stockyards market; and the refrigerated car, in use since 1875, enabled dressed carcasses to be hauled long distances. A calf costing five dollars might be fed on public-domain grass and sold a few years later for forty or fifty dollars. In the Far West many cattle companies were declaring annual dividends amounting to 25 percent and up to 40 percent of invested capital, most of it money from Britain. In Wyoming alone in 1883 twenty cattle companies largely foreign-owned were capitalized at twelve million dollars.[1]

For the Closes, winter feeding of livestock depended on the price and supply of corn, and since 1877 was a good grain year, ample quantities and low prices were anticipated; "feeding cattle cheap and selling them dear equals big profits," William reported. He discoursed fully on the long-term plans for the tract he and Fred had just purchased. Next spring they would try to put 600 acres into cultivation, building six or eight small houses and leasing them to tenants with a contract calling for the renter to break an additional 20 or 30 acres. Crop costs and profits would be split with the tenant. The main lesson European immigrants had to learn was that careful attention to a small plot of ground, which they were accustomed to doing, did not suit the American farm scene; instead, "it pays more to cultivate larger tracts less well." Of course he hoped to get mostly British settlers, for the German immigrant, although good at farming, did not seem of the right social class and often lived in low fashion. "Outside their cabin all is untidy and in a mess. No attempt to keep the cabin they live in distinct from the farm—pigstyes close up to the cabin and pigs scratching themselves on the doorpost, chickens running in and out."

By mid-August, it was time to buy feeder stock, and sixty miles east of Denison Fred discovered the cattle he wanted and bought them for a good price. He wrote William to suggest he help on the cattle drive home. "So, arming myself with my brand new cattle whip, and a toothbrush, I started on my mare, Polly." William practiced using the whip, which was twelve feet long, cracking it over his head as he would a hunting whip, but he nearly hit Polly's head. After she calmed down he tried again, only to have the whip crack on Polly's flank. On the third attempt, hoping to produce the pistol-shot sound, "I succeeded in bringing the lash smartly across my face. Ah! didn't it sting."

As William approached the town where he expected to rendezvous with Fred, he heard shouting and whip cracking and discerned two men on horseback trying to keep a herd of cattle out of unfenced corn. William assumed it was Fred, but as he neared did not recognize him, for both these men wore dark suits while Fred had left in a light grey suit. He was about to pass by, "when a voice, unmistakably Ginger's, shouts: 'Where the (ahem) are you going to, can't you help us?'

"Is this black, grimy-looking mortal, covered from head to foot with mud, mounted on a wretched Indian pony, that gay, fascinating brother of mine? Yes indeed, it is he.

" 'Look sharp, get to the centre.'

" 'All right, my general,' and I get to the centre. My advent turned the battle, for although I was not a very formidable operator on their hides, still the cattle did not know it just then, and kept a respectful distance from me."

Next day they rose early, taking advantage of the cool part of the day to herd their eighty-two cattle toward Denison. William found the task "most horrid, dirty, tedious, and slow," with dust penetrating eyes, nose, ears, mouth. He had to wipe his spectacles frequently and had a gritty sensation in his throat that no amount of water relieved. It was a blazingly hot day and no breeze blew to cool them. The Mexican saddle with its high pommel seemed very uncomfortable and he missed the lean, neat English saddle. They finally reached home after thirteen hours on horseback, and because William had fully experienced the legendary (even then) cowboy role of cattle driving, he concluded, "there is remarkably little romance . . . and a great deal of weariness and dirt."

He felt the same about farming, once he got into it. They finished constructing cattle and hog pens, which were situated in a sparse woodlot with a small stream running through it to water the livestock. They now had 169 cattle and about 100 hogs; the latter had to be dosed with sulphur and charcoal ashes to ward off cholera, and all had to be branded. "Ginger was operator in chief." It was becoming increasingly clear that while "Ginger worked like a nigger . . . I preferred superintending." This was an important discovery for the brothers to be clear about, for while Fred actually enjoyed the physical work in farming, William relished the planning and management. They would have to conduct their future partnership accordingly.

In his journal William mingles accounts of their recreations with reports of their business pursuits. Their father's brother, Uncle Thomas Close, age eighty-one, responded with enthusiasm and attentiveness, keeping track of their purchases in land and livestock, offering advice, and reporting that their older brother James, now looking after Brooks's banking in West Africa, might very likely turn up in Iowa one day.

William's spirits remained high, and these letters from the outside world helped sustain the pioneering venture. An audience was necessary to make the going easier. It was Indian summer, with warm bright days and cold, dry nights. "I am still wearing my summer clothes," he wrote in October, "I cannot tell you how jolly one feels being out on such days." And the natives' customs continued to amuse him—oddities, like the passion for playing croquet, which even farm laborers took up. It was perhaps the first sport to be played by both men and women of all classes and was sometimes referred to as "the courting game." Once, coming down the hill toward Denison in the evening after tending to cattle, William noticed dozens of lights moving about and it took him some time to realize it was "nothing more than croquet players carrying their light—it looked as if a lot of fireflies were buzzing about. . . . I have several times been dragged into playing that horrible, hateful game."

The better educated people in the community were eager to enjoy the company of the lively Close brothers; their learning and manners were greatly admired. How could these talents be put to use for the good of all? A school-teacher invited them to visit her one-room schoolhouse near their farm. They found the little scholars hard at work and the room itself well equipped and exceptionally clean (the teacher, according to contract, was always responsible for janitorial duties). As they sat down and listened to lessons, some of the answers given greatly amused them. One small girl was asked what an amphitheater was and answered that it was the place where the "Roman Alligator fought." Another was to explain the meaning of *canine*. "She was sure of her answer: 'men who eat men!' " The teacher tried to get William and Fred to tell the children something about the many countries in which they had lived, but they couldn't think of anything appropriate or illuminating, "it was . . . a sort of *embarras de richesse*—didn't know where to begin."

Membership in the Episcopal church helped knit the Closes into the community. William served as superintendent of the Sunday school and Fred was a mainstay in the choir. Their religious upbringing had been conventional, without fervent overtones; their father, according to their mother's Commonplace Book of 1855, was a man whose religion consisted of charity and good works rather than faith.[2] The Denison church had been damaged by a tornado, and since it was already encumbered by debt, William found belonging to the Episcopal church was an expensive proposition. One evening a mum sociable was held: "For an hour and a half whoever made the slightest noise or spoke but a word was fined five cents, which went towards the paying off the church debt." At Christmas special solicitations for various funds were made, always requested by the ladies—and how could he refuse? "If they'd only send men around . . . it ain't fair to send ladies."

A few of his neighbors' lives seemed poignant—particularly the Wygants, whose seventeen-year-old daughter Carrie had been horseback riding with him. Mr. Wygant, a lawyer in Denison, was discovered using trust money for his own purposes; he fled, abandoning his wife, daughter, and two sons. All of the Wygant property was seized except the family homestead, an 80-acre piece on the edge of town, which under Iowa law could not be claimed for debt since it was not mortgaged. The Wygants were highly respected, educated people, and William found "Miss W. decidedly...the best of the young ladies around, and withal rather pretty; she plays the organ, leads the choir at church, and is an active teacher in the Sunday School...." With no means of earning a living except to farm, the Wygants sold all the possessions they could spare—among them Carrie's organ, although she loved music—to raise capital to buy stock and equipment. William was fascinated to learn that the townspeople did not regard the family as disgraced. "No one thinks the less of them because Mr. W. was a scoundrel and they are reduced to poverty, but on the contrary they are greatly respected by all." Each of the Wygant children shared the farm work. William observed Carrie driving in the cows, and when one of her brothers had to go off to attend to business matters, she took his place on the mowing machine for the day. Although she served as church organist and directed the choir for two years, she received no money since "money is very tight," and William suggested contributions from his correspondents would be thankfully received.

Carrie Wygant and her friend, Miss Seyers, claimed to be experienced riders, so one day William rode out into the country with them to test their abilities. He proposed a canter, and their ponies began racing. Miss Seyers, a poor rider, clutched the pommel, crying *"woa, woa"* and soon fell off. Twenty yards farther, Carrie also tumbled off. "As I come up to the rescue, I think: 'Is this Iowa riding?' " Miss Seyers, pale and groaning, thought she had broken her arm. Meanwhile, Carrie in emerging from the ditch, tripped on her riding habit and fell into the ditch again. She came out holding a broken stirrup leather, the cause of her accident. Her habit was badly torn, she was covered with mud, and in the headfirst fall, exactly half her face was jet black, "the line passing as if painted, right up the bridge of her nose...the indignant expression of her countenance and her eyes flashing (she has a pair of A.1 eyes) was too much for me, and I fairly roared with laughter." She was alternately amused and angry with William for laughing and asked how *he* would like to fall into a ditch that way? William begged her to look into a mirror and *then* she would understand his amusement. The three of them sought the hospitality of a nearby farmhouse and examined their wounds. Miss Seyers had a sprained wrist, while Carrie, "after washing her face, discovered a lump on her forehead, and her upper lip had swollen to twice its normal condition." She now forgave William for finding her appearance funny. He sent for a carriage to convey Miss Seyers home, and then he and Carrie Wygant continued their ride, "and I found she could ride well."

That a respectable young lady of seventeen and a gentleman of twenty-four could ride alone together and not be talked about in scandalous terms was now such a normal thing to him that he did not even bother to explain such circumstances to his journal readers. Chaperones were impractical in a frontier town, and with many women expected to do almost as much physical work as men, the social conventions were impossible to observe. A girl of good family, properly brought up, could never be suspected of succumbing to sexual improprieties with a gentleman companion — in a world where one was either a "good girl" or the other kind. Since these flirtations and casual companionships could not endanger a girl's honor, young men might enjoy genuine friendship with unmarried females — an aspect of the American social scene that Fred and William appreciated enormously.

William's pleasure in the lively company of Carrie Wygant occurred on the brink of his engagement to Mary Paullin — and he seemed hardly aware of it. Between the letter of 13 October describing the horseback-riding episode and his Christmas epistle of 11 December, he had been "a month or so" in Quincy, followed by a stay in Des Moines to study the latest land-market news. In his journal he spoke of the Quincy interlude as a trip "to get my warmer clothing, which I had left there," but to intimates he sent private letters announcing his engagement.

The Wygant family understood that Carrie and William were "keeping company" — it was generally known in Denison. But Carrie was a gallant, impecunious Iowa girl, and her marriage prospects — emotional involvements aside — were not in a class with the well-educated, pretty daughter of the rich landowner, Daniel Paullin. Nobody in Denison seemed to know about William's betrothal for several months, although he may have told Carrie. Obviously, he was extremely fond of her; he seemed to have been the one who decided their relationship would come to nothing beyond friendship. A few weeks after William returned from Quincy and Des Moines, Carrie was introduced to Fred's Virginia homesteading companion, H. Hyndman Wann, newly arrived from a visit home to Belfast, Ireland, and their courtship began. A pun in reference to this romantic shift has come down through the years in the Wygant family: an uncle said to Carrie, "I see Will Wann is getting closer."[3]

While William's engagement was still secret, he played the role of eligible, fun-loving bachelor and escorted a local lady to a dance Fred organized:

COTILLION PARTY
Yourself and Ladies are cordially invited to a
Cotillion Party
at
McHenry's Hall, Friday Evening, Nov. 30
Music by Field's Band of Council Bluffs
Per order Committee of Arrangements

The band was due to arrive on the 8:30 P.M. express, with the dancing to begin by 9:00 P.M. As it turned out, the train was delayed and the party probably wouldn't begin until 10:00. The twenty-five couples waited patiently, but at last someone suggested rousing the local band; "But the local band's feelings were hurt at the importation of the Council Bluffs band. Besides, with the thermometer at 10° below zero, the local band utterly refused to leave his bed, and the deputation was unsuccessful. N.B. The Local Band consists of one piece—a fiddle."

When the grocery store clerk claimed he could play the concertina, all urged him to fetch it at once, which he did, but one of Sankey's hymns was the only tune he knew. Another boasted he could "strum a Quadrille on a guitar," and although he hadn't played for a couple of years, believed he could do well enough for them to dance to his music. "But when he brought the case and opened it, it was found the guitar was minus three strings, and his genius did not rise to the occasion of playing on two strings."

Ten o'clock and still no band. Finally, near eleven, they heard a train whistle; the ladies in the cloakroom sent up a cheer—the band was arriving! Although William expected about a dozen instrumentalists, "instead, enter Mr. Field with a violin case, followed by a one-eyed youth with a cornet, and they hurry to the platform. 'Is this the entire band?' I ask one of the Committee.

" 'No indeed,' says he somewhat indignantly. 'There are three pieces,' and sure enough, as he speaks the bass is seen pushing his way in, puffing and blowing, for no time is lost.

" 'Promenade!' shouts Mr. Field, and we all follow-my-leader round the hall and execute various maneuvers. I don't know how the unfortunate 'band' stood it, but between the dances there was only time to drop one partner and pick up another before the next dance began. There were 26 events on the Programme, 'and we are going to get through every one of them,' quoth the Master of Ceremonies.

"*He* certainly did not allow of any delay." Quadrilles took up two-thirds of the numbers, with only a few waltzes, much to Fred's disgust; "but as Ginger, the livery stable keeper, and the ready-made clothier were the only gents who could thread the maze of the giddy waltz, it was thought the others would grumble. . . ."

The only man at the affair wearing a swallowtail coat was Mr. Moses Goldheim, "one of the leaders of fashion here, and the ready-made clothier." He told Fred and William that "he was obliged to appear well-dressed (save the mark!) because it was a good advertisement for his business!. . . he wore a huge flaming red satin sailor's knot necktie with a very low waistcoat."

Mr. Field, the determined master of ceremonies, would not hear of anyone sitting out a dance. "You were always wanted to complete a set—or, if you went outside, you had to freeze." Every quadrille was somewhat different, and with Mr. Field calling out signals, "one was continually on the *qui vive* to know what he meant. I was informed by a lady to whom I ventured to ask for an explanation of some of his terms, that unless I knew how to speak French I would not know the exact meaning.... She understood, however, sufficiently to go through the correct evolutions, as did most of them, luckily for me.

"At two o'clock supper was ready, and not to create jealousies, lots were drawn as to which couples should go in first. Oyster stew the principal staple. After supper, dancing was renewed with increased energy, and all were supremely jolly and boisterous—only from their own animal spirits, however.

"At about half-past four one lady gave out, which left an odd man, a circumstance I took advantage of...but as the lady I was escorting was only beginning to thoroughly wake up to the occasion and looked as if she would never tire, I knew I was in for the finish....When a kind Providence so directed it that the lady gave out, I sat out the rest of the dances, which remain a blank to me. All I know is that at about six o'clock my fair charge 'guessed I must have been having pleasant dreams,' and would I be so kind to take her home, and I found everyone streaming out."

As Christmas neared, the pace of social life increased. One of the liveliest organizations was the Cremation Club, made up of fifteen young ladies of Denison who met weekly to have a good time. "As they naturally could not have that without some plentiful mixture of black coats, they would invite fifteen of the sterner sex...to bring that...necessary garment. Necessary, however, in the mind of the Western 'gentleman' only when he is attending church or a sociable. At other times it seems impossible for him to do anything with it on—to eat his dinner or attend his store. He must be in his shirt sleeves or else I verily believe he thinks his dinner would choke him in the first instance, or his customers out-trade him when at his store."

The Cremation Club girls enjoyed blindman's buff with their gentleman friends and other parlor games of which William soon tired. He suggested that somebody oppose him in a contest of "cock-fighting," a sport unfamiliar to them, and one young man took up the challenge. Both were bound and the signal given. William's opponent wore a pair of regular western boots with box toes and "well retroussé heels." Without much difficulty William knocked him off balance—"crash into a heap of ladies—not only onto his back but still further, so that when he recovered to his surprise he found his toes were resting quietly on one of the girl's laps. He retired from the arena after that, and in answer to my challenge, one more venturesome youth...accepted, and being tied up, placed himself about two feet from the wall of the room, thinking the wall would support him. But when his head came into contact with the wall, I guess he wished he had not been so brilliant."

A few days before Christmas, William helped decorate the Episcopal church. Since no evergreens grew locally, they sent for a tree from Council Bluffs, seventy miles away. When it arrived it turned out to be a couple of four-foot high shrubs bound together; so they improvised, using a bare oak tree. They threaded Indian corn in great ropes and strung cranberries on strands, but still it was a curious looking Christmas tree. Quite unorthodoxly, the tree was set directly in front of the altar, but since the church hadn't yet been consecrated, William figured that this pagan throwback probably did not matter.

He sent Christmas cards to all his Sunday school students, adding a little comment exactly opposite to what would have suited each pupil. "For instance, on the card I gave the girl who paid the least attention, I wrote: 'to Miss so-and-so for her unqualified attention, from her late S.S. Teacher. Then to the girl who 'cut up' the most, 'for her general good behaviour.' To the one that never could answer a question, 'for her knowledge of the Bible,' and so on. To the one who really did know something about the lessons and was always attentive (an English girl by the way), I gave her card, 'for bad behaviour.' "

The next day he received a parcel from a messenger boy, for which he had to pay ten cents. Inside he found a framed card, on the back of which was written:

> To Mr. W. B. Close, late S.S. Teacher
> from Miss Carrie Wygant, for his unqualified attention
> from Miss Lillie Barr, for his knowledge of the Bible
> from Miss Ada Fanekonen, for his general good behaviour

winding up with:

> from Lizzie Sherwood, for his bad behaviour.

"*That* was their repartee."

As the year 1877 ended, the Closes' worldly prospects looked as fat and promising as the livestock in their yards. If prices held, they planned to ship their cattle to market in January, though they could easily afford to hold them, with corn at $0.14 a bushel. Although they bought their hogs too small, the animals were thriving, but an epidemic of cholera could suddenly wipe out envisioned profits. The excellent crops meant that land values were on the rise, and farmers were coming in steadily, looking for land. The Closes had bought theirs at a fortuitous moment. In the spring the breaking of the sod would add $2.25 per acre to the total cost of the land, plus an additional $1.00 per acre spent on erecting farm buildings, which brought the full expense to an estimated $6.50 per acre. "From that outlay we shall yearly receive an income of $2.50 per acre, which is a large percentage." Such a figure was positively dazzling, considering that land in England was then returning a bare 2 or 3 percent and sometimes not even that much. Thus a wonderful opportunity existed to sell others back home on the financial returns possible.

While Fred became increasingly interested in farming and even hated to leave his cattle for a necessary business trip to Virginia, William was beginning to think of following Daniel Paullin's land-speculator career, as originally outlined on the hotel veranda at Cape May the previous year. Certainly his involvement with Mary had something to do with it, for immediately after their engagement he announced plans of spending time in Des Moines to brush up on the legal aspects of land transactions. Investing in raw, undeveloped prairie and selling these acres to actual settlers required a different knowledge from that he had gained on the Denison cattle and pig farm. Mary was a cultivated young lady, ill-suited to an existence as a farmer's wife. After all, her father had made himself rich by buying and selling lands in remote regions, while his family lived comfortably in a civilized town. Perhaps William's reversion to his original career plans did not come about merely because of his anticipated new, responsible role as a family man—or even because of the powerful influence of Daniel Paullin. It may well have been the August cattle drive that did it.

CHAPTER   THREE

The Prospect before Them

ILLIAM'S shift in career from land-owning stockman to businessman and trader had some disquieting aspects—the people he encountered seemed a low sort. In Des Moines as an intern in the Iowa Loan and Trust Company he noted a cheerful vulgarity in the social life, a great deal of mixing-up of privacy and one's business affairs. There was even a shortcut available for courting for "clerks and such like" on New Year's Day. Ordinary unmarried girls assembled in groups of six to thirty and waited to be called on by hordes of men, whom they'd never met, looking for mates. "There is a grand spread of good things, and the happy gentlemen are waited on by these same ladies." The calling cards left (some of them fantastically printed in several colors, usually emphasizing the man's business and worldly importance) are regarded by the women as trophies of a kind. Indeed, the incidence of such inappropriate commercialism hardly surprised William anymore. "One of the first questions you ask a man on meeting him, and one he appreciates the most is 'Well, how's business?' And a stranger will not hesitate to...discuss with you his business...and tell you all about it."

At the Iowa Loan and Trust Company William learned the rudiments of how to make money by investing in raw prairies and shared the information with his relatives. He realized he needed to know more about laws pertaining to land titles. The company located the tracts, negotiated the price, and refused loans of more than one-fourth of the land value. For investors with cash, putting money in land was exceedingly safe—the return about 9 percent. William himself would select the best property, should the readers of his journal be interested. "Ahem—if anyone wants further information, glad to supply it." In this lighthearted fashion he launched a proposal that developed into his principal business activity in the forthcoming years. He hoped his readers would regard him as a shrewd potential money maker, for with the capital they commanded, he might do great things.

A few weeks in Des Moines sufficed. By 20 January he was writing his journal from the Paullin home in Quincy and had begun to study law with the distinguished elder statesman, Orville H. Browning. Browning was a close friend of Lincoln, served in the president's cabinet as secretary of the interior, and before that had taken Stephen A. Douglas's seat in the Senate. He had also served as U.S. attorney general before returning to his Illinois law practice.

William found Browning "courteous to a degree and very refined in his manners and conversation" and curiously dressed in the old style, with swallowtail coat and frilled shirt front. Along with his studies of United States law, William became familiar with the key political and economic issues of the day, about which he discoursed with his journal readers. Silver would probably become the legal standard before long, he predicted. The Panic of 1873 and the subsequent years of economic depression had been caused by "over-production, especially in the iron line."

Underproduction, particularly in manufacturing, was actually closer to the problem. Once the factories tooled up and began to produce consumer goods, the boom of the 1880s would be on. William recognized that there had been a pause in the economic development, but he attributed it to the overbuilding of railroads, which had gone on at a madcap pace, stimulated by great gifts of federal lands. Too few settlers were following the railroads, growing crops to ship to market; and so the justification of an extensive track system was being questioned. For William's projected land buying and selling to work, homesteaders were needed; therefore he tried to understand the domestic economic situation.

His winter idyll in Quincy came to an abrupt end when he received a letter from Uncle Thomas Close, who not only disapproved of William's engagement but had serious doubts about the viability of Iowa farming and all other American land schemes. Uncle Thomas found it strange if Mr. Paullin was worth about a quarter of a million dollars, as William indicated, that he was unwilling to provide a dowry for Mary. "I cannot sanction a marriage which I am sure that had they been living, both your father and mother would have disapproved of." William's business prospects were not only uncertain, they were "doubtful," and though he was sensibly learning about land transactions at the Iowa Loan and Trust Company and apprenticing himself to the Hon. Orville H. Browning, the outcome looked hopeless. The distrust in England "in every United States enterprise" was so general that "there is no chance of persuading people in England to look at United States investments."[1]

William's response to this blow was characteristic: immediately, he set out for England with Mary Paullin, so that his family might make her acquaintance, and at the same time he could convince them face-to-face of his acumen in American land matters. They sailed on 16 February, Mary accompanied by her Quincy friend, Mary Ball. It was a rough crossing and most of the passengers succumbed to sea sickness. "Miss Paullin was the only lady at dinner that evening, and the gentlemen might have been numbered on one's fingers." Her strong constitution displayed on this occasion ran counter to her later posture of a weak, sickly, Victorian lady, half-invalided much of the time.

On 2 March they arrived at Cap d'Antibes and stayed at the Close family home, now occupied by William's sisters and sundry relatives, "the Gynarchy at the Cape." It was the perfect time of year for lovers to be in the south of

France. "Oh! that month!" he later wrote. Early in April William embarked for England, leaving the two Marys at Antibes, where they would remain several weeks and eventually visit other parts of Europe before taking a leisurely trip home in late spring. William hoped to arrive in London for the annual University Boat Race but missed it. When he sailed from Liverpool on 16 April, he was in a blithe mood, his battles won, and his confidence extremely high. He felt closer to his readers again and dispatched his thirteenth journal installment, begun on the ocean voyage. "I had to start back for these regions," he added later from Denison, "in order to get some more land before the breaking season was over."

Fred had built "a residence" for them in the meantime, and when Fred opened the door in his nightshirt at 6:00 A.M., "I found myself in a spacious billiard room. 'Bravo!' said I, 'this is good. Now let us proceed onward and view the other apartments.'

" 'Well,' said he with proper pride and a nightshirt, 'this is the other apartment,' " and flung open a door disclosing the remainder of the residence — one long narrow room. "Fred occupies the South half and I the North half." Carrie's mother, Mrs. Wygant, had been engaged to cook for them. She was not the kind of boarding-house chef who put great emphasis on show, but she knew how to prepare mutton and substantial English fare. The custom of many American hotel restaurants was to disguise bad food by a pretentious use of dishes, "each bit in a tiny dish of its own. These are arranged in a semi-circle around you, one large plate being given you wherewith to discuss all these small items." The five oarsmen from Cambridge one evening in Philadelphia had counted fifty dishes on the table in front of them.

Best of all, Fred had contracted to have 1,200 acres of their joint land broken up for only two dollars an acre, twenty-five cents cheaper than the going rate. The procedure of breaking, William explained, involved turning over prairie grass so that weather could rot the roots and the soil would be left until fall, when it would be "cross ploughed," with the sod finally broken up and ready for spring planting. The first crop of grain on virgin land often paid for the cost of the breaking; but since they planned to have tenants farming, their return would not be quite so immediate. Many prospective tenant farmers had applied to the Closes, but it was important to choose bona fide settlers, not tramps and deadbeats. "We take a mortgage on all the renters' goods and chattels, and if caught decamping they are sent to the penitentiary."

The spring of 1878 was wet, but by 1 June half the breaking was done and William let out contracts for house and barn building. Their bachelor digs proved comfortable and inexpensive. Mrs. Wygant cost $3.50 a week for three meals a day, and a cleaning girl $3.00 a month. "A boy rubs down our nags (after a fashion when Fred is not there) for $2 a month, and stable rent is the same sum." The rooms of their house had been decorated "with all the magnificent and gay embroidery Fred was lucky enough to have worked for him by sundry fair ladies in England." The natives were rather in awe of such splendor, and the billiard table, which had caused such a stir when it was moved in (the youths of the town ogling as they strolled past, half-expecting to be invited in for a game), was now an accepted fixture, and the boys "have learnt...that hints are not taken."

The two brothers shared some domestic chores: Fred attended to the stables, fed and watered the horses; William kept the household supplied with water and trimmed the lamps and filled them with oil. The well was fairly deep and "it is quite a labour on a hot day to draw the water," but they could not justify hiring a houseboy to attend to these simple living matters. "It is undoubted economy to live out here, and I should advise anyone wishing to practice that disagreeable operation to come out to these parts where it can be done without much roughing. Happy to show anyone the trick." This invitation would be publicly extended the next year, and the Close organization would come to be in loco parentis to hundreds of young men, many of whom were not serious about learning the economy trick.

They continued active in church affairs, William serving as godfather to several infants and now and then conducting services. He and Fred had almost had their fill of ice cream socials to benefit the church. The American passion for this confection, "one of the great institutions of this land of liberty (?) and corruption," was amazing. "I don't believe there is a small village in all the...United States that does not boast of its ice cream saloon, and for 10¢ you get as much ice cream as any ordinary mortal could possibly swallow, and generally excellent." William tested to see how much ice cream his Sunday school pupils could eat, if he paid for it. "I am sure they must have all been very ill afterwards, but just now I am, I believe, the most popular at the Sunday School." The yield came to $40.00 for the event, helped a bit by Fred's sideshow attraction—he owned a small air pistol that he lent for target shooting, raising $3.60. He also posted a sign in the billiard room of their home: "Anyone swearing or using bad language is fined ten cents for the benefit of the Episcopal Church." William noted: "It has a very improving effect on the vocabulary of our Westerner, and for once his language is quite chaste. But a few fines have been necessary and Ginger puts them down in the church's Treasury Book: 'To swearing in Close's room...ten cents.' Some future treasurer will be rather puzzled by this announcement."

The local paper, filled with distorted news, misinformation, misspellings, and assorted diversions, was a constant source of amusement to the brothers. In addition to Republican and Democrat weeklies, Denison, like other towns its size, had a daily paper. The editor of the *Evening News,* who also served as postmaster, was a German who had to hire a subeditor "to write English for him and pick up the news," most of which consisted of items such as the information that the barber had installed a new table and "the ice cream man has a new flower pot." The Closes had a hearing before the county board of

supervisors—"it is magnified as a great legal contest. . . . I told him to advertise
for half a dozen breakers, and he puts 100 wanted."

One day when Fred stopped in the post office for his mail, the German
editor greeted him: "Vell, Rost Beeve," to which Fred replied, "Hullo,
Sourkraut."

"The fat little man immediately drew himself up as big as possible,"
William reported, "and answered: 'Vell, sir, if you can't talks like a shentlemans to a shentlemans, vy you had better not talks at all.' "

They fully expected a hostile blast in the next *Evening News,* but by this
time the Close brothers were too popular and economically important in the
town to be harassed. They were exemplary citizens and participated in community events, even an impromptu football game. One day in the courthouse
square, the mayor, county sheriff, city marshal, district judge, "in fact all the
high-sounding titled officials" got together for a spirited game. Fred's dropkick
went over the largest building and right down the steep hill toward the Denison depot, spooking a horse attached to a farmer's wagon and nearly causing a
runaway. "Say, your brother is no 'hooper' at kicking a ball," a player said to
William. "What a hooper is I have yet to learn. Western language is not learnt
in a day. I imagine it must mean a 'duffer,' for I find they have not that word in
their vernacular. I was asked yesterday why our crew got so beaten this year [in
the University Boat Race]. I answered, because they were a set of 'corkers.'
'What's that?' 'Oh, duffers.' No wiser. Remembering the expression of my
friend on Ginger's kick, I tried 'hoopers' with very satisfactory results."

William's dropkick hit the deputy county surveyor in the stomach,
bounced away and knocked the hat off the ready-made clothier, Mr.
Goldheim. The ball then hit a member of the board of supervisors. Goldheim
was equal to the occasion. "Picking up his hat, which was slightly damaged (a
new one on the helmet system). . . he remarked in a loud voice that it didn't
matter, he had just received a large stock of new hats at $2.50 a piece, just like
the one he had on." The game ended when Fred threw his knee out of joint,
attempting an even grander kick, but he recovered in time for the Fourth of
July celebration.

The town had planned Independence Day contests such as climbing a
slippery pole, catching a greased pig, foot racing, shooting at glass balls, and of
course, "the usual stump orator will deliver his stump oration in the style
suited the yokel mind." Most curious to William and Fred was the medieval
tournament that was to take place: knights armed with spears were expected to
ride horseback tilting at a ring, and whoever took the ring would be able to
choose the Queen of Love and Beauty, the next best knight picking the Maids
of Honor. Jousting tournaments of this sort flourished in rural regions of
America and are still held in some places, most notably in Prince Edward
County, Virginia. The custom derived from the fascination with knights and
chivalry that followed publication of Kenelm Digby's *The Broad Stone of*

Honour (1822), and the celebrated Eglinton Tournament of 1839.[2] In its Iowa transplantation, only the dimmest resemblance to neomedievalism remained. Excellent riders though the Close brothers were, they would have no part of it. The Knights of Denison would include the butcher's boy, stable hands, field laborers, and lumber haulers. William observed them practicing. "O shades of Chivalry, is this what you have come to?" Not a coat worn by any of them, and their lances were common laths, "as to their steeds, Rosinante would have made a creditable appearance among them."

The Fourth of July began with firecrackers exploding outside the Closes' bedroom window—rebel armies attacking the British—and only after "the young imps" ran out of ammunition did they begin to retreat. "Ginger had just got his pants on, and if one believed his words, there would be an end of small boys with crackers did he have to go out."

The day's first big event was the parade, with the city marshall leading off in "a glorious scarf...smoking his weed to show he was calm"; then came the Denison Cornet Band in a farm wagon, trying desperately to play, although they were jolted by the ruts. The band was followed by a procession of country people in wagons who had "come into town in their 'store clothes' and were anxious to show them off." After that, masquerades of leading personalities in the town, the best being a wagon labeled "The Denison Cornet Band" with a bunch of youths in masks "playing on combs, kettles, penny-whistles, and the like—their music certainly was not much inferior to the originals." Then came someone dressed as a baby pushed in a small handcart. The baby sucked a bottle violently and finally swallowed it, resulting in fits, "a variety of contortions that I thought only Ginger was capable of." He caught hold of nearby boys, got a whacking from his mother, cried out. "Ha! those strains are familiar!" The baby was dumped "and disclosed to view a pair of legs clad in...greenish grey continuations that could only belong to my brother Frederic, the cloth of which he had given him by Uncle William Brooks."

"Next came the secret societies represented by two or three men with a banner on which was represented some mystic letters such as M.U.M.S. T.H.E. W.O.R.D., or such like." After them, the tatterdemalion Knights of Denison, still without coats. The procession continued to the lower part of town, but upon its return, the baby was gone. "The mother had mutinied and refused to push it up the hill any further, and the baby had to get out and walk home."

The crowd began to gather under the cottonwood trees of the courthouse square to hear the Independence Day address and listen to music by the Denison Cornet Band. A Baptist minister offered a prayer for the Republic, which consisted of many *Oh Lord*'s, and the glee club sang what William first thought was "God Save the Queen" until he remembered the American rebels had appropriated England's official anthem. "I know at all events of two who sang the right words to that tune."

By the time the speeches and official entertainment ended, Fred had changed to overalls for the greased pig contest. He won by seizing the porker's hind legs so quickly that someone in the crowd shouted: " 'Oh, give the pig a better show,' " and Fred released his grip. "The pig went trotting òn quietly and when it had got some fifty yards away, the signal was given and again Ginger came up to the pig first, who again quietly surrendered. This was too much for Ginger, who with the utmost scorn, flung the pig away. 'Pshaw,' he said, 'I won't go after such a pig! Why, it won't run!' And after that the pig trotted home and was officially awarded to Ginger." He also received the promised five-dollar prize. "Ginger, who is a connoisseur in the pig line, says the reason it didn't run was that it had had so much grease put on it that with the hot sun, its stomach got out of order."

The Grand Tournament proved a disappointment, for after watching all the runs aimed at carrying off the ring, the livery stable keeper, who was proclaimed the winning knight, did not get to crown the Queen of Love and Beauty after all, "that part of the programme was left out." Meanwhile, dancing was in full swing under the cottonwood trees, most of the participants country people. "*We* town folks were above that sort of thing, but it was amusing looking on. 'Ballencay to your *honey*' is the way I heard the Master of Ceremonies give out his directions in the quadrilles." William noticed that among the dancers, different nationalities were represented, especially Scandinavians and Germans.

In the glass-ball shooting, Fred again won first prize. As the day wore on, the beer drinking increased, but there was remarkably little drunkenness and only one case of assault, which amounted to little more than knocking off one another's hats. Firecrackers punctuated the night air, and the two tired English gentlemen returned home to privacy. "The Fourth of July, 1878, is a thing of the past, and I am glad of it."

THE improvement of Close-owned acres was so fully underway that further virgin tracts were needed if William was to emulate Daniel Paullin's route to riches. Whenever he heard of cheap land, he set out to inspect it. Sometimes he had to sleep two-in-a-bed with a stranger, and if he refused such arrangements the host was offended, and he could never stay there again. "The people as a rule are not nice in regard to their bedding. Charges of light and heavy cavalry are conspicuous—luckily both Fred and I can't be very sweet morsels and the cavalry do not inflict much damage on us."

In June William bought 420 additional acres, and in July he was often out scouting while Fred minded the livestock and saw to construction activities on their farms. Since most Americans had only met Englishmen who were tradespeople or common farmers, they assumed the dropped *h* was characteristic of all classes and that William must have lived in the United States for some time to have broken the habit. For the most part, when he put "England" after his name in a hotel register, he got immediate respect. His costume of high leather boots and riding breeches, scarcely the coolest apparel for Iowa in July, was nevertheless practical for horseback riding, crossing sloughs, and as a protection against rattlesnakes. One old Irishman "went into ecstasies" over William's boots—"for 36 years, he said, he hadn't seen anything that did his heart so much good. I must needs turn round and let him see the little button at the back that kept the boots up."

Daniel Paullin wrote he was seeking to buy land for his sons Ed and Henry and proposed that William join him in the hunt. They toured six counties in northeastern Nebraska, discovering "splendid lands" at the low price of $1.50 to $2.00 an acre, but the country had few settlers and there would be difficulty finding good renters. Most of these tracts were heavily taxed, since each county voted its own rate of taxation. Speculators from the East often held title and the local settlers wished to bleed as much tax out of the absentee landlords as they possibly could. They built "splendid school houses where often not a farm is in sight." Bridges to nowhere were erected in mock fulfillment of taxes levied. All sorts of skulduggery was possible, given the circumstance of absentee owners. When a railroad sent investigators to determine why so much tax money was demanded on the company's land, they discovered the county supervisors were more numerous than citizens of the area and "blind contracts were let out in all directions, which were never fulfilled." Not being able to locate the schoolhouse that had cost $2,000, the inspector was ushered to the loft of a farmhouse, where he was shown benches, textbooks, maps, a globe. Since a portion of school funds could be allotted to fuel, the farmer had his house heated free; his three children were the pupils—the only pupils—and the farmer's wife the teacher at a salary of $30 a month.

Taxes ran as high as 7 percent of the land value, making many speculators and railroad companies eager to dispose of their holdings, no matter what the price; in this way true settlers would finally arrive and begin to work the land. "So the swindling that goes on, strange as it may appear, does really do good to the country, by obliging non-residents, whose lands are not improved, to sell at low rates to farmers who will improve them."

The county seat of Wayne County, Nebraska, La Porte, though located on wild prairie, had a handsome red brick, domed courthouse. "Every American official building must have a dome; it would be nothing without. On one side of this huge pile were three little houses, two of which were stores; and this was La Porte. The entire population of the county numbered this spring 308, and yet they build themselves a $20,000 Court House, hauling the brick over 50 miles." This was faith in the future to the point of folly. It was also part of the wholesale scheming to get rich; everyone in the county appeared to be in on some variety of con game. Underwritten by tax revenues, "the dozen or more officials use the Court House as their dwelling house, cooking and sleeping there and concocting fresh plans to skin the unfortunate Eastern holder. This city of four houses publishes its paper, but that, the Editor informed me, was to secure the county printing, for which he receives a handsome bonus. These swindlers are looked upon as nothing more than smart men by the settlers in general."

William and Daniel Paullin decided to leave Nebraska alone for the time being, though in a year or two they might reconsider. When they reached Sioux City, population 6,000, at the juncture of the Missouri and Big Sioux rivers, the moving water made William long to "scull over it." Wide, fairly calm, about twenty feet deep, the Missouri seemed perfect for future regattas. Travelling east along the Little Sioux River in Iowa, "we came upon what may turn out to be the lands we are in quest of." He had examined enough midwestern soil to be a judge, even without Paullin's aid. "The lands I am speaking of made my mouth water as we drove over them. Nothing could be finer. Gently undulating, just enough to carry the surplus water away and prevent any swamps, perfectly watered lands, too, abundant springs in all directions, splendid dark, rich soil, 'many a farmer in England would fill his pockets with it and roll in it for delight'—the agent who took us round told us, was what an Englishman had said when he first saw the soil."

On the hills the topsoil was four to five feet deep, in the valleys "twice that depth." Even the subsoil could grow a crop, as he noted from a field planted where a road had been cut through and subsoil remained. The land had natural fertilizer in phosphates of lime. It was incredibly good land; the only reason it hadn't been taken as yet was the grasshopper scourge, which cleaned out earlier settlers. Perhaps it was a price the landowner had to pay every few years—and was still worth it. When the region was cultivated in different crops the grasshopper cycle might be broken. It was also in a tornado belt. "I suppose with the growth of trees they will become less frequent," William wrote. He was completely sold on this site; "only a strip of land 50 miles wide on each side of the Missouri River...has this wonderful formation, but these lands near Sioux City are extra fine, both in the way they lie and in the richness of the soil." A New Yorker and a partner held 14,000 acres which would probably be sold in its entirety, at about three dollars an acre, "bigger bait than we can swallow." But perhaps a piece of it might be bought, if not the whole thing. "As soon as the lands we want are bought, I shall depart for Europe...."

William needed considerable cash backing to become a land buyer on this scale. Uncle Thomas had warned that English investors were not likely to trust funds to an American agency. To get around that prejudice, he decided to set himself up as a land agent and form a company: Close Brothers, Limited, with offices in London and Iowa. On the West Fork of the Little Sioux River, a small stream with beautifully shaped, sloping hills on either side, the Close brothers would establish personal stock farms and found a town. Though William was a thorough expatriate by now and affianced to an American, he would never forget the necessity of keeping a firm base in England for his enterprise. In this respect his land-buying and selling operation resembled that of any other colonial business venture. The ties to the mother country were the lifeline, never to be cut, for these always offered the promise of a way home.

CHAPTER FOUR

Going Out to Iowa

HILE negotiations were being completed for purchase of "the promised land," William enjoyed his last months in the role of gentleman-settler. He read services in the Episcopal church, attended more ice cream socials, joined in songfests, and accompanied Fred on excursions for prairie chickens, which were plentiful and provided a delicious alternative to "the horrid, tough beef that is sold here."

One delightful interlude occurred in September when a convention of schoolmarms descended on Denison and were quartered in houses throughout town. During this session of the institute, they were instructed in classroom methods and took examinations to win their teaching certificates. They came from all parts of the county and had their "dissipation as well as the course of lectures," most of these pleasures consisting of croquet parties and church "sociables." "We are blessed with four of these School Marms boarding here. Farmers' daughters, raw unsophisticated girls, full of life and fun, and as Ginger is likewise, you may imagine the noise." That these two young bachelors would be asked to put up young girls for a stay gives some idea of how well the conventions of morality held for "respectable" people.

While Denison life could be lively and attractive if one enjoyed what the country had to offer, there were certain drawbacks that became increasingly annoying for a permanent British settler, among these, the abysmal standard of hygiene. William had not forgotten how sick he became from imbibing Philadelphia water. "Everywhere throughout the States you will see the same carelessness shown in regard to sanitary measures and everything is left to fate." Pigs were kept in pens around many Denison houses, and there were numerous open cesspools. Infant mortality was high. "They are ready with any amount of sympathy when anyone loses a child, still the almighty dollar is too strong for them. They pretend not to believe that diphtheria has anything to do with bad drainage.... They prefer running the chances of losing their children to doing away with their hogs."

A neighbor set up a pigsty on the edge of the Close property in Denison, about fifteen feet from their bedroom window. William complained to the marshal, who took action, but the remedy involved turning over the dirt, "and the stench was ten times worse." The only recourse was to buy out his neighbor's pigs (at an exorbitant price), with a contractual agreement that there would be no more pigs. "But it is not all that can afford the luxury of buying a man out."

How much pleasanter for all British incoming settlers if they could associate with their own kind, create a society as much as possible independent from some of the more grating aspects of raw western American life. The colony idea evolved naturally as an outgrowth of William's land-buying and selling plans. If purchasers of his land were British of a class used to associating with each other in England, all the more pleasant.

During this period the Closes' most important visitor who might affect their long-range plans was their older brother James, recently returned to England from West Africa. Twenty-seven-year-old James was still at loose ends, seeking an appropriate future. On this trip he seemed largely preoccupied with touring and stayed in Denison only one day, since he had been invited by a shipboard acquaintance to join an expedition to the Rocky Mountains to view the eclipse of the sun from a spectacular vantage point. Upon his return, however, he inspected the new land near Sioux City that William was undertaking to buy and was equipped to make up his mind whether or not to join William and Frederic in their venture.

On 1 October the huge land deal finally was put together, drawing upon the financial resources of James as well as Fred and William—and Daniel Paullin, although his participation was made possible by a loan provided by William. Since Paullin had been instrumental in giving William a chance to find this land and had bargained with the owners, William no doubt felt obliged to include his mentor and future father-in-law, even though this distinguished, supposedly rich land speculator was surprisingly short of cash. Perhaps it was a gesture of friendship on William's part—in romantic style he would do a favor for this beloved's father, a sign of his devotion to all the Paullins. However it happened, the lands of John Bloodgood and Mrs. Edmund Stanton were purchased for $34,740, not all of the cash delivered on the day of sale but a due date for the total was set for twelve months hence. The Closes and Paullin, by buying such a large amount of land, were able to get the very low price of $2.40 an acre for fertile, extremely desirable property, some of the finest agricultural soil in the world. The increase in value of this land, once it was broken and after buildings were erected, would be the basis of the Close brothers' fortunes. Although they would go on to buy and sell hundreds of thousands of acres in the following decade, they would never again get such fine land for so little money.

When news of the sale of the Bloodgood lands became known, the *Le Mars Liberal* headlined the story, "Hail Britannia!" Close Brothers would locate in Le Mars, opening their office in February 1879. Obviously, everyone in the area stood to gain, for rich British settlers would soon be coming in. Le Mars was somewhat smaller in population than Denison, but like the latter, a county seat and therefore the business center. The town was located at the junction of two major railroads serving northwest Iowa, the Illinois Central (then called the Iowa Falls and Sioux City Railroad), which joined Chicago with Sioux City, and the Sioux City and St. Paul, which connected those river cities. The name, Le Mars, had no French origin but was made up of the first letters of the Christian names of six ladies on board the first train to enter town. Although as early as 1869 Le Mars had a post office, one house, a wheat-grinding mill, and a railroad station, only in the last five years had it really begun to flourish. By the time James Close opened his office it was a bustling community with hotels, restaurants, churches, and a full line of businesses serving settlers.[1]

William returned to England in October 1879 to begin selling land to prospective emigrants and investors. The more British "of the better class," as he put it, went out there to live, the nicer it would be for everyone concerned.[2] "The Prairie Journal" ended, for he was no longer a bona fide pioneer. The journal had been addressed to an intimate audience sharing the adventures of two young Englishmen in the fabled American West. Such a mode of communication was no longer suitable from the rising entrepreneur, William B. Close of Close Brothers, Limited, with offices at 23 Cornhill Street, London; Manchester; and Le Mars, Iowa. In the early years of the organization, Manchester even more than London would be William's center of activity, for the Closes had their best foothold and family connections there — particularly among the Brooks's banking friends — and it was where brother John Close and his family lived.

ONE early convert to the Iowa emigration idea (though not a purchaser of Close-owned land) was Captain Alexander K. Barlow of Manchester, who went out to Sioux City early in 1879 and bought 3,000 acres about a dozen miles southeast of town. He did not follow the sage advice of William because the pamphlet of Close Brothers on northwest Iowa — rich in detail and practical, describing the step-by-step way emigration should be accomplished — had not yet come from the printer. Captain Barlow knew little about the Iowa climate, the soil, or any other of the essentials necessary for making a success of Iowa ranching. His land consisted of bluffs overlooking the Missouri River, which lay five or six miles in the distance. These picturesque, loaflike bluffs, so strange in appearance compared to the hills created by retreating glaciers, had been fashioned by continental winds blowing across the plains eons ago (only portions of central China contain similar land formations). Unlike the rich soil William discovered in the valley of the Little Sioux a score of miles away, Barlow's land had little agricultural value, but he had paid from six to eight dollars an acre for it.

The setting was dramatic; a splendid place to erect a baronial mansion, he thought. He hired an old family friend from Manchester as master builder. A local contractor with a crew of twenty-five began construction. The native brick mansion with twenty-seven rooms would be remarkably English looking, Gothic and Tudor in style, a replica of a Northampton country house: a large central hall, carved woodwork, stained glass windows, and fireplaces in most rooms. Ox teams from Sioux City struggled across the open prairie, forded the rampant streams of Big and Little Whiskey creeks, and labored up the yellowish loess bluffs with building materials all during the summer of 1879. The bricks were baked on the site (rather inadequately); the slate for the roof was imported from eastern Iowa. Brick barns were constructed to house Barlow's livestock, the best in bloodlines, many of them shipped from England.[3]

Captain Barlow was more interested in style than substance and did not seem to realize his methods of attacking the frontier were foolhardy and bound to end badly. Economic success with his cattle raising hardly mattered, for he was rich enough to withstand reversals for awhile. More important to him was that his 3,000 acre ranch be of an appropriate scale to suit his station and be commensurate with his income. He would buy his way into becoming a western gentleman, and it would have to happen all at once.

On 16 October 1879, with the mansion still not finished, an unseasonable blizzard swept across the prairies. The builders nearly perished, for they had no shelter. The storm lasted three days, closing off all roads, all food, and sources of supplies. To keep from freezing to death in their makeshift tar-paper shacks, the men burned most of the wood intended for the construction—the flooring, siding, and panelling. A rapid thaw immediately followed, warm Indian summer weather, and the floods were so sudden and severe that twenty-three horses drowned. It was too much for Captain Barlow, waiting impatiently with his family in rented Sioux City quarters; he quarreled with his contractor, fired him, hired another.

Misfortunes continued. The well digger and his crew worked for months but were unable to find an adequate water supply. Barlow felt he was being cheated by these crafty natives and yet knew he was helpless, for there was no alternative way of accomplishing his grand design. The roof was barely on when all the crates of household goods began arriving from Manchester: tooled oak woodwork for window frames and fireplaces, leaded glass, furniture, antique armor, paintings, carpets, and ancestral silver and china. The Barlows had no choice but to move in and live there for the winter, although during the worst of the weather only a caretaker held out. By summer the house was at last finished; in the keystone above the front door the initials A. B. and the year 1880 were carved. It was the grandest manor house any British emigrant to the area would build—in setting, landscaping, and general design.

When the Close Colony reached its heyday, the largest homes would be erected in towns, particularly Le Mars, in architectural styles generally conforming to American middle-class luxury houses of the time. Those that remain blend in with all the other 1880s houses still extant and do not particularly suggest English origins. The British country homes, even the large ones, were usually wooden, some with mansard roofs or Queen Anne cottage style; none of these early homes remain intact now. Their very size was impractical for heating and upkeep. Later owners who bought out the British cut them down to manageable proportions, using the lumber for barns and corncribs. If there is one talent a farmer must have it is carpentry and general construction abilities. The large wooden country houses of the British, if not destroyed by accidental fires, were easily dismantled.

But Barlow Hall, constructed of soft native brick, was another matter. A cobblestone and brick drive wound through Scotch pines. At the Gothic entrance a footman in full livery greeted guests who arrived for the many parties the Barlows gave in the early months of their tenure. According to a local newspaperman, who wrote of Barlow Hall at the time of its demolition in 1943, the legends people repeated involved Captain Barlow, who with "his guests sometimes rode their steeds into the wide hall, and that fox hunts and polo games in keeping with the best English tradition were staged in the vicinity of the Hall. Leaping flames from the massive fireplace are said to have lighted many social gatherings." Heat from such fireplaces was insufficient to get residents through a frigid Iowa winter, as the Barlows soon discovered; in typically stubborn English fashion they refused to install central heating.[4]

Captain Barlow's ranching enterprise did not amount to much. Soon he turned his attention to downtown Sioux City real estate opportunities. By July 1881 work on the foundation for Captain Barlow's new block of brick stores was begun.[5] Barlow did not become an integral part of the burgeoning Close Colony, not even joining the Prairie Club, but he did participate in county fairs and horse-racing events, entering prize horses from his stable, and he took part in regattas on Spirit Lake, serving as judge on one occasion.

The Iowa climate was not to Mrs. Alexander Barlow's liking: winters too severely cold, summers overwhelmingly hot and humid. Their friends in Sioux City lived too far away for easy transportation to and from Barlow Hall. The Barlows took to wintering abroad; only Captain Barlow returned for the summer. The servants tried to maintain the Hall standards, and the butler's query when a local visitor called, "Tradesman or gentleman?" aroused a mixture of awe and ridicule. These servants displayed a lower-class version of Captain Barlow's arrogant attitude toward the neighbors, his disregard of posted areas when he was out on a hunt, and his insistence on doing exactly as he pleased — even to the extent of stringing fences across public trails and removing bridges he didn't approve of. These actions resulted in constant litigation, most of which he lost, with damages.

After a few years Captain Barlow returned to the Hall only once in a while, but not because his disputes with the locals soured his Iowa existence; he seemed to thrive on these controversies. There were rumors he had benefitted substantially from a will; his wife preferred living at their new country estate near London. Barlow began to sell off livestock, polo ponies, and other horses, and finally disposed of all household goods. The only traceable artifact from Barlow Hall is the tall oak clock in the Sioux City public library. After Barlow sold the Hall he tried to establish himself in Africa, then South America.

Misfortunes befell all who tried to make something of Barlow Hall in subsequent years. A man was killed in a shooting there; another hanged himself from an attic beam. For awhile in the 1920s the Hall was a chicken-dinner roadhouse, situated conveniently as it was on the principal highway leading southeast from Sioux City. Later, tenant farmers tried to live in the Hall and farm the poor soil but without success. Bats and rodents took over the building and it finally had to be knocked down; everything of value in it had been looted or vandalized.

Barlow Hall was one of the first follies of the region. By choosing to erect a mansion on an exposed bluff, Barlow quite clearly was challenging the elements to do their worst. More sensible pioneers built tidy, small, heatable houses and "toughed it out" until larger dwellings could be constructed. Barlow Hall signified that its owner felt he could conquer this new, empty region of the earth merely by arriving and being his own Manchester, England, self. He would be the rock and the flow of life would have to be around him. It was just such an emigrant venture — a waste of effort and money — that William Close hoped his new settlers would avoid; therefore, he set down careful instructions in his *Farming in North-Western Iowa*. The brochure expanded on his letters to the *Times* of London that appeared in the fall of 1879 and his magazine article in *Land and Water* of the same period. It also firmly established the concept of an Iowa British colony in the making.

THE idea of forming a colony in order to sell land certainly did not originate with William Close. Colonization schemes based on land development had flourished in the United States whenever new regions became available for settlers. These promotional efforts were fundamentally different in purpose and character from colonies based on religion, such as the Mennonites, or on social and political ideas, such as Robert Owen's community at New Harmony, Indiana, founded in 1825. As early as 1817 two rich Englishmen, George Flower and Morris Birkbeck, announced the opening of a colony in southeastern Illinois along the Little Wabash, centered in the town of Albion, in what came to be known as "the English prairie." About 4,000 of the original 14,000 acres were developed into small estates typical of rural England at the time, and a pamphlet advertising the colony went through eleven printings. But the colony did not attract a sufficient number of settlers.

In 1838 Henry L. Ellsworth issued a brochure describing his tenant-settler plan for 18,000 acres he owned in the Wabash Valley near Lafayette, Indiana, which mostly drew settlers from small New England farms. The alluvial plains of the Middle West did not have to be cleared of trees or rocks and seemed perfect for large-scale farming; with new machinery being developed, Ellsworth hoped to interest landowners who considered themselves future gentry—not grub-staking small farmers. No actual colony came into being, however.

Victoria Colony in Ellis County, Kansas, was more nearly a prototype of what William Close had in mind. It was founded in 1873 by a Scotsman named George Grant, who the year before had purchased nearly seventy sections (about 44,800 acres) from the Kansas Pacific Railroad near the present town of Hays. Grant himself was interested in raising purebred cattle and sheep and hoped to be joined in his enterprise by "upper-class Britishers of means." He set up land offices in Edinburgh, London, and New York for the Victoria Colony.

Throughout Europe in the seventies American western railroads were busy promoting lands for sale, issuing pamphlets filled with lush promises and glowing descriptions of the countryside. Most of these fliers were aimed at the small-stake homesteader with just enough cash for the ocean voyage and a small amount to put down on new land. George Grant's "haven for British Gentry" would be quite another thing, and the price of land was a good indicator. He had paid between $0.40 and $0.80 an acre, but he would generously let it go for $5.00 to $17.50 per acre, 20 percent down and the balance due in four years at 6 percent interest. True, the price was higher than most land in those parts, but the newcomer should realize the advantage of belonging to Victoria Colony, where congenial associates could be found.

The peak year of Victoria Colony was 1876, when 300 British settlers lived there. Crop failures that year, grasshopper invasions, and much more severe weather than expected discouraged the colonists. Soon even the social tone began to falter. One investor sold a large tract to "indigent English workingmen and farm laborers," and by 1880 the census reported only 128 British-born residents in the whole county. Collapse of the colony came about after the death of Grant in 1878; a group of Russian immigrants took over the site and called it Herzog Colony. William Close seems to have known about the existence of Victoria Colony—it was well publicized—and he used the same techniques in promoting his own. In 1884 Close Brothers bought 100,000 acres in the county just west of the old Victoria settlement.[6]

SINCE William could not personally be the colony leader in Iowa, it was important that he recruit likely candidates who would help develop the concept. Everyone who bought land from the Closes had a stake in the success of the colony and might be called upon to aid the company in its efforts. One of the earliest of these was Robert G. Maxtone

Graham, who was twenty-two when William made his acquaintance in Manchester, where Graham clerked in Brooks Bank. Robert was precisely the sort of lad William sought: a youth of good family forced by financial or social circumstances to seek an occupation, who possessed some money on his own or had access to it, and who could be talked into the adventure of a career in the American West. By February 1879 Robert Maxtone Graham arrived in Le Mars. Through the help of James in the Close Brothers office, a few months later Graham owned a sizeable piece of black-earth prairie.[7] On 9 October he responded to William's request for a testimonial to run in the brochure: "As you know, I have been out here some eight months. Your recommendation and the talks we had together . . . were the cause of my coming here, and so I wish to tell you how thoroughly satisifed I am with the country and all I have done here; more particularly with my investments in land. I enjoy the life, and find myself much better in health than when I was in England."

The Grahams and Maxtones had figured in Scottish life for centuries, Maxtone land having been granted by charter by King James I. Robert's father was the thirteenth laird, an overbearing, powerful, authoritarian man, whose eight children alternately feared and loved him, in Biblical fashion. The senior Graham had some of the oldest herds in Scotland in bloodlines; he served on the Scottish agriculture and fishery boards, was a friend of Gladstone, and was active in public affairs. The eldest son, Anthony, would succeed to the title and family estates after the death of the father; thus Robert, the second son, and James, Jr., the third, were without prospects. They were educated at minor schools and tutored in vicarages, and no attempt was made to seriously prepare them for an occupation. Their father "considered that there was no chance of any opening anywhere for younger sons," according to a family chronicle, "and they were expected to remain at home, as the five daughters would, too, unless marriage changed their prospects." No female could think of a career outside the home without being regarded as eccentric. "Each daughter in turn took on the household management for two months at a time, but as there were 16 indoor servants and an excellent housekeeper, this could not be called arduous."[8]

Robert and James, Jr., rebelled, the latter finding a position in an accountant's office in Edinburgh and Robert with Brooks Bank. William Close's encounter with Robert—his success in persuading the young man to emigrate to Iowa—took place only after the father had left for Germany with his family for reasons of health. Having reached his majority, Robert commanded funds sufficient at least to purchase Iowa land. His early helpful role in the Close Brothers organization was crucial, for he was more than just a colonist. William wrote James on 4 November 1879, nine months after the Le Mars operation began: "let Graham manage the small farm work, you only supervising."

But Robert did not remain in agriculture long. In mid-July 1881 the *Le Mars Sentinel* noted: "Preston and Graham of the English Colony are opening a commission stockyard and house on Fourth Street, Sioux City. . . . It is their purpose to handle all kinds of stock and agricultural implements, and to fill orders for anything that may be needed by a farmer, from a hand-rake to a threshing machine." Although the firm flourished for a time, competition was severe and Graham moved farther west to New Mexico, where he bought a ranch and raised cattle. Freedom of movement bore a direct relation to means available. Graham, like other restless gentlemen from Europe on the loose in the West, moved about considerably. James Cowan, who along with his brother farmed in the Close Colony in the 1880s and then raised horses in Wyoming, wrote his parents from Rawlins 2 Nov. 1885: "A fellow called Graham I took a great fancy to. I have never met a fellow I fancied so much on such a short acquaintance . . . has a good deal of money . . . a ranch in New Mexico. He's only 27 but a most perfect gentleman and the quietest, nicest mannered fellow I have ever met, I think, awfully well up in everything and awfully good company, quite a contrast to most of the Iowa crowd."[9] The following year in August Robert Graham visited the Close Colony again and participated on the losing side of a cricket match. By that time his New Mexico ranch venture may have ended; California beckoned.

He never made a spectacular success of any one thing; his fate was to live many wandering years away from Scotland. His estrangement cannot be attributed to the sheer distance in miles he lived from his Highland home; he could have afforded more frequent trips had he cared to make them. In contrast to the lowly steerage-class emigrant, forced by necessity to cut a new way, hoping for a better future for self and family and no easy out once the decision was made, the gentleman emigrant had vaguer shorings. After a privileged childhood, now cast upon the world, he knew a bit too much about how society worked, but this knowledge was of little consequence as he attempted to establish a place for himself in alien surroundings. Social forces, not economic necessity, had ejected him from the parental fold. He could never be sure that the eviction had been absolutely necessary, and it took a strong character indeed not to become embittered by the experience. Victorian parents tried to manipulate the destinies of their often too numerous male offspring by setting a scenario dictated by social custom — putting faith in the system. To a son's eyes this eagerness to conform sometimes appeared to contradict professed parental love. It was as if his parents were saying: we love you and have high hopes for your welfare and success, therefore you must live your life thousands of miles from all you know and those you love. You may only come back when you have earned your new place and your presence can be adequately explained. If you are truly manly, as we hope, you will not object to any of these conditions.

When Robert Graham married his California landlady (of the rooming house where he lived) in 1902, he brought his bride home to Scotland to meet his relatives. By that time both parents were dead. It was to be his last visit home, for now "it would seem that Robert . . . had definitely adopted America as his country. But life there has always worn the strangeness of exile to one whose heart is rooted in the old associations and the old remembered places," according to a family historian, who could not conceive of one member of the Maxtone Graham clan turning his life so resolutely away from the "old associations."[10]

Robert sired one son, Robin, who when last heard from was a taxi driver and proprietor of a garage in Albany, California.

William B. Close as a child.

William B. Close, student at
Cambridge University, ca. 1875.

William B. Close (*back row, second from left*), captain of the Cambridge crew, and crew, 1876.

(*left*) William B. Close, Iowa period.

(*right*) William B. Close, ca. 1920

(*bottom*) Close family house, interior, Antibes, France.

(*left*) Frederic B. Close as a child.

(*right*) Frederic B. Close, Iowa period.

(*lower left*) Frederic B. Close, 1890, shortly before his death.

Margaret Humble, ca. 1881

(*lower left*) Eric Gordon.

(*lower right*) Margaret
Humble Close Gordon,
ca. 1890s.

Margaret Humble Close Gordon,
ca. 1890s.

James B. Close, Iowa period.

Margaret Humble Close Gordon,
June, 1898.

James and Susan
Close's home,
England.

The three surviving
Close brothers: Wil-
liam, James, John,
and Arthur Close-
Brooks, 1907.

CHAPTER FIVE

Landed Gentry in the Making

ECAUSE of William Close's promotion of the colony during the winter of 1878–1879, "northwestern Iowa became far more familiar to the politer British ear than it ever had been to the American," according to *Macmillan's* magazine.[1] One reason for his success was his understanding of the aspirations of the upper middle class, since he came from much the same background himself and was aware of the plight of younger sons of gentlemen.

No youth emigrating to Iowa to become an apprentice farmer or a land-owner would climb a notch higher in social position, but William Close made it possible for them to emigrate without compromising their social standing. Therefore he primarily appealed to modestly situated gentlemen, especially clergymen, who were already existing on fairly small inheritances, whose families were frequently large, and whose sons were almost as full of the devil as their fathers were full of God. In the normal course of things these boys might eventually come into an income of only a few hundred pounds a year and were expected to augment it by taking up a socially respectable occupation—the armed services, the church, or civil service. They couldn't afford to marry unless their fiancées possessed incomes of their own. Young bachelors moved about on the good network of railroads to country houses throughout the kingdom and back to London clubs, aimlessly pursuing leisure. This idleness would be beautifully offset by a rugged sojourn in the West of the United States, or by army service in India, or in some other testing place where a boy could become a man by enduring trials of fire of one sort or another—which would build character and toughen moral fiber.

Fathers of such lads saw William Close as an attractive model to emulate. He was a famous rowing "Blue" of Cambridge, whose feats on the river were widely known at a time when the mania for sports was reaching its height. Outstanding oarsmen became public personalities, written up in special magazines such as *Oarsman's Companion* and *Rowing Almanac,* complete with steel-engraving illustrations. The concept of modern athletic contests and sports journalism came into its own during this period in Victorian England. Among athletes, oarsmen were especially esteemed. The rigorous training produced physiques impressively manly—what a true gentleman should look like. Bodily good health was easily equated with moral strength, for Charles Kingsley's "muscular Christianity" was very much in vogue.[2] William's role as a

Sunday school Bible class teacher and occasional preacher in the Denison Episcopal Church made his credentials even better. True, he was "in business," but
like his father, William found nothing incompatible about being a gentleman
and earning an honest living. Get-up-and-go was increasingly viewed as an
attractive attribute, honorable in anyone. William's mother told her children
that their father never tried to circulate among those "who fancy they belong to
a superior class in the social scale." He had too much self-respect to allow
himself to be patronized by such persons — "a pride which rebels at the idea, or
fashion, that because a man is a merchant, or engaged in trade, he is not fit for
the best society in the world."[3] But William knew he could promote his colony
among those who still adhered to the old class prejudices.

The prospective life of a young British landowner in Iowa, which William
described to his clients, seemed of a piece with traditional gentry concerns.
Owners of farm property the world over were always held in high esteem, and
this would surely apply to America as well. A youth might establish a base
quite easily, acquire several thousand acres if he wished, provided he came to
learn something of how to run a stock farm and supervise overseers. The young
squire's removal to Iowa need not be permanent; once the ranch was established, he could return to enjoy the London season or shooting and hunting
on country estates and all the other pastimes to which he was accustomed —
where he would meet his friends. William did not present quite such a frivo-
lous interpretation of the proposed emigration, but many of his clients saw it
that way. Iowa was only twelve to fourteen days away; a good number of young
Britons never forgot that. With money to travel, some of them returned home
almost every winter. One boasted of having made sixty-five trips across the
Atlantic in the course of a decade.

Any thought of entering a young man in agriculture at home (should land
or a situation be available) was largely out of the question, given the dire state
of British agriculture from 1875 to 1885. The cumulative effects of a policy of
free trade in agriculture resulted in low prices for crops, and the shift from
hand labor to machines meant an oversupply of help and general rural unrest.
Added to this, terrible weather: in the wet year, 1879, England had a mean
temperature below the thirty-eight year average for all months including summer. Crops did not mature — there were heavy frosts as late as the end of
March. The year 1880 was almost as bad, with a rainy summer, floods, and
deep snow in winter; and 1882 was known as "the sunless summer."[4] As a
consequence, Iowa as described by William Close in *Farming in North-Western
Iowa* seemed like paradise. The thirty-two page brochure was printed in Manchester and distributed by the thousands.

The colony was intended "to combine Western farming with some English
society. . . . " Close Brothers would attend to every detail of arrival arrangements, inspection of lands, or investment capital for a small commission. "We

have also arranged with a number of farmers in our neighborhood, with any one of whom a new-comer, by paying for board and lodging . . . could stay until he had made up his mind whether the country and mode of life would suit him or not. Or, if he should be totally inexperienced, we would help him to find a stock farm, where, if he makes himself sufficiently useful, he will be boarded and lodged in exchange for his work, and in time perhaps get wages; thus he could, before laying out his money, get a practical insight into farming."

Close Brothers promised to advise on choice of lands, verify land titles, and arrange the best terms for breaking and building construction. A minimum of £1,000 ($5,000) was required of all who wished to belong to the colony, and Close Brothers' commission was 5 percent. Before leaving England for the colony, £25 must be deposited to be refunded if the emigrant was dissatisfied with what he found. And should a young man wish to become a pupil on one of the Close brothers' personal stock farms, the fee would be £100 ($500) per year, but that sum also included the commission on property the client might later buy through the Close organization.

In Canada, before the decade of the 1870s, a number of retired British army officers and other socially acceptable gentlemen enjoyed a pioneer life that involved a little farming and a great deal of hunting and fishing. Once settled, they sometimes took in paying youngsters of proper background who wanted to learn about frontier life before deciding to settle permanently. This "pupil" idea, which the Close Colony developed so extensively, had been in practice for some time and opportunities to "go out" circulated in the English public schools. Even the fee — £100 per year — was a figure that William Close must have taken into account as the going rate.

In his brochure William tried to strike a truthful tone and yet make the venture sound attractive. The colony region, while largely unsettled, had many of the advantages of civilization, a climate that was "particularly healthy," adequate rainfall, winter cold that was very dry, "very little snow," and summers that "those who do not like much heat may not like . . . but, again, it is a dry heat, and not oppressive." In fact, winter usually brought a lot of snow and Iowa summers were typically high in humidity and temperature, excellent for growing corn.

He explained why such superior land happened to be available: speculators held it at artificially high prices, and grasshopper plagues, now a thing of the past, scared off settlers. Drawing upon geological surveys, he described the soil of the Missouri River watershed, which he compared favorably with that of the Rhineland. "It does not 'bake' or 'crack' in dry seasons . . . it stands unchanged in form when exposed to the weather. Wells dug in it require to be walled only to a point just above the water line, while the remainder stands so securely without support of any kind that spade marks remain visible for years."

This sort of personally observed detail made his pamphlet very convincing.

He doesn't mention the infamous bogs, into which he had fallen so often, claiming "the roads are uniformly good." Any kind of crop, especially corn and wheat, could be grown, but the raising of sheep, cattle, and hogs might be the principal aim. He described how he and his brother built a stock herd, the use of open prairie for grazing, and how quickly profits could be realized on hogs. Tables of statistics showed a typical three-year period of hog and cattle production (more years than the Closes had been in the farming business). The most attractive aspect of the pamphlet was its succinct yet comprehensive coverage of the whole subject, with sections on "Breaking," "Western Farming," "Agricultural Productions of the State of Iowa," "Fuel," "Educational Advantages," "Laws," the system of land surveys, an accurate diagram of the farmhouse Close Brothers would build, markets, railroads, domestic servants ("there is always a demand"), medical help, and sport. It ended with "Our Experience in North-Western Iowa," which supplied exact financial information and quietly stressed the enormous returns that the Closes found could be as high as 54 percent on investment in a single year.

Surely any smart, well-educated young Englishman could learn about American rural matters quickly. William Close himself had no farming experience prior to the Iowa venture, as he made clear. If *he* could do it, why not anybody? He used this pitch to the gentleman's code adroitly, flattering his readers that their good sense would always serve them well. Farming in the West was often carried out in a crude manner, with little attention to soil conservation, "but good farming always pays; and an Englishman, who knows how to combine some of his old country farming with the best points of American farming, will easily double the average yield, and must turn out a successful man." Testimonials from early colonists helped sell the message. This opportunity ought to be seized now, since lands were becoming more expensive and settlers from other countries were moving in fast. Going out would cost from seventy-five to ninety-five dollars by first-class steamer and train, or sixty-five dollars by intermediate class. Late winter was the ideal time for emigrating since breaking began in spring and a newcomer should be somewhat familar with the region by then.

WILLIAM'S brochure was distributed widely in the spring of 1879 and new print runs were ordered. During the summer he returned to Iowa to oversee improvements on his wonderful new farm on the West Fork and to check on his and Fred's stock farm near Denison. He had been separated from his fiancée for half a year; now visits to Quincy were part of his busy schedule. His Plymouth County stock farm was not yet a suitable home for a man to bring his bride. Given William's need to travel constantly to promote Close Brothers, a home there might not be feasible; nor would it seem a suitable setting for Mary, at least until more colonists arrived with wives to create a decent society.

By September he was ready to return to England, this time with Mary along, her brother Ed, the youngest boy Bert, and Mary's sister Ada. It was not a happy trip. Serious disagreements arose between William and Mary when they reached London. She ran up bills amounting to £350 ($1,750)—an extravagant sum in a very short time. Whether this excessive spending was a symptom of the stress between them or a cause of it cannot be known, but suddenly Mary broke off the engagement and returned to Quincy. William wrote his brother regarding the financial aspect of the rupture: "Also, there were a great many expenses connected with Miss Paullin, which rather than that she should leave unpaid, I paid through Ed Paullin. She does not know I paid them, Ed simply telling her he had the money. *She must not know I have paid them. . . .* Ed has signed a note for himself and his father, which I don't think is worth much legally."[5]

The second blow also stemmed from the Paullin quarter. William received word from Quincy that Daniel Paullin had suffered a severe accident, incapacitating him. Since he could not tend to his affairs, he would not be able to come up with his portion of the cash due William on 1 October, which William had expected in order to make the final payment on the Bloodgood lands. This news couldn't have come at a worse time. Close Brothers was geared to swing into full operation, with James in place in Le Mars, William in England scouting up likely prospects, and Fred serving as farm manager and agricultural adviser (though he was not yet a partner in the firm). The home base for Close Brothers, Limited, at the moment was John's house in Manchester. From there William wrote a series of letters to James, giving him advice, informing him of business activities on the European end. He also had the unpleasant task of making Mr. Bloodgood aware of his financial predicament. "Will it be convenient for you to grant an extension of the payment to the 1st of January next?" He posted a similar message to Edmund Stanton, husband of the other owner: "My inability to meet my notes arises from being disappointed by the Messrs. Paullin not having been able to pay me for about 4,000 acres of the lands." He tried to sound businesslike, explaining that as soon as he knew of Mr. Paullin's injury he wrote to Bloodgood, but embarrassment shines through the sentences. Such excuses were commonplace and no substitute for faithful payment on time.

A month later, in a tone of frustration and anxiety, William wrote to Robert Maxtone Graham in the Le Mars office, informing him of prospective farm pupils he had signed up. All colonists should pool their wisdom and indicate how the pamphlet, due at the publishers for another printing soon, might be improved. More testimonials should be included, fresh witnesses to the virtues of Iowa, back-up comments verifying the facts set forth, all complete with names and addresses in case anyone wished to check. It was good to hear the railroad had reduced rates for colonists. "Most of the fellows want to pass by Niagara Falls," which suggests the half-touring nature of the Iowa emigration for many of them. If through his personal contacts Graham inveigled a lad to emigrate, William thought he ought to get a commission.

At this time the choice Iowa property in William's mind was the shore of Spirit Lake, eighty miles north of Le Mars on the Minnesota border. John Close first aroused this interest by ordering the purchase of lands for himself there. "I am just telegraphing to stop the purchase for John of Spirit Lake," William wrote Robert Graham. "He can't go the whole hog. It is such a good thing that we ought to try and swing it ourselves. Everyone wants to go to Spirit Lake. Can't we swing it ourselves? You, Jim [James Close], Court [Roylance Court, Jr.], and I? I can take 2½ sections and probably get more to join here. I shall wait three weeks & if you can't take it, shall go on selling it, unless you telegraph that you will take it." He knew John was only interested in the lakeside property for speculative reasons and would never actually go there to live. This gave William a moral right to see that bona fide residents were not denied the splendid opportunity. A lakeside ranch, with plenty of rowing and sailing, seemed an ideal place to combine business with pleasure. He envisioned a home there for himself, though at the moment no bride was with him in the picture. William did not scrutinize his feelings regarding the two sorts of land buyers—the speculators and the settlers. And yet when the issue arose over the Spirit Lake tracts, he had no compunction about outmaneuvering his brother John's merely business interest, since he and his friends were contemplating homes there and a community. "It would be very nice to have headquarters there. You have no idea how the lakes take in people's mind." Obviously, the lake areas were more attractive than the flat prairie. But in the end Graham did not communicate an interest in buying.

During the fall of 1879 young men from England began arriving in Le Mars to become part of the colony; by December one newspaper reported that "Le Mars is beginning to look like London."[6] But for William the threat of financial disaster still loomed. If Paullin hadn't been able to come up with the coin by 1 October, why expect him to pay three months later? William wrote Paullin asking if he should try to get a mortgage on his own to raise the needed cash—an idea clogged with emotion and illogic. Why should William mortgage his lands when Paullin might do the same and take care of the problem? It was fairly certain that neither could get mortgage money from the Bloodgood lands, the title being too unclear at the moment. The matter was further complicated by William's painful awareness that James and Fred had put their own money into the deal. "I must free James and Fred at any cost. It is not fair to keep them from disposing of their lands. James wants to sell and is powerless to do so." Perhaps it would be best if Paullin wrote directly to James in Le Mars and sought the opinion of the firm's attorney; or William might try to dispose of the Paullin part of the lands for about $3.25 an acre, which would reflect a tidy profit over the purchase price. "Are you willing to let them go at that? Please answer by return."

Then he wrote to James in Le Mars: "Ed Paullin, his sister, and the rest start today." Ed expected to be put to work by Close Brothers, overseeing breakers and supervising improvements of farms. "I spoke very plainly, there must be no underhand work...also told him that you had no confidence in Henry [Paullin] at all, and told him what Henry had done." If James felt uneasy about entrusting Ed with a major assignment he might say: " 'Here's a job for you. Improve these 5,000 acres and you'll have so much cash down for your trouble.' " Ed's help might be needed if their whole enterprise began to boom. "I'm afraid you will not get on with Ned—you can yet try." Ed and Henry Paullin hoped to start a stock farm. "Would I send him boarders," Ed had asked. William, anticipating this request would not go down well with his brother James, added: "perhaps we could chance a premium and divide with him," allowing Ed a few boarders but splitting the fee charged.

Whatever unfair pressures the Paullins were bringing to bear on William, Edward and Henry were bent on becoming stock farmers in Iowa. For them even the question of clear title was not so important—if it could be settled eventually—for they were not planning to sell their land immediately, as were the Closes; they were true settlers. They even managed to lure a railroad to their part of the prairie a few years later, and the town of Paullina, Iowa, was named after them.

William flung himself into his work in order to stop brooding over his painful breach with Mary Paullin. Letters to and from America would cross, leaving questions unanswered; maps and leases shuttled back and forth in a somewhat chaotic manner. William criticized James's imprecise handling of business affairs, but by wildly firing off orders, suggestions, and queries, he only caused his brother bewilderment. "You say acting on orders you have bought 100 head of cattle and they are disporting themselves at the farm. Are those for my tenants or are they ours or whose?" And James went ahead and purchased land for a client whom William said was only tempted. "He does not bite; however, you can easily turn that farm on to someone else." The lag between orders and executions was frustrating. "My telegram to you was *Acheter blé,* which latter is French for Buy wheat," but somehow James got the idea his brother was ordering 26 lots of city property. Too late to do much about it. "Surely I have money to buy 26 plots if you have bought it," and he would simply unload them quickly on someone else. The confusion arose because William used personal funds for portions of his investments, yet at other times transactions involved the capital of the firm. James was expected to handle

William's personal business affairs, in addition to the company's, and to see to the operation of William's stock farm—or arrange for Graham or someone to manage it.

William urged James to invest further cash toward enlarging his own stock farm to justify the $500 fee charged a boarder for becoming an apprentice. The pupil or so-called pup should feel he was receiving a broad farming experience. If these lodgers (who after all didn't see much of the Closes) became dissatisfied with their situation, word might spread back home. Graham could attend to the expansion, and the lawyer should be engaged on all leases and legal matters. "Play the people and the companies off against each other and get rattling low prices."

Plenty to do—William was so busy he didn't have time to brood over his disappointing love life, nor did he contemplate an early return to America. "Thanks old chap about what you say about not going out. I don't know if I could stand it when she is so near." James was asked to look out for the youngest Paullin boy, of whom William was very fond. "Bert I particularly wish you should use as if he were my brother. He is a sound little chap and if not spoilt will turn out well."

William put up at Trinity College, Cambridge (his old college), for about two weeks in mid-November 1879 and found himself in proximity to a number of likely emigrants. One successful catch usually landed another, for a youngster going out to Iowa desired company. "I don't think I shall lecture as I am afraid I would make a botch of it—we Closes are not oratorically gifted by nature." Ostensibly, his reason for being at Cambridge was to coach the rowing crew. "Of course by coaching the trials I keep myself before the fellows." He mailed information on his colony to every member of the varsity and interviewed thirty or forty undergraduates. In his enthusiasm he went a little too far and sent a circular to "every clergyman in the Kingdom," giving his address as Trinity College; subsequently, he began receiving forty to fifty letters a day. "I got into hot water with the Master of Trinity for dating it there and had to see him." But the Close charm worked. "He said I had behaved very handsomely and he was glad to have made my acquaintance."

He definitely netted nine pups and "at least ten who are negotiating with parents. . . . At all events we are now very fully known in Cambridge and for years have a good accounting around there." Meanwhile, his letter to the London *Times* about farming in Iowa had been reprinted "in hundreds of papers & receive daily many letters from farmers, etc." Business was so lively that William commissioned agents to help, among them Henry Garnett of Wyreside, Lancaster, whose son Gerald had departed for Iowa in October. William instructed Garnett to insert notices about the colony in various newspapers. "I've had them printed to save the trouble of writing a number out. . . . In your reply to the applicants for information, send them a pamphlet and a line saying: 'Mr. W. B. Close has left this neighborhood (quite correct) and has requested me to make a list of those who'd like a personal interview and when. He will return before long and see you.' Words to that effect."

Should Henry Garnett turn up a young man who actually emigrated to become a pup, paying £25 ($125.00), the commission due would be £2.10s. ($12.50). "The commission is not to be paid until the man pays us the £25." These meagre money considerations seemed hardly worth making a fuss over, either by William or Garnett. But by paying attention to even the smallest of financial matters, William hoped to establish his credibility as a good business-man. Much larger sums would be due Henry Garnett if he were instrumental in finding British capital for Iowa land investment, "10% on our net profits for a term of years we have not yet fixed."

The Garnett ranch a dozen or so miles west of Le Mars became a popular hangout for the young British during the next four years, for Gerald was a leading sportsman in the colony, vice president of the Prairie Club, prominent in all activities. Meanwhile, in England, his older brother Robert, educated at Cheltenham (as was Gerald), married a gentleman's daughter in 1880 and came to enjoy the privileges of the primogeniture system. In due time he inherited a large portion of the Garnett family fortune, became squire of a manor in Yorkshire, and served as magistrate for Lancashire and the West Riding. Both sons followed their father's plans designed to assure they were well set up in life.

WHILE Close Brothers was still a fledgling company, William chanced upon a potentially large client. Richard Sykes of Manchester, an acquaintance of John Close, expressed interest in buying several thousand acres. William knew enough about Sykes's resources to realize he was a serious prospect. The only extensive Close-owned land available at this time was the Bloodgood-Stanton acres, and William instructed James to proceed with documents of transfer. He wrote Richard Sykes that the land, with the cost of breaking included, would come to $27.50 an acre (a steep markup, since the Closes' paid about $5.00 including breaking). The sale would be "null and void if we cannot provide you a good title in four months."

Naturally, this seemed odd to Sykes. William tried to clarify: "I do not for a moment think there would be the least trouble about your title, but acting as agent I want to be very careful, and the reason I put the clause of four months is that supposing you were unhappily for all your friends, to retire to a better world," and in such a case Sykes's executor could not press Close Brothers for damages. It was all really a very small consideration, "for it is only a question, whether Mr. Paullin pays up by January 1 or not. If he does not, I have the power to seize his lands at once, but I do not want to hurry him if possible, as his capital is somewhat locked up." It isn't hard to imagine what a shrewd Manchester businessman thought of this ingenuous line of argument.

Part of the problem was that Close Brothers was undercapitalized. Fred, still not in the firm, was involved with a potentially rival land office company operating along similar lines and headed by a man named Plaice, whom James and William regarded as fishy indeed. They hoped soon to bring their brother around. But how solve the problem of insufficient cash in the organization? William thought the time had come to go beyond the family and felt perfectly comfortable taking a partner who hailed from the university brotherhood of oarsmen. Twenty-seven-year-old Constantine Benson, son of a Lancashire merchant, had gone to Eton and Cambridge and was a rowing "Blue" in 1872. He possessed many of the physical and intellectual attributes of William himself, moved in similar circles, and would be effective promoting Close Brothers. "I took the bold step," William told James, "of saying that if he came out to us, we would take him in partnership with us, provided he could command £15,000 [$75,000] to invest with the firm." With such an infusion, the company could move grandly with the land market and proceed with the large design William had in mind. "I told Ben you must ratify my proposals—but without hesitation I would accept him, and with Ginger we should be enough. I hope he elects to go out." Benson would of course want to visit Iowa before deciding. And in a postscript: "I suppose Fred will see the error of his ways and join with us, but he must give us undivided attention to the business."

Sykes continued his inquiries, perhaps sensing a chance to profit handsomely if he could manipulate the twenty-six-year-old, inexperienced William. "By enclosed letter from Sykes, you will see he means to go it big and actually talks of 11,000 acres to his own tune. Find out the best you can for him, for say about £15,000 [$75,000] worth, and let me know particulars. . . ." The farms Sykes already owned that the Closes now managed were to be rented out on half-shares for 1880, "and he wants nice groves and orchards of apples. If you have rented his farms, try and make fresh leases." But how could James suddenly furnish fruit orchards? James is merely expected to take care of all contingencies, including management of William's Crawford County farm, which he now owns separately, having disengaged from partnership with Fred. "Also, I have no objection to renting my farms for half shares again, if the tenants like it, and you can provide wheat for all my new farms. I suppose no hoppers have laid their eggs." How exasperating for James to receive such orders and queries! William felt compelled to unload all his anxieties and transfer as many problems as possible to his older brother in Iowa. It helped relieve the pressure of his solitary course.

William also had a suitable domestic couple ready to sail; the husband could be farm manager for someone, the wife housekeeper. She was "young, lively, good-looking and ladylike, yet plucky and full of work and go." When James failed to respond to the possible services of this pair, William sent them out anyhow. "She and her husband cannot wait longer, as they cannot live. I am sure she will be most useful and is experienced. Lots of our pups will be only too glad to snatch them up." They embarked with Aimee de Pledge of Gloucester, who planned to housekeep for her brother Guy, already a prominent colonist. Soon after arrival she met the son of an Irish baronet, Montague J. Chapman, Oxford graduate, and they were married the following year.

William envied the excitement of these young people "going out" and still doted on the Spirit Lake site, which might make a fashionable "Saratoga of the West." He told James, "I want only one improved farm and it must be either *on* the lake, Spirit or Okoboji, or very near it. I may want to make it my home in the future." But with whom and under what circumstances, he could not foresee at the moment. "I'm gradually giving up the idea of returning next spring, as I expect to be far too useful here."

Inquiries regarding the colony were pouring in daily. Several railroads had gotten in in touch with James to ask if Close Brothers might act as their agents. It might look all right in Iowa, but William worried that a British investor might be suspicious of collusion over prices; "people here may think we're acting for the railroad," whereas they were committed to look out for the welfare of the settlers. The Sioux City and St. Paul line offered their disposable lands to the Close organization for $12.50 an acre, which could be resold for enough profit to make it worthwhile. The east-west line from Sioux City to Chicago offered their lands at $25.00 per acre, ridiculously high. "Write very strongly about it . . . explain the advantage of having good English farmers in the neighborhood." All of these maneuverings with railroad agents made William nervous about the reputation of Close Brothers. Their credibility with prospective pups and land investors might suffer, for rumors abounded regarding speculators who played both sides against the other. "I have come to the conclusion that we must not make anything on the railway side but act entirely for the pup. What we make from the railroad we must give the pup the benefit of. This is the important thing." A remarkably honorable private stance to take in the era of robber barons!

Constantine Benson visited Iowa and seemed about to join the firm as a partner. Perhaps he could be most effectively used as the partner solely responsible for shipping interests. "Think what a lot of earth our pups and ourselves will have in a year or two, besides wheat, flax, etc. No one could be better connected with what we want than Ben." His uncle was one of Liverpool's largest cattle importers. "Not only would we ship over our produce, but we would turn into shipping commission agents for others." Benson's Manchester friends were expected to buy a shipload of live fat cattle from America the coming spring, and if it worked successfully, more orders would be forthcoming. However, the exact terms under which Benson would enter the Close partnership were still to be determined.

More and more pups expressed interest in training on one of the Close personal farms, and what seemed to be evolving was an agricultural school on the plains. Instead of deferring to James's concern about the maximum number of pupils the Closes could accommodate, William replied, "you will have to build dormitories." Every young man should be urged to "write his impression of the country and of the people, say a fortnight after arrival." Furthermore, one of them might send a dispatch to the *Field* magazine describing the shooting, fishing, "any blessed thing that will keep us before the public — not forgetting to mention us, say he dates: 'With the Close's, N.W. Iowa.' "

James had been plagued with ill health, which worried William but did not stop him from issuing commands and insisting on prompt answers to questions. "Try not to overwork, old chap. Use others. If you cave in there will be the devil to pay." Orders were coming in nicely: £1,000 ($5,000) from a Cambridge professor and another £350 ($1,750) from William's Cambridge agent, who was scouting for pups and clients.

As the first of the year approached, James reported that Daniel Paullin still could not come up with the cash. William proposed "cutting adrift from him, pay for the lands ourselves and pay him for the improvements...give him a bonus of say 50¢ an acre for the good lands and nothing for the bad lands." Some settlement had to be reached over the breaking already done and Paullin's expense accomplishing it. "My first duty is toward you and Fred. I cannot allow you two to be hampered in the way he has been doing." By now William had hardened his thoughts concerning the Paullins. If James deducted the loan William made to cover Mary's European expenses from the profits Paullin would realize in disposing of the Bloodgood lands, "I think Paullin is sure to go to law and try to bluff you. Never mind that, but see he has sufficient bonds for court and no men of straw."

Part of William's new stern stance reflected his reaction to James's disgust. "Yes, of course, you have a perfect right to have your lands freed....I have no intention that you should take any risk in the Paullin-Bloodgood matter....I don't want you to have any dealings with him, unless you see it is to your advantage. Break with him if you like. It is useless my trying to control your activities."

By now William was probably able to scrape together the total owed Bloodgood and Mrs. Stanton. Although disabused of the Paullins, William could not resist chiding James for his remark about Bert Paullin, which he found "most unwarrantable and unjust: 'Sooner or later blood and gene must show itself.' It is a horrible thing to say of anyone." Particularly because the snide comment would have to include Mary Paullin, with whom William was still in love.

With such a profusion of requests, leases shuttling back and forth across the Atlantic, James would have done well to answer William line by line and keep an exact record. Ordinary laborers and farmers with little capital were writing Close Brothers in England by the hundreds, but could anything be done for them? And what about "helps"? Were servant girls needed? And what would be the rent in Le Mars for a house for a certain period? How much did food cost and "how many cubic feet go to a ton of hay?" Since farm laborers received 15*s*. ($3.75) a week in England, would they do better in Iowa — or was the labor situation taken care of by the pups, who provided so many extra hands for a farmer? How about married couples with experience in stock raising; if such couples with little money were sent out, could they be placed? William begged James to please answer — at once. Properly executed deeds should be sent forthwith, since the new owners were anxious; ditto, all leases, accurately set down. At the same time James should not "do chores, and don't tire yourself. Let Fred have the surveying department to do; you keep cool and direct. Use others."

Fred finally and definitely decided to join Close Brothers, though a few disputes about commissions remained to be settled. And, another excellent turn of furtune occurred: the Close siblings won a lawsuit involving the settlement of their inheritance. "It was a near go. How lucky I was in England." Now there would be more capital for all of them soon. William wrote to Fred on 10 December 1879:

> I heartily welcome you into our firm and am sure you will be most useful. When you and Jim discuss matters, remember not to try and thrust each other's opinions down each other's throats, and don't think each other fools because you don't agree. . . . Also, don't crow over each other when one of you is right, and for goodness sakes don't say "I told you so." Such things only breed disagreable incidents between you.
>
> Your affec. brother and partner
>
> Wm B. Close

William dispatched a brief note to John Bloodgood, informing him that by 1 January, "or a day or two after, I shall be able to meet my notes." Money was pouring in. His Cambridge scout had just turned up another investor with £600 ($3,000) to send to Iowa. No longer in a financial bind and free of the threatened collapse of Close Brothers because of Paullin's default, William wrote his former mentor. Communication was obviously painful, a mixture of business and emotion — and anguish over a friendship sullied. He explained why he had to act in a responsible, businesslike way, especially because of his partnership with his brothers.

> Ed has probably told you. . . I have paid all your daughter's expenses and debts and both their journey money. This comes up to over £350. I enclose the account. Of course, it would be right I should be paid this money back as soon as possible; therefore, I should keep that amount back out of the sum James and Fred may agree to pay you for improving the land, etc. I suppose you concur in this. I have told James in the utmost confidence about my having paid Miss Paullin's expenses, and you, he, and Edward are the only ones who know anything about it. I trust it will not go further, and the last one whom I should wish to know about the matter is Miss Paullin herself. You may understand why.

She is long ago with you, and I hope you find her much improved in health. I have no longer any right to allude to her by her Christian name and must accustom myself to speak and write of her as a stranger. In view of what has happened, I shall not return to Iowa, at least not for some time to come, until I shall be better able to remain with calmness in the same neighbourhood as herself. I am very glad that from present appearances, it seems that I shall have enough business to keep me occupied here.

William urged his brother James to be lenient in adjudicating the Paullin share of the coming settlement, allowing Paullin 5 percent for having "negotiated the purchase and shouldering the trouble of improvements. Remember in negotiating the purchase he saved us $4,000, for I should have been content to have taken $2.50, but D. P. stuck out for $2.25 and got it. [The price was actually $2.40 an acre.] I think $2,500 or $3,000 not too much. Then you are once for all home. No more dealings with them."

But such was not to be the case, for Ed Paullin kept trying to lure away pups that the Close organization had placed on other farms. "I am sorry you did not take my plain warning, *viz,* not to meddle with our pupils," William wrote Ed. Two particular young men he didn't mind giving over to Paullin, "although you had no right whatever to them and really should not have asked for them." Now Ed was asking for others. "Why are you so short-sighted? I speak to you as a brother, openly and plainly; answer me as such."

FIRST reactions from the colonists in Iowa ranged from dismay over the extremes of climate and general living conditions to foolish overenthusiasm, and both caused trouble for Close Brothers. An older emigrant, R. P. Kay, hated Iowa and quickly returned. "I hear Kay is back," William wrote James, "and...calls the country all the bad names he can....How stupid Mrs. Kay must be—she will ruin her husband...however. Remember, I am not urging the common farmers to go out, only pups go out now." The Kays' behaviour indicated that they were not the right sort for emigration. They should have taken the challenges of the new country in stride and triumphed over adverse circumstances. A year and a half later the *Field* reporter in Le Mars noted that "discomfort is laughed at, inconveniences chaffed at, and hardship ignored. Though much hard work is done, the picnic air pervades all of it, and the unfortunate who does not conduct himself honourably and in every respect like a gentleman is placed instantaneously in Coventry—Boycotted...."[7]

William got Kay to make amends for the damage he may have caused Close Brothers. In the next issue of *Farming in North-Western Iowa* Kay explained: "I must tell you that it was with great regret that I left Iowa. I only did so because Mrs. Kay could not settle there. It is, as you told me, rather rough for ladies." He praised the country for its cattle and sheep-raising potential, knowing of no better place "where a single man could find more profitable outlay for his capital and labour, and enjoy himself, particularly if he is fond of shooting...and if I was a bachelor would return there at once."

The pups of the first wave were beginning to show their mettle. Some liked the country, another was "a devil of a spy on everyone," James informed his brother. Robert Maxtone Graham continued to flourish—"I did not know that Bob was a pigeon shooter," William remarked. And using a phrase from rowing: "I am sorry Grayson proving weak at the first trials. He told me he would rough it any amount."

Serious damage to the firm's reputation could have been the result of young Alfred Shaw's excessive haste in wanting to buy land. "I say," William told James, "you must not be in such a hurry to advise young fellows like Shaw to invest. His people didn't like the telegram. Looks too much as if we hurried them.... Shaw is in the light of a son to you, and you are to look after him and restrain him."

In Liverpool William ran into Mr. Shaw, who was very much agitated that three days after the boy arrived in Le Mars he telegraphed for money on James Close's advice. "If a fellow wants to invest at once, let him write on his own account," but try to persuade him to hold off for a bit. Mr. Shaw had been talking angrily to his friends about this, annoyed also that his son spent £45 ($225) on the trip, when William said it could be done for £25 ($125). Now Mr. Shaw would not let his son buy even one farm, and yet William had heard that young Shaw did buy one. "Where does he get the coin from? Shall I write to his father and say...that we will reimburse him if he transfers it to one of the investors?" In the future the firm had better emphasize that it was arranging for young men to go to Iowa primarily for stock-farm experience, not so much to buy land, which was so highly speculative. Eight weeks ago Mr. Shaw had been talking of investing from $10,000 to $15,000, "and when I saw him last, he did not even mention the subject. I am afraid he is not pleased."

The role James should play was becoming clearer—at least to William. He was to judge the character of a young man; "you are to be somewhat in the light of a father...and look after their morals." He was to keep tabs on all of them. "Their money is placed with us, they draw on us; it is your business to see that it does not go too fast. In fact, you must look after these raw and inexperienced young men or boys." And if things weren't going right, "you must advise the parents...."

Among the early colonists, Roylance Court, Jr., of Newton Manor, Middlewich, Cheshire, seemed similar in calibre to Graham and Garnett, who were adjuncts to the Close Brothers staff. A number of pups were delegated upon arrival in Le Mars to go under "the Court plan"—he took special charge of them. Plat records show that Court and William Close owned land jointly, early on. But it was soon clear to James that Court was not working out, and he informed his brother. "One idle man will contaminate the whole lot," William replied. "You must speak to him and show him what a responsibility rests with him. I hear he and Shaw spend the day walking arm in arm. Shaw's father laid great stress on his being *made* to work." Threaten to have their money withheld, if they didn't cooperate. "Pupils are sent to us as much for our moral influence as for anything else." William had been telling parents that if a young man didn't work, he was shunned by others. Days were so well-regulated that the newest greenhorn had to get up early in the morning to feed the horses, whereas the more experienced enjoyed privileges. He was loosely borrowing Dr. Thomas Arnold's system at Rugby, the sixth formers being on top and the lower levels obliged to perform certain duties. "Also, we must not let our stock farms degenerate into rowdy places, but their character must be kept up. No swearing, drinking, and so on." Roylance Court, Jr., as it turned out, shaped up nicely. During 1880 and 1881 he virtually managed William's stock farm on the West Fork, then returned to England and became a barrister.

Some contemporary critics of the agricultural pupil system felt the $500 the Closes charged for tutelage by people like Court was much too high. William asked his brother if the pups thought their money was well spent, "or would they rather have saved £75 [$375] and gone onto some neighbouring farms?" In addition to James's in loco parentis role (which was an extension of William's tendency to take on parental obligations), were the Closes making good on promises? "The fellows are sent to us to drill and be well looked after. It delights the parents' hearts to be told that they are forced to work. They must be taught plowing, etc., and there must be no idling." But how to accomplish this aim? James couldn't be expected to run an agricultural school in addition to his other duties. Someone else would have to be found. Even some other *place* was needed, not the Close stock farms, which were located more than fifteen miles from Le Mars.

William found his solution in the person of Captain Reynolds Moreton, who had commanded a British warship for nine years and at forty-five was looking for a pleasant, challenging retirement. Moreton's first wife had died in 1865. The following year he remarried—a daughter of an Irish clergyman, whose seat was Dromore Castle, County Kerry. Reynolds Moreton was the fifth son of the second Earl of Ducie, a title dating only from 1837. When Captain Moreton settled in Le Mars, he was hailed in the press as coming from a family famous for its herds of purebred cattle.

In May 1880 Moreton purchased an improved farm overlooking Le Mars for the astonishingly high price of thirty-four dollars an acre. The site on which the buildings were located commanded a view of ten or more miles in most directions—a perfect place for the colony's major establishment. The enormous price tag sent ripples of land-fever excitement throughout the Northwest. Everyone, including the seller, was taken completely by surprise, for the asking figure was far out of keeping with the prevailing cost of land, and he "had no thought that he would be accepted."[8]

Captain Moreton must have realized that the proximity to Le Mars and the grandeur of the elevation made the property unique; by owning it he would immediately become the principal squire in the Close Colony. It was here on Dromore Farm that the Prairie Club came into existence on 1 December 1880. The first county telephone is believed to have been strung from Captain Moreton's home to the House of Lords tavern in Le Mars, so that the captain could keep tabs on his carousing pups.

Moreton immediately spent $20,000 to remodel the house, enlarging it to seventeen rooms; all the floors were solid oak planking. The handsome walnut staircase had a niche on the landing for a coal-oil lamp, and in the upstairs bedrooms, flat English-style wardrobe closets were built, with pegs for the pups to hang their clothes. The two-story clapboard structure had a mansard roof and several attractive bay windows. To enhance the setting, a large grove of elm, spruce, walnut, and various fruit trees was planted. The outbuildings were done over on a scale in keeping with the house: a sales pavilion and four barns — one for cattle and hogs, another for sheep, a third for horses, a fourth for polo ponies.[9] Captain Moreton imported Shropshire and Southdown sheep from Sussex, a strain that flourished and continues today on western ranches. British efforts to transplant livestock bloodlines came to be an important contribution to American agriculture. Their shorthorn cattle and Poland-China and Berkshire hogs, bringing high prices at the Sioux City and Chicago slaughter houses, convinced other settlers to stop thinking of wheat as their main product and to turn instead to livestock raising.[10]

Moreton fortunately had the services of a good superintendent to run the many departments of the farm. By February 1881 he had ten pups in residence, not merely to provide free labor; these young men were actually involved in agricultural training. They learned by doing and paid Captain Moreton, brother of an earl, for the privilege of boarding with him.

That first winter the Moretons lived on Dromore Farm, the weather was more severe than the Closes had prepared colonists to expect. It was one of the bitterest winters on record. But Moreton thought it fortunate in the long run that the initial winter of the colony's establishment should have been exceptionally severe, for by this lesson no newcomer would be fooled into taking inadequate precautions to protect livestock or have an insufficient quantity of feed on hand. "Let the lads always prepare for a long hard winter, and be thankful if it turns out a short and pleasant one." He was an amiable, imperturbable optimist, whose years as a sea captain sat easily; he enjoyed being in charge of young men.[11]

George du Maurier's cartoon in *Punch* on 12 November 1881 was thought to have been inspired by tales of life at Dromore Farm, where most of the pups were either sons of aristocrats or scions of well-placed families. Captain Moreton set a good table for his privileged boarders: English cooking in every respect, with home-cured hams and frequent legs of mutton. "We'll never forget the dinner bell," one guest recalled. "It hung at one end of the porch, and when the hostler rang it, it could be heard over the entire farm." At one point Moreton had twenty-two pups under his supervision. They slept in the small upstairs rooms referred to as "the dormitory." After dinner the first floor rooms were opened for billiards, chess, and cribbage, or one could browse through the latest British magazines and newspapers in the library.[12]

Portly, genial Captain Moreton looked the part of country squire and played his role with considerable zest. He was the moving force behind the agricultural fair of 1881 and personally canvassed for premiums to be awarded. "Let the farmers themselves now do their part. Prepare at once for a grand display, and let us show the world that Plymouth stands in the very front rank of agricultural counties." The county fair tradition, once established, became an annual event, and the competition for prizes was intended to enhance local farming efforts. Excellent show animals, along with splendid fruit, vegetable, and grain produce on display helped set the standards. Farmers could see for themselves what their neighbors were accomplishing and perhaps learn how to better their own production in the future.[13]

In the fall of 1881 a reporter visiting Dromore Farm found Moreton actively at work overseeing the laying of 350 feet of iron pipe from his new artesian well (the first to be dug in the region) to the boiler house. He drilled the well so as to be certain of a more steady, adequate supply of clean water than the shallow, surface wells could provide. The arrangements in his barns and sheds seemed very efficient, with double rows of stalls, wide aisles, and haylofts overhead within easy access. Four hundred feet of wood fencing enclosed the lots. Hay and straw stacks immediately behind the sheds provided a windbreak and shelter in blizzards. Of the ninety head of cattle, nine were blooded heifers and one a "magnificent full-blooded bull." Captain Moreton bought the area's first steam engine tractor, a ten-horsepower vehicle that "ran around the streets" of Le Mars for everyone to see, driven by Henry, the captain's twenty-two-year-old son. In succeeding years, Moreton's superintendent and Henry custom threshed for many of the neighbors with this machine. Five hundred bushels of wheat or oats could be threshed in a single morning. The steam engine was also useful in grinding livestock feed, which was cooked before being ladled out into troughs. Not only did his animals enjoy hot meals, they were also housed in barns at night, although life outside in the yards would make them "better sheltered...than most stock in this country."[14]

Captain Moreton, like a number of other officers in Her Majesty's service, displayed an evangelical streak, perhaps because military duty forced one to consider life and death. Moreton stepped to the pulpit whenever anyone asked him to, delivering sermons in the style of his American contemporary, the evangelist Dwight L. Moody. Sometimes in the local press he was called the Reverend Moreton. The captain himself furthered his ecclesiastical claims, but he may have been exaggerating when he said the Episcopal bishop of Iowa thought Moreton should be ordained pastor of the Le Mars church. He founded a YMCA by raising $1,500 in subscriptions among the colonists, all of whom could easily be persuaded that young pups needed a place of Christian atmosphere to offset the influence of the saloons. Moreton's Bible reading classes and religious discussions on topics such as "The Relation of the Church to the Second Coming of the Lord" were a regular weekly feature and well attended. His guest appearances in Congregational and Presbyterian pulpits drew wide followings. His spell-binding oration one Sunday afternoon attracted an overflow crowd, "one of the largest audiences ever assembled in the church." On 31 July 1882 he addressed parishioners on the subject of Daniel's character, "his determinedness, his standing by his 'No' when he said 'No,' " and mesmerized his listeners as surely as if Daniel actually stood before them. "How many Daniels are there in Le Mars, aye, in this congregation?" As his fame as an inspirational preacher spread, Moreton travelled great distances to fill a pulpit, his wife often accompanying him. Dromore Farm was often the scene of religious gatherings for young and old. One fine June day in 1881 wagons and carriages transported all the Congregational Sunday school children from church at 10 A.M. to the orchard Moreton had planted when he first arrived. Picnic tables were set under the trees; in addition to the lunch each child took along, the Moretons provided ice cream, lemonade, and cookies.[15]

With Fred and James Close moving about in connection with land purchases and William living mostly in England, Captain Moreton became the colony's nominal head. When correspondents from Europe or Poultney Bigelow writing for *Harper's* arrived in Le Mars, it was to Captain Moreton's they were sent. The *Field* reported: "Captain Moreton is a father to the Colony, a good religious man, with great influence over all the young fellows....these Moreton boys are taken specially good care of; but, of course, admission to the captain's establishment is not an easy matter to procure. His boys do all the work of the farm. Lord Hobart, when I was there, was mowing, assisted by two of Lord St. Vincent's sons, and the hon. captain was feeding a thrashing machine. It was hot, but everyone looked happy....And again the picnic aspect, despite the real hardship and remunerative work, struck me irresistibly." Lord Harris was expected to arrive soon, "to revive the highest standard of cricket."

Captain Moreton told the *Field* visitor that those who did not succeed in taking to life in Iowa, who had "breakdowns," were largely victims of excessive drinking habits and partakers of bad food. "No young English gentleman could work hard on a diet of beans and bacon, such as he gets in the house of the western American farmer. So the captain keeps a generous table, and his boys are certainly a credit to his system: clear-eyed, bronzed, and muscular, in the highest health and spirits. How much more sensible and useful lives they live here than they would do if at home!"[16]

Even the ultimate aim of this new life was boldly illustrated by Moreton's citizenship action. He took out naturalization papers in September 1882 and thereby decisively set an example of how to solve a problem that continued to haunt the gentlemen immigrants. Should they stay in this country? Why? Should they become American citizens and meld into the classless, egalitarian society here, when as offspring of British gentlemen they enjoyed a position in English circles, their names recognized—everything except livelihoods?[17]

CHAPTER SIX

Some Difficulties Surmounted

 N the early stages of Close Brothers, William attempted to make money on all aspects of the operation—tutorial fees, land-sale commissions, percentages on improving raw prairie, banking personal accounts, and farm management for British investors who never intended to become colonists. In the latter category, Richard Sykes, John Close's friend, was the biggest client and the most trouble. Sykes asked William for impossibly detailed information: when his land was to be broken, what buildings were to be erected, and where and exactly who would manage the farms, and how the half-share system worked. "You understand," William wrote James, "that he wants all rents on half-shares, so send estimates for amount of seed required, value & how much to be in what and how much in corn." A simpler way would have been a cash-rent agreement, so much per acre going to the landlord, the tenant making what he could on his own. Share-rent management of farm property for fussy clients like Sykes was simply not feasible for Close Brothers, although William was not yet aware of this.

Furthermore, Sykes was delinquent in paying. "As you have failed to pay in the money I am forced to decline to act as your agent in this purchase and have wired the facts to my brothers," since "they do not keep such sums as £1,200 ($6,000) idle to suit the convenience of clients." Almost by return mail Sykes sent £800 ($4,000), instructing Close Brothers to purchase land to that amount. "I am fast getting into a quarrel with Sykes," William wrote James. "He is most slippery." Sykes requested William to withdraw his statement that he would not act as agent. "I see nothing...to withdraw—that we can't buy land unless the money is paid up. He accuses us one and all of being most unbusinesslike, so for goodness sake hurry up and send his title deeds [for lands purchased already]....He complains much about that. I have him, though, on the hip. He alleges that he could not pay up for Spirit Lake because he was *too busy?* By the way, he says that his first investment through you was entirely in a philanthropical spirit to help a young man starting in the world."

Sykes also had to be made to understand that to purchase the choice Spirit Lake lands, he must agree to have Close Brothers improve them for the usual charges. If he were merely interested in buying lands for speculative purposes, holding them and then selling, some other tracts would have to be found. Because of these difficulties with Sykes, William began to clarify the difference

77

between a settler and a speculator—the former to receive prime consideration. "You are mistaken," William wrote Sykes, "in supposing that you are to have the whole list of lands before you and that you are to have your choice. All I promised was that as you and John had your names down first for anything that might turn up, James was to give you two the first choice for an improved farm, i.e., the two best improved farms to go to you and John respectively. The rest will be divided equally by James and Fred out there. It is perfectly impossible for me here to divide the lands." After receiving further infuriating notes from Sykes, William sent back the £800 check, "in order that if you were willing, we could start afresh with a proper understanding between us."

As it worked out, Sykes finally purchased about 30,000 acres in the extreme northwest corner of Iowa. Much of it had belonged to the Sioux City and St. Paul Railroad, which Close Brothers sold for them. By 1881 fifty breaking teams were at work creating quarter-section farms upon which the necessary buildings were erected. Sykes and his friend John Close arrived for a visit in the spring of that year—John's sole trip to Iowa. After the farms were ready to be worked, Sykes hired good overseers, and in this way he did not have to be in residence except during the nice weather. The Sykes home, "Larchwood" (later the name of the town), was one of the most impressive in the area. He enjoyed playing the grand seigneur with the local folks, and one Larchwood resident recalled the excitement in school when Mr. Sykes of Manchester, England, dropped by for a visit, passing out oranges and candies to the children, looking very grand and important as he strolled about the classroom. "I still possess a 'drawing slate' he brought me on one of those occasions, and some specimen beads from strings of 'Irish beads' he brought to my somewhat older schoolmates."[1]

Sykes's stock farms dealt principally in Galloway and Black Welsh cattle, his heifers and young bulls highly prized. By 1888 Sykes was selling some of his land on a ten-year term basis. He had gained the reputation of being a tough customer for anyone having business dealings with him. The widow of the Close Brothers' attorney had to go to court to wring legal fees out of him; it took her four years to secure a judgment of $1,500. When it became more profitable for Sykes to unload the higher-priced land on new settlers, he relinquished all of his Iowa holdings and by the turn of the century no longer had any connection with Middle West farming.

While clients like Sykes added greatly to Close Brothers' coffers, it was the colony itself that increasingly absorbed William's attention. How were the young lads doing? Did they like the country? James must continue to "be their advisor or mentor to whom they can turn for instruction, so that they are not cheated on arrival. . . . Of course, all extra expense, buggies and so on, they must pay, and lawyers' fees. Your principal work should be sitting in your office and dispensing advice." Had James made arrangements with the lumber companies, the furniture suppliers in Chicago, with the machinery people? "I have some 35 booked to sail in the next six weeks, and goodness knows how many are thinking about it." He had been working too hard. "Every night up to twelve or one o'clock and all Sunday." The total sum already paid in by clients came to over $100,000. "I feel very tired but can hold out until Con Benson returns [from Iowa]."

Mrs. Harriet Humble seemed like an ordinary parent-investor when she deposited a premium for her son, William, embarking from Liverpool 22 January 1880 aboard the *City of Richmond*. As a £25 pup, he was to be settled on some suitable farm in the colony. "He's a young, inoffensive smug of 18," William wrote James. Mrs. Humble was only recently widowed; her husband had been a large landowner in the Midlands, with several farms in Yorkshire, a hunting lodge in Scotland, plus "financial interests in the United States," according to his grandson. There were eight Humble children, four girls and four boys. One girl had married and was living in Wales, but the rest of the children's futures had to be somehow managed by Mrs. Humble. The attraction of the Iowa British colony was surely that her son William would come under the supervision of an older man—to make up for the lost father. Once the boy got settled in Iowa, he wrote lively letters home describing farm life, with the result that his sisters decided to visit, as well as Mrs. Humble. Since they were extremely attractive girls, they were immediately noticed in the colony and widely introduced. According to octogenarian T. J. Maxwell, once the groom of Fred Close, one day while out horseback riding Fred spied two of the Humble girls bathing in a stream. He was so struck by their beauty— particularly Margaret's—that he fell in love on the spot. However the romance started, it quickly became serious, and Fred married Margaret in the fall of 1881. The other sister, Susan, married James Close on Christmas Day, 1885, in Chicago. A third sister, Annie, married a later Close Brothers partner, Samuel Houghton Graves.[2]

With William Humble on board the *City of Richmond* was W. White Marsh, whom William characterized as a "gentleman son of a Rev'd, been sheep farming in Australia and wants to get onto a sheep farm." Marsh's brother, Arthur, and his wife shipped out a few months later, but instead of remaining in farming he became an ordained Episcopal minister, serving as rector in Blair, Nebraska. His son, upon graduation from the University of Nebraska, won a Rhodes Fellowship in 1905 and studied theology at Oxford. In this fashion the transplanted Englishman, Arthur Marsh, was able to follow the advice of *Blackwood's* magazine (March 1889): whereas a well-educated gentleman who had once known civilization and the stimulating company of congenial friends could live a rustic life for years, his offspring could not. "If an emigrant has children he ought to pinch to his last farthing to give his son an education in Great Britain." When young Marsh returned to Nebraska after Oxford he became vicar of St. Paul's in Omaha, but died in France in 1917, serving as chaplain with the American troops.[3]

The Honorable Henry Frank Sugden sailed a few days later than Humble and Marsh from Liverpool aboard the *City of Chester.* Sugden "intends to pick out a piece of land and improve it through our firm," William reported. How much he was to be charged William left to James; special consideration ought to be given because Sugden had been serving as a Close agent, receiving a £2.10s. commission on every pup he persuaded. "He takes two out with him to view the country."

Frank Sugden was the grandson of Lord St. Leonards, an eminent law reformer, sworn to the Privy Council in 1834 and created Baron St. Leonards in 1852, the birth year of the future British emigrant to Iowa. Frank's father was a clergyman, a second son who did not inherit the title. Frank had already spent considerable time on the southern Minnesota border as a sheep and cattle farmer. When the Close Colony formed, he endorsed William's prospectus, speaking from his Middle West experience. One year later, all set up on the West Fork near the Close stock farms, Sugden was heavily involved in raising sheep. In January 1881, 400 of them died, more than he had ever lost before, although in Minnesota he had carried as many as 3,000 sheep through a winter. His losses were attributed to inferior Missouri-bred sheep, which he'd purchased cheaply the previous fall. "He is satisfied that it is bad policy to bring sheep from the south to winter here," the local paper reported, "no matter how tempting the price may be at the time."[4]

A sister kept house for Frank, but in 1882 they decided to return to England; the whole Sugden establishment was put up for auction, "a large lot of horses, cattle, implements, and household goods." However, the following year the Sugdens were back and continued to play an important role in the colony. When Frank's father died in 1886, rumors spread throughout the English settlement that a new baron was in their midst. Miss Sugden sent word to the press that such was not the case. The confusion among the transplanted Britons perhaps arose because of the cause célèbre following the death of the first Lord St. Leonards in 1876, which some may have remembered. Frank's grandfather, author of the *Handy Book on Real Property Law,* was "one of the most learned real property lawyers who had ever sat on the bench," and there were eight codicils to the will, set down in precise, technical language, as if Lord St. Leonards in a parting shot would demonstrate what a brilliant attorney he had been. His grandson, offspring of the first-born male, inherited the title, but his daughter Charlotte, "a lady of great ability," who had "largely assisted her father in the preparation of his legal treatises," saw to it that her brother, the Reverend Frank Sugden, and herself were designated to receive the bulk of the estate. Naturally, the new baron protested. But Charlotte and her brother won the case. When the judge, Lord Brampton, died, the *Times* obituary referred to the suit: "It was probably the most singular instance in the annals of our law of the establishment of a lost instrument by secondary testimony," most of it accomplished "on the evidence of Miss Sugden." Although the Iowa Frank Sugden did not inherit the title upon the death of his clergy-man father in 1886, his financial situation was considerably changed for the better. Thus "Old Sug," as he was called, left Le Mars and returned to England.[5]

                                    THE colony would be attractive to settlers only if word of mouth were favorable, and William was distressed that a couple of brothers had complained about sleeping two to a bed. "With the premiums they pay, they must be provided with a bed each. Don't overwork them." Another wrote "a vicious and unwarranted letter. We don't wish any of this to get out. He says the country is not fit for darkies—the cold is awful. He runs down everything."

William was beginning to realize that some of the rambunctious young bachelors fresh from the public schools were not "taking" to rugged prairie life and needed the settling influence of solid, older married couples. These seasoned homesteaders would become the bulwark of the colony. "Capt. Mount Batten, with whom I am staying now, will probably go out next month [February]. He is sick of farming here and Madge is all on fire to go out—and would tomorrow if she could.... Looks like it is all not that ladies can't go out with their husbands, and the sooner we get some ladies with real go in them...the greater our colony will be. I can't see any objection to ladies as long as we can get a dozen...at a time and in one place." Spirit Lake might be settled with such English families; "we can soon get it a fashionable American watering place and make it a very paying concern by selling lots and building hotels." Captain J. C. Cooper and Mrs. Cooper, already Le Mars residents, were another stable couple, "having been a captain in the army, he's always a good reference"; furthermore, Cooper and Batten had served in the same battalion and were old friends. So was Capt. W. P. Bridson from Manchester, who booked passage soon after reading William's letter about the colony in a local newspaper. To this group of ex-service officers would be added Col. James Fenton and his wife, who initially requested Close Brothers to find an im-proved stock farm near Le Mars. "He has ten children and therefore must be near schools," but now "he would like to go to Spirit Lake." Another eminently suitable pair were Mr. and Mrs. W. McOran Campbell. He was thirty-three years old, son of a wealthy Scottish landowner who was magistrate for the counties Dumbarton and Lanark and Lord of the Barony of Tullichewan. These married gentlemen immigrants would "form a capital nucleus for your society [William says *your*, not *our*], and then by judiciously starting a small hotel we could make a lot of coin by making it *en ville de pleasance*. People coming back somewhat complain of the hotels. Why don't you run up some addition to your Le Mars establishment and make newcomers comfortable on their arrival?...You could charge a reasonable amount until the pups are stowed away. Men like Batten and Campbell it would pay to put up free and make reasonably comfortable."

The *Field* correspondent visiting Le Mars in the summer of 1881 found the hotels the worst feature of the "rising and stirring little town." Nothing even in West Texas or Nevada could rival the Le Mars hotels for "general discomfort and bad cooking." The only good to be said of them was that "the proprietors are very civil, and do not pretend to think they do the thing well, which is some mitigation of their offence."

In addition to his other duties, James was not to neglect the management of William's personal stock farm. "I shall invest all I can in sheep and stock. I want to have 3 or 4,000 pounds [$15,000–$20,000] in sheep and stock...reinvest all my seed [unused seed was to be sold] in my stock farm." Had James arranged to "sell my wheat as soon as there is demand for spent seed? Don't let it go too late, for the moment the demand for seed wheat is over, there is a fall in price. Will a bicycle be of any use to you to go from farm to farm? A man who is a good bicycle man wants to know. His name is Dalton." Obviously, William had totally forgotten the state of most Iowa roads or he would not have asked such a question. Bicycle or not, several Daltons emigrated and soon were highly visible in the colony—with a town west of Le Mars named after them.

The pressure William put on James also reflected his anxieties regarding the Paullins and pain over his broken engagement with Mary. Love and money were so intertwined he could not separate them, and the Paullins appeared to be aware of his vulnerability. Then a letter arrived from James with the surprising news that the Paullins had managed to scrape together the needed cash after all. They had saved their piece of the Bloodgood-Stanton lands, and now Ed was his old boasting, braggart self. He ridiculed the Close Brothers' purchase price for the Spirit Lake tracts, telling James that it could all have been bought for $8.75 an acre. William consoled his brother: "He only wanted to show you that you lost by not dealing through his father. He told all sorts of untruths in the same way" to several others. James would have to decide on the ownership assignment of the parcel, with the Paullins receiving title to acreages for which they actually put up cash. William took some satisfaction in specifying that along with other parcels, "the Paullins are to have...the worst 40 in S.E. of 24.89.43."

But William's bitterness evaporated when he received a different kind of Paullin communication—this one from Mary. The letter arrived in late February or early March, an epistle so winning and conciliatory that suddenly, as far as William was concerned, the courtship was fully restored, perhaps stronger than ever. Up to the moment he received Mary's letter, William stated no intention of returning to Iowa in the spring of 1880. He had all he could do managing the London end of Close Brothers. The suddenness of his change of plans suggests the depths of his feelings toward her, but just what brought about her change of heart long puzzled the Close family and aroused numerous suspicions. William's niece, Anne Eaden, who transcribed "The Prairie Journal" and for years served as unofficial family scribe, claimed she understood how it happened. "I am in a position to know," she wrote, for she'd been on intimate terms with her Uncle Bill. In Anne Eaden's view, although William was "deeply in love.... She did not return it."[6]

Why then did she make the crucial move that brought about the reconciliation? Anne Eaden believed (implying that it was finally her Uncle Bill's opinion) that "Her father for financial reasons wanted the marriage: eventually she gave way." It was not merely the $22,500 debt various Paullins owed William, but if this interpretation is correct, Daniel Paullin shrewdly realized that Close Brothers and the partners involved were on the verge of an enormous financial success. Paullin had been instrumental in bringing it about, having befriended and trained William in land purchasing. Such an investment in a promising young man's career should not be lost just at the point where substantial gains for the Paullins might be realized. Fathers often prevailed upon daughters when it came to marriage arrangements; even educated, emancipated Mary seems to have bent under this paternal coercion. To mitigate the crassness of such scheming, Paullin could take comfort in the notion of how pleased William would be to have his bereft, lonely condition alleviated, his love finally consummated. These months since the break, William had continued to demonstrate his emotional involvement with the Paullins, and certainly the family appeared to need a bulwark like this gifted, enterprising young man. Daniel Paullin was entering the last year of his life. Health failing, he may have exerted particular effort to secure the well-being of his children who would soon be orphans. The boys' future lay in farming in northwest Iowa, but what of the girls? At least Mary would be handsomely taken care of by a good man already on his way to riches, who wanted nothing more in the world than to make her his wife.

Mary played her part convincingly. William sailed from Liverpool aboard the *Celtic*, disembarking at New York on 20 April 1880. He routed his train trip west through Quincy but only visited Mary a few days; on 26 April he arrived in Le Mars, ready to undertake the last full season of his tenure on the prairie. Now that he was about to achieve all that he had been striving for—successful in his marriage suit and rapidly becoming a wealthy businessman—the "trials" were over. The rest of his life would unfold directly from this destiny of his own making. But his best years had involved the struggle itself, not the realization of his dreams.

CHAPTER SEVEN

Gentlemanly Activities

AMES Close acted upon his brother William's suggestion and renovated a Le Mars hotel, naming it Albion House, so new arrivals would feel more at home, but he could not serve as housemaster for the entire colony. Responsibility for the behavior of individual pups lay mostly with the host farmer who had received a sum for tuition or who employed the youth as a hired hand. Whereas most Le Mars citizens seemed pleased by the influx of settlers with large quantities of cash, when the so-called better class turned out to be intractable youngsters, antagonism against the British began to mount.

One young Close colonist wrote a supercilious letter to his hometown newspaper, the Manchester *Courier:* "Now as to the 'helps,' though they don't call their mistress 'Mum,' yet they are kept in perfect subjection. Of course among men the tinker and tailor calls one by one's surname, or even by one's Christian name if he happens to know it. To that you get used. Also in hotels all dine together, the working man and the swell. To us English it is wonderful how civil all Yankees are, nothing could be too good for us. They opened doors for us, carried our bags, and never took a 'tip' during our travels; but there the English, as a rule, carry revolvers and now and then use them, which creates respect." An Iowa paper, picking up on this story, commented: "Is this fellow a saphead, or is he only trying to come Mark Twain on his English friends?"[1] Still, carried away by the idea of being in the West, a few Close colonists dressed in pointy-toed boots, cowboy hats, and wore guns at the hips to dramatize life for themselves and friends.

Near the end of his life, William looked back on this period: "I was young and I did not know what I was doing, for although we had some splendid fellows join us, yet a number of parents seized the opportunity of loading on to us sons and relatives that were an embarrassment to them here, and who never would make good, so we had our hands full, as you may imagine."[2]

One such black sheep in the Close Colony was James Reginald Nash. Young Nash, a student in St. John's College, Cambridge, was sentenced to one month in prison for perjury at a Cambridge Assizes. He had sworn before the magistrate that he was not in Jesus Lane at the time of a "rag" after the Newmarket races, April 1880, when in fact he had been. After Nash was released from prison, he was too much disgraced to have around, so his family

84

shipped him off to Iowa. There he seems to have been a subdued member of the colony, not a party to some of the high jinks that went on.[3]

In mid-May 1880 a Le Mars citizen and his wife were out driving when suddenly their team bolted, frightened by a drunken English youth. The driver, a cripple, was thrown from his carriage. Later the Close Brothers' office wrote the *Liberal,* denying the truth of the published account, only to have the complaint pounced upon with relish by Editor Leidy: "We do not... hold the Close Brothers responsible.... We do feel that our people have been outraged by the drunkenness and rudeness of some of these new arrivals; we do wish that somebody could be held responsible for them...." The editor drew a contrast between these brash youngsters and the sober, responsible Britons with families who had recently bought farms. "Indeed, we know that the better classes are as greatly incensed at the indecent manifestations of the 'bloods' as are our own people, and they are as anxious as are we to have it stopped." There would be serious trouble unless something were done soon, for other incidents of a similar nature were constantly occurring. It was ridiculous of Close Brothers to object to newspaper coverage; "we will continue running our paper as suits us.... likewise hoping that there will never be other occasions for us to make mention of the bad actions of Englishmen on our soil."[4]

Frontier journalism thrived on controversy, and although Leidy knew that the influx of wealthy Britons was good for regional development, he could not resist stirring things up, particularly since prohibition sentiment was quite strong and the British tended to be drinkers. An unidentified correspondent to the *Liberal* (probably the editor himself) asked if something couldn't be done "to abate that miserable nuisance styled the 'House of Lords'.... Last Sunday while passing from church, I counted no less than twelve drunken young men standing in front of that shebang, and the door being opened I thought I saw a number of women inside jerking drinks for the ungodly loafers who were reveling there. Cannot this be stopped? Will not the respectable, Christian men of Le Mars combine to rout this last infamous place?"[5]

To which Editor Leidy replied: "To gut the place, as our friend suggests, is out of the question," but its collapse should come about because of "its flagrant violation of all law and all decency." Unfortunately, no "decent Christian men" of the town seemed ready to do anything. Should they identify themselves as being against liquor, it would harm their businesses, as Mr. Leidy knew, because he had been taken to task by reporting "the drunken sprees of the silly English lads who have come over here to get from under paternal restraint." News of the presence in Iowa of rich young "lords" also brought wantonly dressed women to Le Mars, who strolled the streets and frequented the House of Lords, the House of Commons, and Windsor Castle, the most popular British hangouts.[6]

The *Field's* correspondent had a far different impression of the House of Lords during his visit in 1881. He found the establishment "one of the most respectably conducted and cleanest of the public-houses, kept by Fred Barrow, an Englishman. Here one can get little luncheons and suppers, and drink— good Bass and Guinness out of old-time pewter. After 11 P.M. the House of Lords closes its doors to everybody; and Mr. Close himself, if belated and thirsty would of a certainty be refused a drink after that hour."

The trouble between the *Liberal* and the young Britons continued, and on 7 June 1880 four of them visited the newspaper office and demanded any apology for the attacks on the British colonists in previous issues. "The editor kindly but firmly refused to make any apology," reported Leidy, "when these blackguards began threatening, swearing that they would 'bust his bloody blarsted head' if he did not take back what had been published." He would take nothing back, and the four visitors left "muttering deep curses upon Yankees and Yankee newspapers. One of the quartet whose yawp was of greater dimensions than the others declared that if the *Liberal* was printed in Hengland it would be suppressed," to which the editor commented that he was thankful to be in free America. He would continue to speak out, "the inhibi- tion of these drunken thugs to the contrary notwithstanding. If the Englishmen who came over here to take advantage of our cheap lands will conduct themselves decently, we certainly will have nothing but good words for them; but such as intruded themselves upon us Monday morning we will hold up to the public censure at all times."[7]

As soon as this retort appeared in the *Liberal*, "the Englishmen held a council of war" and decided to punish Leidy. "As we hear it," said the *Sioux City Journal*, "five of the especially aggrieved drew lots to see who should inflict the chastisement, and that duty fell upon J. Wakefield, Esq." Jack Wakefield, twenty-two, was the son of a country squire of Sedgwick House, Kendal; his mother was an American, daughter of James Haggerty, at one time U.S. Consul in Liverpool. Educated at Eton and a graduate of Jesus College, Cambridge, Wakefield had already been in several escapades. On one occasion the proctor at Jesus caught him "at a wine in Malcolm Street" and he was fined; a few years later Wakefield again encountered this proctor—now a clergyman—who had just invested in 1,300 acres of the Close Colony.[8]

Wakefield and his three companions, armed with a horsewhip, accosted Leidy on his way to the post office, which was located in a drug store. Two of the Englishmen grabbed Leidy as Wakefield was about to "apply the butt end of a carriage whip" when the druggist himself came to the rescue of the hapless Leidy, and so attention suddenly was turned "to the man of pills," who in turn had to be rescued by his partner, another druggist. In the scuffle Leidy managed to escape into the rear of the store, "and when Wakefield not to be balked of his vengeance, rushed after him, he ran afoul of a bunch of fives of a stalwart butcher, which caused him to see more stars than there are in the star spangled banner.... Wakefield received the clip just behind the left ear." The druggist's partner was also "somewhat hurt in the scrimmage," receiving a bruised shoulder and a jammed hip.

The *Sioux City Journal,* under the heading "War Between the Races," declared that these young men "may be 'gentlemen's sons' in England," but here they seemed "more like 'Baltimore roughs' or 'New York rats.' " The trouble arose because they "have plenty of money, a superabundance of animal spirits, and being thousands of miles away from home and among strangers, go in for what with them constitutes a 'good time.'. . . They accept as a literal fact that this is the 'land of the free.'. . ." And while Leidy may have exacerbated the situation, the latest affair further damaged the British immigrants' reputation, "and I fear that a repetition of today's occurrence would end only in a young Bunker Hill."[9]

The battle involved not only a clash between citizens of two nations—two "races" in the newspaper's term—but a contest as to what kind of settler should develop this part of the country. The chauvinistic, self-conscious settlers who were already in residence—some of them only recently from Europe—accepted being an American as enthusiastically as they embraced its future. They resented the insistent Englishness of the Close Colony, for it seemed to imply that the United States was not an amalgamation of all sorts of "races" and cultures but that one group intended to make it an outpost of *their* civilization.

The *Sioux City Journal,* in recounting the troubles at Le Mars, referred to the English as "guests" on American soil and as such they would do well to respect their hosts. They were not to presume to make the locality into a replica of England. Earlier that year the *St. Paul Press,* the largest, most influential daily in the upper Middle West, launched an attack upon the concept of the Close Colony, particularly the premise that only those individuals possessing at least £500 to £1,000 ($2,500 to $5,000) could join. This was not regarded as the American way; immigration should be open to all who were healthy, willing, and eager to strive for a better position in life. Anything other suggested a class system of the sort America could well do without. "If the Close Brothers were to use as much influence toward obtaining some of the laboring class from the manufacturing districts of England, or from some of the suffering counties of Ireland, they would bestow a greater blessing on the northwest than they do by bringing over capitalists, for capital can live anywhere," but manpower was what the upper Middle West needed to develop its potential.[10]

To some observers the callow Britons displayed an appalling ignorance of farming matters and did not seem of the stuff to learn. The very fact that they were public school and university educated meant that hauling manure, milking cows, feeding hogs, and laboring in the fields ill-suited them. Such occupations were best left to the half-illiterate peasants who traditionally worked

the land, because that was all they knew how to do or could ever learn. Jack
Wakefield might be the son of respected gentry, but he did not appear likely to
make a go of Iowa farming. He didn't take it seriously. On one occasion,
playing the role of true Wild West man, he rode his pony directly into the
House of Lords and ordered his drink from the bar without dismounting.[11]

With such strident displays, a certain amount of answering was bound to
be forthcoming from the local "American" boys. The newspapers enjoyed reporting these dustups.

> A young Englishman and a couple of chaps from the country got up a
> good sized show on Tuesday afternoon. They had all been taking budge
> promiscuously, when one of the country lads thought to make it interest-
> ing by giving the Englishman a clip behind the lug, which he proceeded to
> do, and then lit out at a 2:40 gait. The Englishman followed to the street,
> but got hold of the other chap and warmed his ears with a pair of beer
> mugs. Then there was a flight to a saloon and a three-cornered bombard-
> ment of beer glasses and knuckles ensued, after which there was another
> retreat, and the pale air was streaked with cuss-words, while the claret
> flowed freely down the necks of the combatants. No arrests.[12]

Often the fun involved merely laughing at an out-of-place young greenhorn, with his inappropriate airs of dignity, mocking him in a fashion Anthony
Trollope caught when he visited America: "that republican roughness which so
often operates upon a poor, well-intended Englishman like a slap on the
cheek."[13] One such incident of ridicule occurred to H. C. Christian, a pup on
Captain Robinson's farm near present-day Akron, Iowa. He went duck hunting
on the Dakota side of the Big Sioux River with the Captain's $300 team and
spring wagon. Since the ferryman wasn't around when Christian returned to
the river, he drove his team aboard and ferried himself across to the Iowa side.
But he forgot to put up the gate of the ferryboat. When the craft touched
shore the team backed off the deck—into the river. Christian hung onto the
harness and went in with the horses. He managed not to drown, however. Next
morning the bodies of the horses were found down river and the wagon was
broken beyond repair; a valuable gun was lost. Such stupidity! How could such
a feckless youth make anything of himself here? Yet Christian learned farming,
became naturalized, and lived in Iowa the rest of his life.[14] But restless, wild,
young Wakefield returned to England for the winter of 1881–1882 and was
almost lost at sea in a bad storm on his return to the Close Colony. Finally,
toward the end of the decade, he emigrated to New Zealand, where he died in
1896.

The best antidote to idle mischief was a large assignment of work, for
there was no end to the amount of energy one could expend in agricultural
labor. Walter Cowan from his newly purchased farm wrote his mother that he
and his brother "have had to work like niggers. We are out at about 5 A.M. and
don't sit down to supper till 9 and you may imagine after that we feel hardly in

a fit mood for letter writing."[15] But some of the gentlemen's sons in the colony got up parties to go bear hunting in Wisconsin, took fishing trips to Minnesota, or simply went on extended sightseeing excursions throughout the United States. In winter, if they did not return to England, they found life in various southern regions more congenial. Who was to stop them? For the most part they were in control of some funds and far from parental eyes. Tuition had been paid, and it bought them their freedom.

A far different type of local British pioneering was also true at that time. Col. James Fenton, forty-five years old, son of a banker from Rochdale (near Manchester) who was also a member of Parliament, brought a little needed respectability to the colony. Fenton had worked in his father's bank from age eighteen, rising to a partner in the firm, but in midlife he sought a different career in another part of the world. His interest in emigrating to America developed out of a trip to compete in an international rifle-shooting match at Creedmore, Long Island, in 1877. He bought 1,000 acres about a dozen miles east of Le Mars; and while the younger children were educated locally, the older ones were placed in boarding schools, following the usual practice of British colonials.

The roomy house and outbuildings of Colonel Fenton's "Carlton Stock Farm" were on a slight rise at the bend of a creek which ran clear and steady year-round—a good auxiliary water supply, should the wells run dry. Fenton, like other Britons, chose a spot for his buildings with an eye for esthetic considerations as well as practical ones. He planted 14 acres of trees, which included a sizeable orchard, erected a windmill, and built a tank capable of holding 2,000 barrels of water. His principal barn, which is still standing, was constructed on a hill slope, so that a grist mill could be installed on the lower level. Teams hauling wagons entered the barn from the hillside; the grain was dumped into the mill below, where oxen in yoke turned the mill wheel.

By 1881 Fenton's holdings included 200 cattle, 24 horses, and 320 hogs. He began advertising "always on sale, high-grade Durhams" and registered Herefords. Fenton's fields were planted in small grains (wheat, oats, barley) and corn. Mrs. Fenton entered the annual agricultural fair with garden and dairy produce and was particularly known for her prize-winning butter, the first British dairy products on the local market. The Fentons were too old and settled to be part of the sports and night life of the colony, but Colonel Fenton was a member of the Prairie Club in Le Mars, where he might meet his countrymen, and they worshipped at St. George's Episcopal Church in Le Mars. Otherwise, they lived a rural life largely self-contained, with interchange among the neighbors mostly confined to cooperative crop gathering and other harvest work.[16]

Only ten miles south of Carlton Stock Farm, on the West Fork of the Little Sioux River, the Close properties were being rapidly developed and were referred to locally as the "upper" and "lower" Close farms. These homesteads were splendidly situated below a roll of land, with fine southern, southeastern, and southwestern exposures and were somewhat protected from the prevailing winter northwest winds. Fred and James's farm (the upper) was owned jointly at first, but upon Fred's marriage their property was divided. Fred's chief barn is still one of the biggest outbuildings in the area, ample for housing cattle below and storing hay above. The three-story frame dwelling (later destroyed by fire) had a full attic and a veranda on three sides. From a rocking chair on this porch one had a fine view of the West Fork valley. Fred always relished domestic comforts, and his house was equipped with water on each floor, a bathtub, indoor toilets, and well-proportioned rooms with fine woodwork and flooring. In 1880 Fred and James were feeding 800 sheep on their 960-acre farm, plus 200 each of Berkshire and Poland-China hogs. Since cattle and sheep were the leading livestock on British farms at the time, most settlers started with them, but Fred soon realized the possibilities of profit in hogs. Furthermore, much to the surprise of Close Colony settlers, the local population did not eat beef or mutton. What meat they ate was strictly pork or poultry, the pork chiefly salt pork.

William's 2,000-acre farm, lying to the southwest of his brothers' place, was managed by Roylance Court, and in 1880 the animal population consisted of 2,000 sheep "graded in from thoroughbred Cotswolds" and 1,000 shorthorn cattle. A newspaper reported that the Closes were "constantly adding to their possessions, and bringing the wealth and brawn of merrie England to this garden spot of the west." Two sheep cotes, each 100 feet long, had been built on William's farm and seven pups helped with the work.

With their farms flourishing, the Closes platted a town named Quorn, which they expected would attract the Chicago and North Western Railroad, then building from the east toward Sioux City and directly on the proposed route. Quorn was named after the well-known fox hunt based in Melton Mowbray, a market town of the Soar valley near Quorndon, Leicestershire. The purpose of establishing a town near the Close ranches was to provide a commercial center apart from the residences and buildings on the Close lands.[17]

The overseer's house and granary became the nucleus of Quorn, and the Closes leased a site for a mill on the West Fork to J. J. Heacock, of English origins, who had a successful milling operation in eastern Iowa, near Cedar Rapids. "He decided to move his mill to the wheat fields," his daughter recalled, "so he loaded the machinery and even the hand-hewn timbers onto a freight car and shipped it to. . .the closest railroad point at that time. From there it was hauled by teams to Quorn. . . . They worked all that fall and winter putting in the dam and building a small frame building. But it was ready for the wheat crop of 1882, which was made into flour on these Buhrs. . . ."[18]

Two years after its 1880 founding, Quorn boasted seven stores, one saloon, a blacksmith shop, and several wooden homes. Oblong blocks were laid out, thoroughfares that were merely dusty or mud roads, with First Street at the river near the mill; then Second Street — there never was a Third; and lateral cross streets named Britain, Main, and Elkhorn. One of the two hotels operating in 1880 was erected by the Closes; they kept the downstairs rooms for Close Brothers business. Known as the Ranch, the inn had three upstairs rooms for guests, and the proprietor could provide food. Such an establishment was convenient for putting up prospective land buyers or visitors who travelled to Quorn to see a pup or call on the Close farms. The Ranch was restored to its original look by Kingsley, Iowa, historical groups in time for the celebration of the nation's bicentennial.[19]

With the founding of this British town, yeomen from Great Britain and elsewhere in the United States were drawn there to settle and ply their trades. Among these were the Maxwell brothers, both of whom found immediate employment on the Close farms. "Fred had a large place with quite a few pups," T. J. Maxwell recalled, "and the boys from Quorn would go down there for parties — strictly stag parties. Will's house was a bachelor establishment, and the pups didn't get much to eat if they went down there. Called his place 'the poorhouse.'"[20]

In Quorn the pups eagerly awaited mail from overseas. The mail carrier would stop on his trips to larger towns nearby. Mail addressed to anyone in the area was dumped into a bin and would-be recipients had to paw around until they found their own letters. Before stores were established in Quorn, Fred Close would arrange for an empty wagon to set out for Le Mars periodically and return loaded with provisions, which the Closes in turn sold to the settlers. "Not for profit — just a service," said Maxwell, "to keep things going."

Maxwell remembered some of the jokes played on newly arrived pups. Once a fresh lad was thoroughly teased and tried — his obvious ignorance about farming a laughing matter for everyone. They even put him on a horse — saddle backwards. He didn't know what was wrong because he had never seen a western saddle before, with its high pommel; consequently, he took a terrific pounding in his rear, much to the delight of onlookers. Another time they sent him off to get "a half-round square." He rode all the way to Le Mars, eighteen miles, and when he returned, was furious: "You're no gentlemen! You're no gentlemen at all! There's no such thing as a half-round square!"

Hanging about the Heacock mill became a favorite pastime for the local working-class British. They could see friends, exchange gossip, and watch the horses Cub and Barney hauling wagons in and out. One of Maxwell's friends was shooting pigeons in the mill rafters one day, but his gun wasn't functioning properly; it hung fire. He turned to Maxwell: "That's the last time I'll ever shoot this gun!" and stamped the stock of the gun on the ground. It went off, shooting him through the chest, killing him.

Disasters and entertainments went hand in hand in typical frontier fashion. One British field hand was struck by lightning in July 1881. A doctor from Le Mars attended his wounds, spending four hours a day twice a week making the trip to Quorn during the next four months. The young man had no money, but the doctor presented no bill; however, the patient did not improve. Better medical aid was available elsewhere for a price, and the physician decided to help raise that money by giving a lecture, "The Anatomical Structure of Man," with the patient as the exhibit, all proceeds to go to him. It was a sensation. "The second lecture was delivered at the Quorn school house last Saturday evening, which indeed was a grand success, the room being packed to the utmost capacity. After the lecture ended, the doctor partially undressed the wounds and unfolded a hideous sight, which, after five months of healing, was too much for some of his audience to look upon." Contributions flowed in, the doctor himself contributing $40.00. Some only gave half a dollar, but a total of $84.50 was raised. Maxwell reported the young man recovered but was "horribly scarred."[21]

THE spirited young pups and the married, more settled colonists could all get together in one joyous, highly approved activity — sports. Interest in sporting events had been steadily growing in England from the mid 1850s and reached a kind of sports fever pitch in the 1880s. The Oxford/Cambridge cricket match in 1883 attracted a crowd of 46,000 spectators, still the record for that event.[22] The Close Colony Britons displayed signs of this sports mania and none more clearly than Fred Close, who seemed to be good at anything having to do with athletic prowess. He astonished the natives by his speed on horseback with which he traversed the distance from his West Fork farm to the depot in Le Mars, testing his mount and his ingenuity as a rider against the railroad timetable.

The colonists were spread over such a vast area in northwest Iowa that only those living near Le Mars and in the Quorn vicinity really saw much of one another even casually, and then most likely at the Prairie Club, in a tavern, or church. Sporting contests, which Fred Close promoted, helped alleviate the "sickness of vision peculiar to these empty plains," as Robert Louis Stevenson expressed it in *Across the Plains,* for on the prairie a man "is in the midst of the same great level. . . one quarter of the universe laid bare in all its gauntness."[23] Sports events dissolved the individual's isolation and made him part of a group. Rowing, in which William, James, and John all excelled, was never prominent in the colony because there wasn't much water around; instead, field sports — rugby, cricket, track, and horse racing. A member of the All England Eleven cricket team was a colonist, and many other local athletes had won laurels in public school or university contests.

The first Le Mars Derby took place on Saturday, 15 May 1880. Since William had arrived from England only three weeks before, most of the planning was done by Fred and James, who put up fifty dollars and a silver tankard for the Le Mars Cup. The improvised setting for the races was a hill upon which a house would soon be built, where for this occasion hundreds of spectators could gather. The divots caused by the horses' hooves and the trampled grass could easily be repaired. The local press, before the Derby, tried to describe a typical English race scene so on-lookers would understand why certain young gentlemen had been seen in trial heats on country roads wearing bright-colored silk shirts. Since the races were potentially dangerous to the participants, the reporter hoped a physician would be on hand to set broken limbs or bind up cracked heads. Only two of the scheduled races were open to Americans; despite urging from the press for American entries in these contests, nobody competed against the British. However, one race was exclusively American: the Hail Columbia Stakes.[24]

The Le Mars races brought virtually all the British settlers in the area together for the first time. "The blue sky, flecked with white clouds, the beautiful green grass just long enough to wave and bend to the grateful breeze, the brilliant sunshine, the animated concourse of sightseers," among them many women in handsome costumes, all contributed to the festivity. The first race, the thirty-dollar West Fork Plate with four contestants, was won by Constantine Benson's bay gelding Petrarch. Benson rode his own horse and showed skill in bringing him to the front in the home stretch, beating out James Close's mare Cora by six lengths. Next came the mile and one-half flat race for ponies under fourteen hands high. The first prize, fifteen dollars, was won by Jack Wakefield's mare Maud, ridden by Alfred Shaw; Benson's pony came in second. William Close's mare Little Wonder, ridden by his cousin Willie Gaskell, beat out Gerald Garnett on his Nellie. The race for the Le Mars Cup, one mile over five flights of hurdles, "the great event of the day," was entered by six and won by Benson on Petrarch, described as "a clean-limbed animal of great promise and comes nearer to the appearance of an English race horse than anything we remember to have seen around this section." [This observation was made by Editor Leidy, as if there had been anything but Indian cow ponies in "this section" before.] Fred Close entered the race but was thrown at the first hurdle; however, horse and rider resumed the contest and finished the course, to a round of applause for pluck. But Fred, it was learned later, had fractured his collar bone and was in great pain. Another accident occurred after the races were officially over: Jack Eller, "while leaping his horse over a hurdle...was thrown and kicked and lay for some time unconscious."[25]

Some spectators who had never seen professional horse racing objected to how quickly "the fun was over" and longed for more trial heats. The prohibitionists decried the excessive amount of drinking, two bars dispensing refreshments; other godly citizens deplored the reckless betting activity, although Editor Leidy observed that the "book-maker with his garments of motley and his hoarse cries of 'three to one bar one,' 'two to one on the field,' etc.," had not yet made it to Le Mars. The day's festivities appropriately ended with "a grand ball," according to journalist Poultney Bigelow in *Harper's*. "The event was a grand success, and partners were brought even from St. Paul, 270 miles to the north, to grace the occasion."[26]

It was an extraordinary day for a small town on the frontier. The expenditure of human energy in sports, when it was so badly needed just to make a living, seemed extravagant. The high price of race horses, which had no agricultural use, flaunted the precarious economic realities of pioneering. The amount of time these British settlers were willing to devote to athletic contests appeared to be incongruous with their true purposes as immigrants. All quite baffling to outsiders, who could not perceive how sports helped unify the colony and lift the spirits of the participants. Many local settlers came to watch the races and bet on horses, but why this show was happening remained a puzzle, for they were not familiar enough with the marks of the gentleman class—not just a matter of having money and leisure—but an attitude toward life itself. However, did it go with Iowa farming? Few in the Close Colony would ever ask that question.

CHAPTER EIGHT

The Faces of Success

HILE the Close Colony was beginning to flourish, another transplantation of Britons was underway at Rugby, Tennessee, under the guidance of Thomas Hughes, author of *Tom Brown's School Days*. Hughes and his backers in the English Emigration Association bought 75,000 acres in the Cumberland highlands of eastern Tennessee near the southern Kentucky border. The new town, Rugby, was eight miles from a railroad depot, the chief means of transporting goods and maintaining communication with the outside world. The land was largely forested and full of game, the winters usually short and mild. Hotel, sawmill, and a store were already built by the time Hughes officially opened his colony in October 1880. Since the terrain was deemed ideal for fruit culture, homesteads of 40 and 50 acres were platted, the emigrant paying 25 percent down, the remainder due in installments over three years. The company, which expected a reasonable return on its investment, took responsibility for erecting church, town hall, and other necessary public buildings; the settlers would lay out a cricket ground, create parks and gardens.[1]

American newspapers warned Rugby colonists that it would take hard work to clear the forest and till the virgin soil, that farming was unlike what they might have been used to; the sooner they forgot they had once been gentlemen, the better. As other ethnic or religious groups setting up colonies had already found out, the confines of a transplanted culture might offer an immigrant the illusion of a safe, familiar world, but eventual assimilation was only thereby delayed. And the children of colonists would feel themselves to be American, no matter what barriers or bulwarks were erected to isolate them.

Mindful of these criticisms, Hughes in his opening-day remarks cited the similarity of principles and modes of life that formed the essential bond and explained that Rugby Colony was not a communist society or interested in experimenting in new ways of handling private property or family life. If anything, Rugby would offer a new perspective on the evils of materialistic possessions. Colonists would have in common a reverence for the beauty of this piece of Tennessee, a feeling that it must be nurtured, brought to flower in an intelligent fashion, not despoiled for the sake of personal or collective fortunes. Long before most Americans (except authors like Thoreau and Emerson) were overly concerned about the rape of their land, Hughes was another

Englishman who noted the scars of industrialism that increasingly despoiled nature. The journalist "Bull Run" Russell, accompanying the Duke of Sutherland on his American trip in 1881, was shown in St. Paul, Minnesota, a library, an opera house, a university, churches, and handsome homes. "The Mississippi groans under the masses of timber and innumerable keels. How much to admire! What energy! What enterprise! But how nature suffered from it all! The Falls of St. Anthony turned into the overflow of a canal lock! The great river converted into a sewer laden with manure and sawdust! The lovely landscape defaced by hideous mills, elevators, factories! How the poets should rage, and the plutocrats rejoice!"[2] Hughes did not want his colony to ruin the land. "We can add little, perhaps, to its natural beauty, but at least we can be careful to spoil it as little as possible."

In reaching for a theme for his colony, Hughes suggested the satisfaction a group might experience by being welded together in a higher esthetic and moral purpose than might otherwise prevail, were they to live scattered and separate. The buildings therefore "should be the expression in timber, brick, and stone of the thought of men and women as to the external conditions under which folk should live."[3] Cornelius Onderdonk, a master builder from New York, constructed Hughes's home, Kingstone Lisle, which still stands—a board-and-batten Queen Anne cottage with dormer windows and gingerbread trim.

The primary rule was no liquor, not even in private houses. Ordinary wants such as food and shelter—"These must all be provided here, either by each of us for himself or by some common machinery. Well, we believe that it can be done best by a common machinery, in which we should like to see everyone take a hand." Freedom to worship would be a matter of course—in one church building all denominations were to use. Christ Church, fully restored today, is wooden with Victorian-Gothic embellishments, a steeply pitched roof, and bell spire.[4]

Rugby Colony was committed to restricting the overpredominance of trade and the trading instinct, which demeaned the human spirit, although it had also been a "potent civilizer of mankind, but only so far and so long as it has been kept in its place as a servant." In Rugby the tyranny of commercialism was never to be allowed to take hold. Such a stricture was ridiculed by the *Field* one year later: "In Tennessee no one very much expected a success, which in every new state and country is very difficult of attainment, but which in Tennessee was rigidly guarded against by the selection of a colonial site with the avowed object of preventing any new arrivals being demoralised, like so many persons nowadays, through a too-rapid and unhealthy influx of wealth."[5]

Hughes said his aim was "to plant on these highlands a community of gentlemen and ladies; not that artificial class which goes by those grand names, both in Europe and here—the joint product of feudalism and wealth—

but a society in which the humblest members, who live. . . by the labor of their own hands, will be of such strain and culture that they shall be able to meet Princes in the gate without embarrassment and without self-assertion, should any such strange persons ever present themselves before the gate-tower of Rugby in the New World."[6]

The Closes harbored no such high-flown sentiments about the dangers of trading or the unworthiness of "that artificial class" — ladies and gentlemen. Both Fred and William relished the intricate maneuverings of a bargaining session and found nothing déclassé about it. William in his "Prairie Journal" described how Fred "got his pocket picked of all his spare cash in Chicago, where he had to lay over for an afternoon, but his smart trading qualities came to the fore. . . ." Fred had bought a gold watch at an auction for $11, and after paying his hotel bill and buying his train ticket, discovered on board that he had been robbed. "He grew hungry at last, and bethought himself of his newly acquired watch, so speaking rather loud, he broaches the subject to his neighbour. 'Don't you wish to buy a gold watch? I am obliged to sell it, as I have had my pockets picked, and I must get something to eat.' " Soon a crowd gathered around, asking how much he wanted; " 'why, I should say $100, but I have to get some money, and I am willing to let it go at half that.' " He was offered $15; he "put on a face of virtuous indignation and turned away from the bidder, who raised his price to $20." Fred asked for $30, just as the train drew up to the stop for supper, and the bidder kept offering $20 but Fred remained in his seat. Finally, on the platform of the car, just as Fred was about to rush forward and accept the $20, the man turned and said, " 'I'll give you $25 for that ticker of yours.' " Both Closes had from early childhood witnessed bargaining in Naples, though William thought the Americans were even more addicted to it than Neapolitans. In Denison Fred quickly "got a great reputation for his trading qualities." He always managed to buy hay cheaper than others and was willing to lose a deal rather than give in on price. Once a trade on twenty-five cattle fell through because of a difference of $12, which Fred would not agree to pay.

Fred was not always on the triumphant end of a trade. As William put it, even "the smartest of the 'traders' gets done sometimes. . . . A neighbour of ours had a very good nag, and wishing to drive him close up to the fence, the horse plunged forward on to the fence and drove a stake into his shoulder. He came to us in a great state of mind on account of his misfortune, and Fred went to look at the poor animal." He bought the horse for $10, thinking the stake had only gone in a little way. "When the stake was pulled out it was found to have penetrated two feet, six inches. Fred sold the hide for $1."

While Thomas Hughes thought Rugby should de-emphasize trading and paid no attention to feudal notions regarding bluebloods and the ranking of gentlemen, the Closes managed to present the life of trading as sharp good fun—and aristocratic settlers as just the sort of people one would wish to have around. Being in a colony where the smartest were—even in such an unlikely location as northwest Iowa—was all that mattered.

When these British arrived at the Le Mars depot, onlookers were astonished, for it "confounded all our knowledge and established traditions of immigrants, for immigrants they are." They were well-dressed, bursting with good health; their children were clean, attended by nannies, "and nowhere among young or old is there a hint of travel-stained weariness or poverty." The baggage platform on these occasions was soon piled high with huge steamer trunks, leather suitcases, japanned boxes, furniture—which might include a high-backed tin bathtub or piano—"until a miniature mountain has been built on the platform."[7]

DURING the summer of 1880, between trips to Quincy to see his fiancée, William furthered many plans he had originated in England. With Constantine Benson now an active partner in Iowa, the firm was poised for a major business thrust. William and Benson were invited to St. Paul by an Oxford graduate and acquaintance of William, E. F. Drake, who entertained them in his home and discussed a business deal that would have a tremendous impact on the future of Close Brothers. This railroad had already made available to the firm a great deal of land at a low rate. These new negotiations were intended to formalize the arrangement. William feared being tarred with the reputation of too close association with the railroads, but by now the firm was known for its integrity. That Drake was an Englishman and very much of their world no doubt helped cement the agreement. William was aware that much of the available prairie was owned by the railroads; to acquire it for resale, Close Brothers had to come to terms with this source. The pact was made. Effective April 1881 Close Brothers became sole agents for the disposition of the remaining Sioux City and St. Paul land. In the next few years the company would sell 96,000 acres acquired through this railroad.[8]

William continued to maintain a keen interest in his stock farm at Quorn, managed by the fun-loving Roylance Court. He was a good overseer of new pups and participated in lease negotiations. However, even to this partner and friend, William did not disclose his exact marital plans. On 3 September 1880 Court wrote to William from the Sioux City offices of their legal advisor that he would be sending along an agreement for approval and suggestions, "but do not post them *till* the 11th, as I may come to talk them over." Court thought he might be able to arrive in Quincy within nine days—but the very next day William and Mary were married in Geneva, New York, with Herbert and Ada Paullin as witnesses. From Geneva the newlyweds (and the two Paullins) proceeded to New York City and embarked for England, where they would live—

mainly in a London hotel—until the following year, when William and Mary returned to Iowa.

Ada Paullin was to become part of the William Close household throughout the course of the ten-year marriage—and beyond. Herbert needed to be placed with a good tutor to prepare him for Cambridge. On 26 October a vicar wrote William: "Our mutual friend, Captain Chapman, told me today that you are looking out for some clergyman to take charge of a young brother-in-law. I think it just possible that I might be of some aid to you in the matter. . . ." William financed Herbert's schooling at the rate of eight guineas ($42.00) a month.

Once settled, William picked up on matters left pending following his sudden departure in spring. More publicity about the colony must be forthcoming. He got Constantine Benson's brother Robert to write a piece for *Macmillan's,* and he may have been behind the articles in *Harper's,* the *Field,* and the cartoon in *Punch.* Benson developed themes William had touched on in his brochure, particularly that the two chief problems facing a country squire in those days was how to make a profit on his land holdings and provide for younger sons—both could be solved in Iowa. Historically, "since the world began," populations had been moving westward and ownership of land had provided the basis for wealth. "So far the colony has had nothing but success," Benson wrote. One did have to endure the lack of good servants; and there were few amenities—one couldn't have shoes blackened by setting them outside the door at night in an inn or household. Beds in hotels might be only twenty-five cents, but perhaps a two-to-a-bed proposition, and Americans often "do not wash." He felt the apprentice-pupil system was working "much better than could have been expected considering that many of the newcomers came out with somewhat extravagant notions, and were as ignorant of how to hold their own in matters of business as they were of practical farming." Climate extremes made some settlers uncomfortable, but surely all would agree that fresh air and regular exercise was healthy for any spirited youth, and there was much companionship to be found in sports. "The absence of good turf is the only thing which so far has prevented much progress being made with cricket and football." This matter-of-fact consideration of a young gentleman's interests suggested the upper-class tone of the colony. The immediate attention to games proved that the picnic air prevailed. Even in Rugby, this aspect was attended to at once, with a challenge for a cricket match issued to Cincinnati soon after Rugby Colony was founded. Benson painted a pretty picture of Iowa life, describing the pleasure of riding the Iowa prairie "through lanes of flowers." All manner of birds, fish, and small game abounded, making the country ideal for hunting and fishing enthusiasts.[9]

Benson concluded that the economic prospects looked equally promising: land values kept rising and returns for crops and livestock were running high.

"Labour is plentiful, and it is not worth while for anyone who cannot command some capital to attempt to make a start in Iowa." This remark repeated William's pamphlet message: the colony was for capitalists, not laborers. In truth, there were few hired hands available for steady employment. A man usually worked only long enough to accumulate sufficient money to strike out on his own. This made for very uncertain labor during crucial harvest seasons and a constantly shifting population. In Cherokee, Iowa, near the Paullin farms, statistics of the period show that the number of men who arrived, then left, over a five-year span equalled the total number of men remaining.[10]

For the most part, Benson struck the note William wanted emphasized most: good land was going fast and anyone interested should not delay. By the time the piece appeared in May 1881, Benson could truthfully say that only southeastern Minnesota really had cheap tracts left. With America destined to become the granary of the world, he explained, crops grown in this region would soon be shipped to all the major markets. A vast network of railroads made transportation costs low and wheat was competitive with any grown elsewhere in the world. The opportunity for investing money — and one's life — was unique.

Since many of William's relatives and friends succumbed to the lure, investing money or sending sons out, when anything went wrong they were quick to hold William personally responsible. His uncle, Thomas Brooks, became increasingly alarmed by his son Sam's long silence and was puzzled by the boy's peculiar itinerary in America. Finally Sam sent a letter from St. Paul. Thomas Brooks asked William what he made of the contents. "He says, 'I have met some very nice men from New York and we have been all around viewing the public buildings and the city, our programme as follows: Morning — Visit buildings, etc., Afternoon — Sleighing, Evening — Theatre & social chat.' This is all very well, but he has been a long time at St. Paul and is only loafing. Your idea of getting a steady fellow to join him is very good, and one I have also thought of — but will he consent? I am terribly anxious about him.... I thought of writing to the hotel proprietors (he has been there a month) but I don't know what sort they are in America. I cannot get him to write, and that's a bad sign. I wish I knew what to do." William immediately wrote to James in Le Mars, asking if anybody had heard news of Sam Brooks. On 14 November James replied: "Sam Brooks much better but do not know what he is doing at St. Paul."

Thomas Brooks appended a postscript: "So glad indeed Mary is better, give her my love. My wife is a little better. She has been *very* ill." Weak, "poorly" wives were commonplace concerns of Victorian husbands. For William the problems of wayward sons and black sheep had been largely superseded by Mary's ill-health and unhappiness. Almost from the start there appeared to have been marital difficulties. His intimate friends were becoming isolated from him because Mary refused to meet them. Bad health was the convenient, catchall, socially acceptable explanation; it masked a multitude of problems. Mary Mount Batten wrote William from Reading: "If I come up to London for a day I shall for certain come to see you and my new cousin, but I'll let you know beforehand, as I am aware how busy you are. When are you coming to stay with us?" William's involvement with his Paullin in-laws may have made the kind of country house touring his friends and relatives envisioned quite impossible. He was gone on business trips frequently, to Cambridge, Oxford, Manchester, and elsewhere, most of these undertaken alone—his frail wife, meanwhile, attended by her devoted sister Ada.

William's relations with his brother John seemed mostly confined to business, John merely noting, in one letter, "There is no chance of our getting to London—many thanks for asking us." At William's request, John promised to send a gun to young Herbert Paullin, though "it is rather difficult to know what will suit him." John's wife Emily had no compunction about bringing up the crucial subject of concern to the Close family: "I am so sorry I had such a poor account of Mary, particularly as she was so anxious to be well in London to be able to study." This reference is somewhat puzzling, since schooling was by now some years behind her, but perhaps a course of study of some sort would be therapeutic and bring her out of her slump. "I wish so much there was something we could do to help her. You did *not* enclose the letter from her after all, so please send it by the next post and don't be so provoking again." Had the intended letter been at the insistence of William but not forthcoming from Mary? "We thought Mary looked so wonderfully better when she left us. Don't you remember what a pretty colour she had? If you think the Manchester air suits her, please pack her off at once & I promise her a hearty welcome and no end of petting and nursing. Has she ever taken any 'Fen de Bravais'? It is the one strengthening medicine in which I have faith."

William's half-brother Henry also wrote in concern after learning that Mary "(how strange it seems to call by her christian name one whom I have never seen) is so unwell that she is obliged to remain in bed...." He thought the dirty, foggy London air might have something to do with it; perhaps the box of game birds he sent "will tempt Mary to eat." In this fashion the family expressed sympathy but remained at one remove from William and his mysterious bride.

Business affairs proved more comfortable to discuss. Henry asked William to please explain the fluctuating market in Reading Railroad shares and bonds, reminding William that their uncle, Thomas Close, was also "heavily in them." Was it bona fide increased profit or only speculative pumping, a bubble that would soon burst? While William's English associates regarded him as the expert on everything American, those in Iowa figured he could be of service at home. The pups tended to see William as the prime intermediary in any troubles they might be having with their families. Young Alfred Shaw, whose extravagant first trip out had caused his father to spread sour stories in Liverpool about Close Brothers was now back home for a visit and wrote William from his father's manor, Arrowe Park, Berkenhead:

> I should be much obliged if your firm in Le Mars could settle the enclosed. I came away & thought I had *nearly* settled with everybody but this most decidedly escaped my memory....When will you be up near here again & what do you think best for me to do when I go out again, which will be *early* in February? This is a frightful climate, I must say, after Iowa. [Shaw must have hoped the remark would strike a particularly responsive chord, since criticism of the Iowa climate was pretty constant.] I have not seen *your Pard* [Roylance Court] yet, although I have been out twice with the Cheshire hounds. My Old Governor has very kindly hired a horse for me to hunt two days a week and has *quite* made it up with me, although we had rather a stormy interview one night, 'but all's well that end's well.'

The Shaw family was still upset over the Closes' treatment of Alfred. Mrs. Shaw felt her son should not have been charged for the expenses of Price, the noted cricketer and son of a Cheshire pastor, who made the train trip to New York with Alfred almost in the capacity of guard. Shaw had gotten himself into some kind of scrape, and Fred Close managed to cashier him out of the colony, but they hoped to avoid spelling it out precisely. They would certainly not welcome him back in early February. As for Price's accompanying him to New York, Alfred complained:

> [Now I *quite* understood that he was going there on business *officially,* in which I think you will find I am right. He had then to go on to Boston...& then down to Tennessee. So I do not think it all fair to debit me with this. There was not the *least* necessity for him coming with me. Fred told me before that affair happened in Sioux City (don't say anything at home about this) that some one was going to New York on business & then asked me if I would not like to go home, as I would have his company as far as New York. I wish you would kindly enquire into this. I am sure you will find I am right.
>
> My Gov. says something about my lending the money I have left out on interest—how would this do? my going & working on some farm. But I think it would be better to buy a farm again & if I worked like I did at first I am sure my old Gov. would make the amount up to £1,000 [$5,000] again pretty soon & then if I went on well would give me more. I should like your opinion on these subjects.
>
>   Ever yrs. Sincerely,
>   BABY SHAW (as you called me)

> I might run up to town some Saturday till Monday & stay at your hotel & have a talk.

Whether or not the interview with William took place, Alfred got his way and was soon back in the Close Colony.

From Le Mars James wrote that Ed Paullin was causing trouble. Boasting of his family connection with the Closes, Ed attempted to syphon away some of the land sale business, posing as an agent on property he had no claim to whatsoever. And since the Paullins badly needed labor for their large farming operation, Ed continued to lure pups from their assigned households. William wrote sternly to Ed and sent a copy of the letter to James, who laconically replied: "Mr. Benson can give you further details of what he heard East" about the Paullins. "Henry Paullin still amuses himself passing off as a Britisher."

William's "Pard," Court, arrived in November and reported to William that he had been to his tailor and to Cambridge for a boat race. He had also been hunting with the Quorn pack and to a dog show in Birmingham. "I have been paying visits at Liverpool and Manchester & getting what hunting I can squeeze in. One of my cousins died most suddenly last week, so that prevented my hunting for a few days. Should like, awfully, to see you but can't say yet when I could run up . . . as long as there is hunting I shall not be much in town. I get four days with the Cheshire this week & Saturday with the Meynell, where I shall stay, I think, till Xmas."

This carefree participation in country pleasures would never again be part of William's life, mostly because of ailing Mary, who couldn't go anywhere. Her role as sickly wife was very likely the Victorian woman's convenient escape route from unhappiness, a kind of revenge, pulling down those immediately around her. She may have already been in the early stages of a psychosis that would worsen in time and eventually bring about her death at a young age. The Close family chronicler, Anne Eaden, remarked years later that her Uncle Bill "did everything he could to satisfy her every whim. Once she fancied a pair of black carriage horses. He bought her the best to be had in London, where they were living at the time. So it went on until she left him to go to someone else."

But one pleasure of his youth continued to sustain William — rowing — and he particularly enjoyed coaching the Cambridge crew in their various trials. The rowing coach wrote William in late November 1880, "I am *very* glad to think that I shall have your advice about the men . . . I think you will find two very fair crews by Thursday, and I have hopes of their doing a very good time at Ely on Saturday next."

After the successful collegiate event, the coach reviewed "the points which you especially mentioned. . . ." The interlude for William was a blessed return to an intense, simplified contest. His love for rowing was an emotional involvement that would never undergo the kind of trials experienced in his love life. He had won the Head of the River Fours and Colquhouns at age twenty-one, and the Cambridge University Boat Club Pairs the following year, when he also participated in the University Boat Race. Three times he had rowed for Cambridge against Oxford and one year was president of the club. Every magazine and newspaper article about him and his colony in later years would identify him as a man "well-known on the river in times gone by as an accomplished oarsman," or in similar phrases. Little wonder that in his final burial rites instructions, according to the *Times*, "He expressed the wish that his Cambridge and First Trinity Rowing Club colours should be carried with him to his grave."[11]

The Colony Portrayed

"IT blossoms like a rose," booster newspapers reported about the Close Colony; land values were rising, and British settlers of means were rapidly building up the country.[1] Land speculation and colonization did not at this point seem incompatible, for the trading of prairie acres always at higher prices helped attract colonists. Since land everywhere in the region increased in price, investments always paid off, should an immigrant decide for any reason to leave.

At the very moment the colony was fully coming into its own, Close Brothers business interests were farther and farther away. In order to handle these transactions in land, James opened offices in two northern tier Iowa county-seat towns, Rock Rapids and Sibley, and spent considerable time in these locations. The firm purchased complete abstracts for entire counties to keep informed on land sales; virgin prairie, which offered the chance of greatest profits, was rapidly disappearing. Close Brothers not only received sales commissions, management fees, charges for bank services to clients, and share rents, but they also arranged the mortgages for tenant farmers who would pay for the improvements the firm had made when buying their homesteads. More staff was needed, particularly in the Le Mars office, which had expanded, taking over an entire floor of the largest British-owned business building. Major Charles Ball, who was also county attorney, had been a part-time legal advisor but now joined the firm. He was a volatile, controversial figure to be functioning in an official capacity—a man who illustrated how thin the veneer of respectability really was and how close Le Mars could still be to the Wild West.

Two years before, in 1879, the town had been treated to a sensational rape case involving a leading physician, Dr. W. B. Porter, who was charged with seducing his fiancée by locking her in his office with him, pouring wine down her throat, and twice forcing himself upon her. Dr. Porter claimed the young lady had trumped up the rape charges following his announcement to her that he wished to break off the engagement. Letters in her handwriting, which he made public, indicated she had offered herself to him "as wife" during the betrothal period. Porter claimed it was a frame-up; she sought revenge and hoped to win back her lost honor. Nevertheless, the jury convicted him; he appealed, and through legal delays kept himself in Le Mars. On 11 July 1880

Dr. Porter was shot in the neck by Major Ball. "When nearly in front of the House of Lords," according to a reporter, Ball "saw Porter emerging from an alley-way. . . . As the two passed, Porter hissed between his teeth, 'There goes the son of a bitch.' " Ball had been the prosecuting attorney in Porter's trial. He turned to Porter and said: " 'Don't you repeat that! I won't stand it.' Porter did repeat the offensive remark, at the same time, making a motion as if to draw his revolver. Ball drew his pistol, a small-calibred instrument, and fired. Porter fell to the pavement, making a great noise and calling for help. . . . Several Englishmen carried the wounded man to his office." Dr. Porter recovered, and since the town was "unanimously with Maj. Ball," no matter what the circumstances involved, charges against Ball were dropped and he continued his duties as county attorney. Close Brothers found him a useful addition to the staff several months later.[2]

At the start of the 1881 season, Close Brothers advertised for 180 tenants. Seed would be provided, and the tenant would get half the crop, pay half the threshing bill, and would be reimbursed $2.25 an acre for breaking new soil; if he backset the stubble after harvest (dressing the field for next year's planting), he would be paid an additional amount; and there was no obligation to stay beyond one year. "Every forty farms or thereabouts are placed under the superintendance of a steward, who is controlled directly by ourselves," William explained.[3] The company had little difficulty finding suitable renters on these terms. By this time many of their farmhouses were plastered inside and were somewhat roomier than the 1879 cabins. There were trees around the buildings and an occasional woodlot. Iowa law gave a $100 property tax exemption for ten years for every acre of trees planted. The Closes ordered 400 trees for their own farms on the West Fork, and in 1882 the company had 1,000 acres planted: box elder, ash, maple, and cottonwood, plus a wide variety of fruit and nut trees. In subsequent years these stands provided windbreaks, fuel, fenceposts, shelter for livestock, and harvests of fruit and nuts.[4] Nowadays large groves are seldom found in this part of Iowa because of drouth years and winterkill. Later generations felt the land was too valuable to fill with trees; even the wild plum brush along fencerows would be grubbed out to make fields bigger and thereby easier to work with large machinery.

FOR the colonist bent on settling, development of one particular spot of prairie could be sufficiently absorbing; and if he were a gentleman, as most claimed to be, his work and his leisure pursuits needed to be handled with the right attitude. "On one farm I met two tall and handsome young farmers whose uncle had been a distinguished Member of Parliament," wrote Bigelow in the April 1881 *Harper's*. "The last time I had seen them was in a London drawingroom. This time they tramped me through the mud and manure of the barn-yard to show me some newly bought stock.

They were boarding with a Dutch farmer at three dollars per week in order to learn practical farming. Both were thoroughly contented, and looking forward to the future with pleasure." How amusing of them to regard their future as here in these Iowa cattle yards! "Another young farmer whom I noticed on horseback with topboots, flannel shirt, sombrero, and belt-knife, was pointed out to me as the grandson of the author of Paley's *Theology*. He was attending a cattle auction at Lemars, Iowa." The *Field*'s correspondent, a few months later, also cited Paley as being a champion bowler at cricket. Philosopher William Paley's grandson was a gentleman immigrant who disregarded the code about what a proper occupation should be for one of his class. He entered the cattle business, not as a fancy breeder in the country-squire style of Captain Moreton, but as a business partner in a livestock commission house. As a sideline he went into the nursery trade with a young man from Nottingham who would enter Oxford the following year—the stint in Iowa a mere interlude. They sold carloads of forest and fruit trees, ornamental and fruit shrubbery, all "especially adapted to this latitude."[5]

At the cattle auction in Le Mars, Bigelow also met the son of Thomas Bayley Potter, "the distinguished honorary secretary of the Cobden Club and M.P. for Rochdale." Since Col. James Fenton's father had also been in Parliament for Rochdale, the Iowa emigration may have come about through that connection. Young Potter "had come out only to take a look at the place, but . . . so fell in love with the life that he decided to invest."

The *Harper's* reporter mentioned encountering a man who "had been an admiral in the royal navy." Probably it was Admiral Sir Arthur Farquhar, an occasional Iowa visitor; his four sons, James, Albert, Mowbray, and William, "together with an austere aunt Jane Farquhar, went out there and formed 'Carlogie Ranch'—Carlogie being the name of their father's place in these parts," wrote Keith Caldwell, a Farquhar descendant. William, Mowbray, and Jane were on board the *Scythia*, which arrived in New York on 8 April 1881. "My father, who married another Miss Farquhar, went out with his wife to Le Mars and stayed with them," Caldwell explained. Admiral Farquhar, whose father also had been an admiral, entered service in 1829, saw action in the bombardment of Acre, and participated in a battle against the pirates near Borneo in 1849. Two years later he married and proceeded to have thirteen children at regular intervals, all sons at first—which made him a prime prospect for Close Brothers. With navy acquaintance Captain Moreton heading the colony, emigration seemed an attractive idea. Sons three, four, five, and eight were the principal settlers at Carlogie Ranch, situated on a small rise overlooking Mink Creek just west of present-day Brunsville, Iowa. Admiral Farquhar bought 1,100 acres from Close Brothers and paid for the construction of a splendid frame house. An attic water tank provided good water pressure and the wide veranda on three sides could accommodate many rocking chairs. There were gleaming wood paneling downstairs, hardwood floors throughout, imported tiles for the fireplaces, and the kitchen-dining room arrangement was suitable for a staff of "helps." An alley of small trees led from the road to the farmstead. The barns and house, although considerably altered, are still standing.[6]

The Farquhars became a mainstay of the colony, and Admiral Farquhar came for frequent visits. Jane helped run the household, at least until Albert married the daughter of the Provost of Aberdeen, to which union a son was born in late February 1888. "The northwestern blizzard heralded his coming, and the surroundings were somewhat chilly for an unclothed stranger," wrote a Le Mars newspaper editor, Charles Dacres, whose father was also an admiral in the Royal Navy. Young Albert, Jr., followed the family tradition of going to sea and was killed in action in May 1916.[7]

All the Farquhar brothers participated in various sporting events of the colony. James for several years was lawn tennis champion of Le Mars. Other brothers played cricket, competed in foot races, rugby scrimmages, and even polo, but their names appeared most often in newspaper accounts related to farming—the prices they got for livestock on the Chicago market or their introduction of special breeds such as the Clydesdale horse. In 1888 Albert bought a champion stallion, "Paul Jones," a highly thought of example.[8]

Gradually, the Farquhar brothers left Carlogie Ranch: James to British Columbia, where he entered business; Mowbray joined the Canadian Mounted Police; and William moved to Joliet, Illinois, upon his marriage to the daughter of a U.S. Navy officer, whose home was Chicago. "Do you think the name Carlogie Ranch still survives?" Keith Caldwell, the nephew of these Farquhars wondered, and answered himself immediately: "I doubt it." But Mrs. Katherine Dickman, one of eight children raised at Carlogie Ranch after the Farquhars sold out—although she did not know the name Carlogie—recalled that her family "was always conscious that we had one of the finest homes around." She was particularly intrigued as a little girl by the pass-through serving window between kitchen and dining room, and she loved the beautiful fireplace tiles, though the fireplaces themselves were not used because central heating had been installed.[9]

Caldwell also mentioned Almeric Paget, "an old friend," who "used to stay with us at Cambridge." Paget's name evoked the high social tone of the colony; his grandfather, the Earl of Uxbridge and Marquess of Anglesey, had married the daughter of the Earl of Jersey. Young Almeric was educated at Harrow and Cambridge. He emigrated to America soon after graduation, having come under William Close's persuasive spell. A gregarious, attractive young man with the very best connections in eastern U.S. society, he frequently toured the country, a houseguest of his parents' friends. During the winter of 1883–1884 Paget spent six months in the East and New Orleans. He excelled in cricket and participated in many colony matches, as well as footraces and other track events. He, too, felt no compunction about what might be suitable for a gentleman to "do" when far from home. Paget bought a soap factory that used the by-products of a pork butchery establishment. Paget and his partners were expected to bring to the business "the vigor and sagacity and at the same time the conservative tendencies of the commercial classes of England, where they received their training." How amused he must have been to read that newspaper account![10] One of his partners, Leuric Charles Cobbe, came from Anglo-Irish landed gentry, one uncle High Sheriff of County Louth, another a barrister, Inner Temple, London.[11] Cobbe and Harry Eller continued the soap factory after Paget pulled out; they, too, were appraised in the press as "men of fine business qualities, indomitable energy, and abundant means." By 1886 the factory, employing nine workers, was producing 50,000 pounds of soap a week, with two salesmen on the road and one in the St. Paul office.

Paget quit the soap factory to join Fred Close in the movement of Close Brothers to Pipestone, Minnesota, where he invested in city real estate and built a large stone building for stores. By 1885 he was reputedly owner of "considerable property" in Pipestone, but he traveled to Le Mars quite frequently for horse racing and cricket. Paget probably returned to England in 1888 when his father died; but he was back in the States again for his marriage to Pauline Whitney in 1895, in St. Thomas's Episcopal Church, New York City. Pauline was the daughter of William C. Whitney, secretary of the navy under Grover Cleveland. The Paget/Whitney wedding was attended by the president and his wife, the governor of New York, two cabinet ministers, and all of New York society. Gertrude Vanderbilt was a bridesmaid and Cornelius Vanderbilt an usher. It was a long way from the soap business in Le Mars, Iowa. Back in England, Paget became active in charitable causes and in 1918 was created Baron Queenborough of County Kent. Lord Queenborough had five children, all girls, and the title became extinct upon his death in 1949.

One of Lord Queenborough's daughters, Lady Baillie, bought Leeds castle in 1926, and with Whitney-inherited money restored the historic crenelated Kentish ragstone structure into what Lord Conway, an authority on European castles, called "the loveliest castle...in the whole world."[12] Henry VIII had brought Ann Boleyn to Leeds; it was also the residence of Eleanor of Castile, the consort of Edward I. Three hundred years ago Lord Culpepper owned the castle when he took the assignment of royal governor of the colony of Virginia at Jamestown. The superb condition of Leeds castle today, a result of extensive funds poured into its reconstruction and refurbishment by one of the heirs of the Whitney/Paget alliance, is an example of what sometimes happened when gentlemen became immigrants.

POULTNEY Bigelow in *Harper's* also reported his meeting with a young man who "had been connected with a Shanghai bank"—probably Herbert Cope, who arrived with his wife in the spring of

1880, settling in Le Mars near his China-days friend, Adair Colpoys. Cope began importing teas from the Orient, "pure tea selected for him by old friends in China and Japan, now shipped directly to him at Le Mars," for sale in a local bakery and grocery store.[13]

Herbert Cope's singular mission in the colony was to prove that William Close's opinions on the best way to farm in Iowa were wrong. Close maintained that western farming—with its cheap, available acres—should be undertaken on a large scale, farming "less well" than a European was used to, but spreading out to encompass a large area. Cope decided instead to apply British small-tract farming to the Iowa situation. "To his practical mind," said a newspaper editor, "it seemed that the rich soil might be made to yield much larger crops than were generally harvested." Greater yield per acre, perhaps, but if the total crop did not amount to sufficient quantity, would this still be the wisest course? Cope tried it both ways, buying a tract of 400 acres west of Le Mars that he planted mostly in corn; and another—only 40 acres—located a mile from Captain Moreton's homestead, where he practiced intensive agriculture.[14] On this land Cope built his house, which was protected from northwest winds by a slight roll of the prairie—and set back from the road on a gentle elevation which provided "a fine view of every acre of land on the farm." He constructed four tenant houses, sixteen by twenty-four feet, almost exactly the dimensions of Close Brothers' houses, two stories high and plastered throughout. Each had a well, barn, and granary, and so few acres that the tenant would be able to concentrate on "a very high state of cultivation." Rural residences such as these might also appeal to those who worked in Le Mars but preferred to live in the country. Cope's home, only slightly larger than those of his tenants, was surrounded by a lawn, with a neat barn, granary, and other outbuildings a short distance away.[15]

Cope planted five acres in Russian white oats, sowed with a slow-growing clover; after harvesting the oats, the clover would be a hay crop, which he expected to cut twice before frost. If indeed Cope's method was new to Iowa, it was taken up by most farmers in succeeding years, with red clover the usual "under" crop. Cope planted his other fields with "rare and prolific plants, the seed of which was brought from England, one being the Prickly Comfrey and the other Lucerne Clover, and both of which make splendid fodder for stock." Several acres were devoted to potatoes, again from special English sources. One of Cope's gentleman tenants, a Mr. Smith, devoted full time to gardens of vegetables; many varieties grown had been hitherto unknown in these parts. Another tenant, Hugh Playfair Chiene, son of Major P. J. Chiene of Ellensborough, Dumbartonshire, had arrived in 1880 and met his bride through a friend, Frank Sugden, whose sister Florence Emily, like so many other sisters of colonists, had come to Iowa to help her brother.[16]

Herbert Cope tried to publicize his agricultural experiments by dropping by the *Sentinel* or *Globe* office with the latest crop specimens. He exhibited to one editor a turnip weighing fourteen pounds, ten ounces, and a stalk of corn seven feet six inches high and nearly one-half foot in circumference. With corn like this Cope expected to harvest seventy-five bushels to the acre, considerably better than the sixty or sixty-five common at that time. On several occasions he sent his overseer with prime examples of produce; often he went himself, having plenty of time as a gentleman farmer.[17]

Cope won prizes at the county fair with his alfalfa and other grasses and grains. He touted prickly comfrey (a forage plant known for its effectiveness against diarrhea and dysentery) for hog-feeding, claiming it helped ward off cholera and other diseases. Cope also persisted in his tea importing, constantly introducing new varieties, such as black tea from Japan. On the whole, his agricultural efforts did not have the impact he hoped. Fellow colonists continued in their large-scale western farming ways, paying little heed to his results. The newspaper editors enjoyed his company, however. "Herbert Cope...showed us the Christmas number of the London *Graphic,* and we confess it to be the finest piece of pictorial magazine work we have ever seen." He was full of the latest news from Hong Kong and carried with him copies of Anglo-Chinese newspapers.[18]

The severe winter of 1883–1884 helped make up Cope's mind about Iowa. In February 1884 he rented out the 400-acre tract and turned over his residence, Troscoed, where his daughter had been born in 1882, to still another tenant, on a five-year lease. He planned to live permanently in England. The tea business? Three days before departure he announced that "his tea business here is entirely discontinued, and that he has no agent for the sale of tea." This commodity could still be gotten from Lee Hoo, who ran a Le Mars fancy grocery. Cope returned to North America a few years later, settling in Medicine Hat, Alberta.[19]

Cope's China-days friend, Adair Colpoys, son of the rector of Droxford, Hampshire, graduate of Trinity College, Cambridge, lived first in China and then Australia, where he happened upon a copy of Close's brochure. When he learned Cope would be in the Iowa colony, Colpoys decided to emigrate, but he had a look at Rugby, Tennessee, first. He chose Le Mars, and not being especially interested in farming, became a businessman in real estate, loans, and finally insurance. Together with another Englishman who also became a lifelong settler in Le Mars (A. C. Colledge), Colpoys insured the property of Britons throughout the area.

With unabashed snobbery, every famous family name in the colony was cherished; it served as the stamp of approval on every other participant's presence. The Jervis brothers, Ronald and Cecil, were pups with Captain Moreton in the summer of 1881 when their sister, Lady Harris, and her husband, a noted cricketer, stopped by on their American tour (a heat wave, the temperature at 102 degrees, made cricket-playing impossible). Ronald Jervis was a third son, twenty-three years old when he emigrated to Iowa with his younger brother Cecil. Their father was Viscount St. Vincent. A career in Iowa agriculture seemed a more solid prospect than basing their expectations on some fluke in the primogeniture system that might bring about a place for them in the Jervis family scheme. They bought a farm for $9,000 in 1882, the same place Alfred "Baby" Shaw had sold in 1881 for $6,000. Cecil didn't stay long in Iowa, however, and Ronald, too, gave up and returned to England and eventually became Viscount St. Vincent, outliving other claimants.

When the *Field* reporter visited Le Mars in July 1881 he was chauffeured about the colony by Hugh Hornby (who would succumb to illness and die six months later). "Mr. Hornby brings up a light buggy and a fast pair of trotters one very sunny morning to the House of Lords for me, and *presto* the capital of the colony is left behind, and, with a passing glimpse of the well-cultivated farm of Messrs. Warren, Maclagan, and Watson, we are on the prairie." They passed many English farms, "and at length drew bridle at the end of twenty miles, to find ourselves at the door of the wonderfully comfortable house of Mr. White Marsh, of Weatherfield, Essex." Close had sent him out the previous January, and by now Marsh had miraculously established himself; house and barns built, fields broken and planted. "We had driven through hay to the horse's knees on this property for some time; fairly good looking sheep dotted the hill some half-a-mile off, and everything had the air of solidity and comfort.... Mr. White Marsh was then an absentee; so on the backward trail we put up at his neighbour's.... English servants, English cooking, and thorough English neatness and cleanliness characterised this property also."

When the reporter stopped at Captain Moreton's — "Lord Hobart, when I was there, was mowing...." He was the only son of the assistant secretary in the Indian Department, and his mother was the daughter of the Bishop of Bombay. For a period in the mid-1880s he served with the British forces in the Sudan, but when his father died in 1886 he became the Earl of Buckinghamshire and lived in England. The *Le Mars Sentinel,* announcing the news of his title, cut him down to plebian size. "He could not fail to take the prize for being the homeliest man in any contest either at home or abroad, but a good fellow for all that."

Two other "Honorables" in the colony, whose names were often invoked for snob appeal, were Eric and Herbert Rollo. Eric was twenty when he arrived in Iowa; his brother, three years younger, showed up a bit later — both Rollos were Moreton pups and Eric bought a farm west of Le Mars. When Eric left the colony his household goods were sold to the purchaser of the farm, who cherished these English artifacts enough to preserve them, and to this day an English tea set of the Rollos, with matching china, remains as a reminder of the elegant style of these pioneers. Eric eventually became Lord Rollo; his brother Herbert ended his days in New Zealand.

THE favorable report on the Close Colony in the *Field* came as adverse reactions to the pup system were being heard more frequently in England. However, almost from the beginning William had received criticism for requiring a premium from pups while they were apprenticed to farmers. "Someone in Le Mars has been working against your firm," wrote a former pup to William, shortly after his marriage and return to England. "If you take my former advice to you and Jim to do away with taking any more pups you will do the best job you have done...stick to the more legitimate one of letting farms, and having your own sheep ranches."[20]

The *Field*'s writer addressed the subject directly: "Most of the 600 Close Cadet Corps brought out £1,000 [$5,000] or more with them, and not a few regret that they paid...for the privilege of working for one of the Close brothers for twelve months. Once knowledge is gained, such a sentiment is not unnatural; but where would be this £600,000 now, if each of the six hundred had landed in Le Mars without a friend or without an anchor, without knowledge and without a guide? I will venture to say five hundred boys out of the six would have been irretrievably ruined; and worse, they would have made a bad and unfortunate start in life...." In America the downward slope was faster than in England, where family might be nearby to help. "I therefore say that the premium paid Messrs. Close is well invested; and whether at the close of the year the boy buys land of Close Brothers or of anybody else, even if he goes out into Dakota, or sacrifices the advantages of society by going in search of milder winters in Kansas or Missouri, even then his training is good, and worth the money, and he is not likely to be imposed upon by anybody."

This ardent defense of the pup system was followed in November 1881 by a pamphlet: *The English Colony in Iowa, With a List of Vacancies for Boarders and Pupils on Some of the Best Farms,* by T. G. Mellersh, addressed particularly to the sons and parents of Cheltenham school graduates. This publication appears to have been a covert advertising brochure originated by Close Brothers. Many of the points stressed were a repetition of remarks in William's *Farming in North-Western Iowa,* including the reminder that sufficient capital was essential. The testimonials regarding life in the colony, such an important feature of William's brochure, were expanded to contain actual requests for young men to apply, the details regarding terms to be arranged by the author, Mr. Mellersh.[21]

What is particularly valuable about the twelve-page promotional booklet is that each colonist who placed a notice for pups had to describe his layout, telling what a young Briton would find and why he should come. For example, one gentleman farmer wrote: "My house is a wooden one, as almost all houses are here, whether large or small. I have two sitting rooms, seven bedrooms, and a bathroom with hot and cold water; every room is heated by a flue from the furnace in the cellar." This married colonist writing in January 1881 described a standard of indoor house comfort well in keeping with upper middle-class Victorian houses of the time, for after 1880 most of these in England had running water and water closets, with basins and pitchers in bedrooms for washing.[22] "Although we have every necessary comfort," the Iowa British farmer wrote, "I should not like to take any young men who were afraid of roughing it, as they would not get on here." He outlined his farming plans: "I shall buy from 50 to 100 more cattle in the spring or as soon as I find how much hay I shall have left. I have seven horses and a pony. I shall have to get one or two more ponies in the spring, before the herding season commences, as I run my own herd." "Ponies" were the native equine strains of the West, wiry and shorter than horses, very intelligent, and possessing superior stamina. "If a pupil wishes to keep a horse of his own, I shall charge £12 [$60] a year for its keep; of course he would attend to it himself. I should not like to receive any young men who were not of good moral character, etc., as my own sons [educated at Cheltenham] are good lads, and I should expect my pupils to obey me as they would their father."

Another advertiser, writing in April 1881, described himself as a married "gentleman, resident in the English Colony...vacancies for two or more pupils...the two that were with me having left a few days ago to start a farm of their own." Candidates must be willing to work, under twenty years old preferred, and if they were not going to take an interest in farming, "I would rather be without them." His holdings were extensive, 1,500 acres with 1,500 sheep, 300 cattle, and 100 hogs. The previous year he'd shipped a carload of Cotswold and Oxford Down sheep (which "thrive wonderfully on the rich prairie grass)...I consider this a most excellent locality for stock-raising, and if properly handled, profits are great, often 100 per cent." The letter sounded like personal correspondence, either to William Close himself or to the author, Mr. Mellersh, that had been skilfully abstracted to make it into an appeal for pups. All of the notices had a similar quality, with a balanced emphasis on profits to be made in farming, the challenge of western life, and the congenial society of like-minded Britons.

Another in the list of vacancies came from "three gentlemen brothers, who settled in North Western Iowa in 1879." These would be the Eller boys; Harry had been appealing to William to send him pups for their labor force. "My brothers...have now a large farm of their own, where they raise cattle, sheep, and hogs. At first only two went out [Harry and Charles], but they reported so well upon it, that the third joined them last year." The prospective farm pupil "can stay a month on my brother's farm, to see whether he likes the life, etc.; if at the end of that time he decides upon remaining a further sum of £——— is to be paid. This will entitle him to a year's residence with my brothers, with whom he will live precisely as one of themselves, and will be taught everything necessary to become a stock raiser himself." The Ellers would act as advisers and friends, similar services to those promised by William in his brochure. "At the end of his year's residence, should he wish to buy a farm for himself, my brothers will themselves give him all the benefit of their experience. . . ."

A clergyman's son farming 5,000 acres near Le Mars needed two pupils. "I have a very experienced American foreman, who would give instructions in the various ways and means of farming in the Far West. The life is rough, and no one ought to come who cannot stand roughing it at times. Shooting—wild geese, duck, rabbit, prairie hens, prairie wolf, deer, and many small birds. Outfit—good strong clothes, saddle and gun; boots bought out here are more suited to the country. . . ." Then he mentioned some of the notables already in the Close Colony.

A sixth Iowa Briton (seven placed announcements) described his farm, the town of Le Mars, and explained there were "about 600 Englishmen, many of very good family and from the Universities, and several ladies. . . so we have the advantage of a society which is by no means without refinement." He described his living situation: "We have a very comfortable house (piano, etc.), and a good housekeeper." Not only were women generally believed to be a civilizing agent and morally superior to men, their presence guaranteed the viability of the colony itself. Thirty years earlier, one writer had put it succinctly: if a colony was not attractive to women it would be an unattractive colony. For men to stay, women had to want to live there, too.[23]

Although the young men going to Iowa were promised a warm, hospitable welcome and friendly advice, in fact they were often adrift, left to their destinies, due to the fluctuating land market and abrupt changes of owners' plans. Ill-prepared to act wisely, too young and far from his family, a youngster was frequently thrown upon his own resources, which might include money in the bank but not so often judgment as to how to use it.

When James and Walter Cowan (who were first pups near Le Mars in 1883) bought their farm and undertook its operation, they needed a good overseer whose wife could do the cooking and housekeeping, plus pups to aid with the farm work. In late November 1883, James wrote his father: "Lane, whom I think I have spoken of before, is coming to board with us through the winter and is to pay us $4 a week. It seems rather scrubby, taking money for board from an old pal, but it seems to be the way out here, and, of course he could not expect us to board him for nothing. He came one day and asked us to board him as his time is up next month with the people he is with and he has nowhere to go for the winter."[24] But the pups were often unreliable farmhands. Although the Cowans had done their friend Lane a good turn, when a fine opportunity presented itself, he departed, leaving the Cowans short-handed again, just as a new season was about to get underway.

The Cowan brothers, luckily, found a loyal English overseer and his wife; however, this faithful pair planned to start farming on their own as soon as possible. James wrote home, asking for a housekeeper to take care of the two of them and two pups for fifteen dollars a month, "which is more than double what they get at home. The Mother, I remember, said something about the cook wanting to come out and she would suit admirably so far as we can tell, if she would be up to the work." The Cowans would pay for the passage out, and it would be worth it to get an English woman to "do" for them; "a Yankee I could not stand. They are almost all so untidy and they cook in quite a different way to what we do, and all our habits are exactly opposed to theirs. I can't endure these western Yankees: the more I see of them the more I dislike them. There is not one man in a hundred whose word you can trust and who is not a rogue. There are only about three Yankees I have seen yet whom I would trust, and I should think as many hundred whom I know to be rogues."[25]

THE Cowans held the common notion of the superiority of English women, but the true difficulty in getting them to emigrate was a class matter. The British Ladies' Female Emigrant Society, formed in 1849, had been somewhat successful in overseeing transport of women who wished to emigrate, with matrons on board ship to prevent the recurrence of any incidents of rape or abuse, which had been widespread. But what the colonies actually required were women who would become the future mothers of the Empire; merely shipping out domestic servants would not solve the problem of mates for gentlemen British emigrants. The irony was that many women of good family were pining away for some useful occupation. There was no reason why only women from the workhouses should go out to the colonies when plenty of idle, educated, attractive women were eager to do so. Dr. Livingstone in his *Life and Letters* pointed out that this denial of female company led "to enormous evils in the opposite sex—evils and wrongs which we dare not even name...." Now was the time to do something about the situation, said a writer in *Macmillan's:* "In Virginia and in Iowa...settlements are rising up, where the younger sons of our gentry go and apprentice themselves to the earlier holders of land, until they, in turn, acquire land and become the gentlemen farmers of the future."[26]

Somehow in the exuberant rush to make profits from new land in various parts of the world and to set the social tone that would perpetuate upper-class ideas, the role of women had not been given full weight. William Close thought the solution lay in older married couples who would go to the West together, but what about the young bachelors if they didn't happen to fancy their friends' sisters? Perhaps a female "pup" system which corresponded to the male might be inaugurated. Feminist groups, church organizations, and other movements on behalf of women banded together in the Women's Emigration Society, founded in 1880, to provide information and grant loans "for the emigration of educated women to the colonies." These women would be called "Lady-Helps" or "Help-Companions." Abhorrent as the idea of domestic service might be, the genteel euphemism was comforting; reports from the colonies indicated that such ladies were treated as members of gentlemen's families. Actually, their situation was similar to that of the pups, whose hired-hand labor was dignified by calling it schooling and who, of course, would soon be land-owning farmers. The gentlewomen going out as "Home-Helps" knew that the life of a char would probably not be theirs for long: they would soon marry the bachelor gentlemen farmers.

A chief enthusiast of the lady-help idea was Rose Mary Crawshay, who succeeded in placing one hundred women in "genteel service," operating out of her Office for Lady-Helps in Portman Square, London. As the movement caught on, an umbrella society encompassing a number of organizations was formed, a network of clergymen's wives and schoolmistresses spreading the word to distressed gentlewomen in their localities. Those espousing the idea were well aware that many in the upper classes would react with horror at the idea of a lady working like a scullery maid rather than exercising her "energy of brain" solely. Yet there were an estimated million more women than men in the United Kingdom and something had to be done. Robert Maxtone Graham's father might with equanimity contemplate no future for his five daughters other than remaining at home the rest of their lives, cared for by the men of the family. But the circumstances in many households of the gentry prevented a similar view. "A woman though she may be well born and well bred, and have an ancestry which dates from the Conquest, cannot hope to be supported by her male relatives," said the *Macmillan's* writer. Furthermore, it was a terrible waste of intelligence, resources, and energy. One schoolmistress, speaking of her educated young ladies, said: "I have lived...to see hundreds of these fine creatures pass through my hands. What are they doing with their culture and their energy?" For most of them no employment possibilities existed. The Brontë governess character was a prototype and dramatized the hard role these women faced.

A few critics of the Women's Emigration Society felt it was a mistake to cater to the social and genteel opinions prospective emigrants entertained; rather, the truth about the difficulties of colonial domestic work should be spelled out. Most of these young women knew as little about the kitchen as their brothers did about agriculture. Later a Colonial Training Home in Shropshire offered a crash course in domestic duties and was hugely oversubscribed. If a gentlewoman emigrant could handle domestic work, perhaps social status would take care of itself. Testimonials from lady-helps in far parts of the world were reassuring: " 'very happy and comfortable, treated quite as one of the family, and dine at the same table.' " In truth, "the ideal home-help combined dignified service with companionship." It was lonely for settlers in the colonies, too, and having someone in the household from one's own class was often seen as a great boon, just as having pups provided companionship for early Close colonists. Of course, a lady-help could go only where a lady already lived—into a married household, not to bachelor digs. The single gentlemen could employ only middle-aged women in their establishments, which was why cook and nanny from home seemed the one solution.

In 1881 only fifty-nine women were sent out by the Women's Emigration Society, which had branches in Queensland, Canada, South Africa, and Iowa, often handled through clergymen in these places. In Le Mars it was Reverend Cunningham at St. George's. All emigrés reported satisfactory adjustment to colonial life, aided by the women already there. With this modest start, it was hoped more women of quality would come "to look upon colonial life in the same way in which their brothers do — not only as an inevitable necessity to be encountered bravely and cheerfully — but as an opening for ability and perseverance, an escape from a constant ill-rewarded struggle to the space, the plenty, the generous abundance, of a new country."

For some gentleman-settlers fully cognizant of the physically demanding work of Iowa farming — extra help unsteady or nonexistent — it was unthinkable to involve a lady from Great Britain in such a life of drudgery. The exhausting work dissipated notions of what civilized life should be, and many colonists were half-ashamed to find themselves in such a fix. They would not dream of having a lady on hand and feel responsible for her misery. James Cowan might tune up his mind a bit by studying Euclid late at night, but it was an act to test just how far his mental capacities may have slipped under the terrible onslaught of Iowa farm labor. Since the typical Victorian gentleman felt ladies should remain on pedestals, how could they become the cheerful soul mates William Close envisioned for his young married colonists? If a lady devoted her energies to the emigration venture, she ran the risk of losing her beauty, dignity, and refinement — at least in the eyes of the prim, inexperienced, and conventional young man who was likely to be her husband.

Many of the ladies from Britain in the Iowa colony first came as visitors to their brothers' farms, met and married someone in the colony. If women of the lower classes, they were sent over to be the "helps" for the gentlemen or as a married pair "doing for" the young settler. "In Iowa one saw a 'lady' about once a year," James Cowan wrote, "although of course there were lots of women."

English servants were likely to be quickly spoiled by American egalitarian ways. Not only did every hired girl expect to sit at the table with her master and his family, but an indignant Isabelle Randall, writing of Montana ranch life, reported that these creatures expected everyone "should sit in the parlor with them afterwards. . . . I don't want to be bothered with any more servants if I can possibly manage to do without them. . . . It is no use trying to have them out here; even *good* English ones would be spoilt in a month. The natives are very queer, independent, and rough; it is no use trying to make them into *servants,* and very disagreeable to have half-educated, ill-mannered sort of people to eat and sit with you; and if you had English ones, the natives would soon make them discontented."[27] Rose Kingsley in Colorado Springs discovered that English servant girls usually married right off, and although Orientals from the West Coast might be the best servants, they were too much trouble to import, so she got along with the garlic-breathed daughter of her laundress.

Knowing what a wife from home would have to put up with, James Cowan had scruples about embarking upon such a venture. "I get frightfully sick of never seeing a woman or anyone that is civilized and going home last year made me worse than ever on this point," he wrote his brother in January 1888. "The only salvation for a man in this country is to marry, but when he can't afford it, he is left, as a Yank would say, and anyhow there is not one woman in a hundred whom one could bring here without feeling you were tearing her away from everything she cared for....People out here [he is writing from Wyoming] always wonder why Englishmen never marry and I think regard the whole race as celebites [*sic*], if there is such a word, and they can't understand a man paying a woman to cook for him when he might just as well marry and get it done for nothing. I have come to the conclusion that nine tenths of the labouring people who marry do it as a matter of business and economy and without any other idea whatever, and half of them value their wives just in the same way one values a horse."

The following year James wrote his brother in India: "There is very little show of marrying unless it is to an American, which is...out of the field of possible events in my case. And you might as well shut an English girl up in John O'Groats House as bring her here. We have been out here for five years now and except twice...we have not seen an educated woman the whole time....A fellow just grows into a sort of bear in time under these circumstances; and isn't fit to show himself in civilised society...."

One can understand why the idea of a lady from home encountering the rough realities of the West jarred his sensibilities. The Cowans' sister Lillias came out for a visit and wrote to her father about it in a somewhat mannered style, tongue-in-cheek, as a little girl. It suggested the kind of woman who would indeed be ill-suited to pioneer life. She journeyed west with her girlfriends, Ella and Henrietta, on the Pennsylvania Railroad. "The cars were so grand. You can sit about in grand plush basket chairs, and you sit on a sweet little balcony at the very back of the train and get the wind and see no end, only you get a good many smuts into your eyes. There was a beautiful nigger ladies' maid and lots of sweet beaming nigger men to attend to us. We had beautiful bath tubs before we went to bed and then got into our nightgowns and went to a beautiful wide bed with sheets, and the Major climbed up on the one above me. Then I had another beautiful bubbly this morning and a grand breky and felt quite swell when we arrived...."

When Lillias reached the Cowan farm at Akron, Iowa, she served as a nursemaid to a colt that had lost its dam. "I have been appointed head nurse and feed her every three hours on sugared milk....I have been doing a lot of bad things one way or another. One of the worst was that I rubbed Mrs. Taylor the wrong way and produced a storm. [Mrs. Taylor was the Cowans' housekeeper.] Ella's diplomacy has however settled her down again. She really is wonderful.... Henrietta is doing sweet little sketches of the farm and its surroundings and she has made great friends with the lady of the millinery store and she has invited us to go over and spend the evening and have some music. She and I go into the city with Budd pretty often and try to get letters and do the marketing. It is very amusing...."

James had foreseen that the visit would probably go this way. He wrote his mother in alarm when he received news of the impending visit, only six days before "Toogie" (Lillias) and her friends were to arrive. "There are five bedrooms in the house and seven people living in it *now,* and five more including three ladies is somewhat of a staggerer and even you cannot at any time have had to face anything like this."

Local residents, hearing of the arrival of ladies from England to stay with the Cowans, began to speculate. "When it got about among the natives that we contemplated building another house [for the overseer and his family] they immediately jumped to the conclusion that Walter was bringing out a wife, and when they see the contingent arrive they will think it is a case of wives for the crowd, in fact an importation of wives—instead of horses, this time." And, showing he hadn't forgotten his wit and learning: "After six months of almost complete seclusion I will be able to quote Byron and say, 'this is not solitude, 'tis but to hold converse'—not exactly with Nature in the correct sense of the word but rather with the 'shock of men'; the two stanzas want to be jumbled up together a little to fit in just right."

Even the local press understood the improbability of ladies from Great Britain adapting readily to the harsh conditions of Iowa, and so when one of the colonists took the bold step of marrying someone from home and transplanting her to the prairie, the news was greeted heartily. Andrew C. Douglass, "the genial young Scotchman" who had a farm north of Le Mars in 1880, traveled to New York in October of the following year to meet his fiancée, Agnes Carmichael, "daughter of a wealthy farmer of Machir, Islay, Scotland." They were married in New York and embarked by train for Le Mars. The bride possessed some knowledge about life on a farm, as the *Sentinel* pointed out: she "has had the advantage of that practical training for housewifely duties that still survives among the better classes in Scotland."

The classic way for different cultures to assimilate was through marriage, and this held true for the Close Colony as well. The majority of Britons who stayed did so because of their American connection via matrimony. Having a wife born to American farm life helped enormously, and it bound the settler to circumstances now beyond his control—cut off possible salvation by help from home, eliminated the possibility of removal to Australia, New Zealand, or elsewhere—and forced the colonist to give up the dream that somehow he would become repatriated or that all his older brothers would die off, putting him in line for the ancestral livings and perhaps a title. His situation was known to him thoroughly, and there was little he could do but accept what circumstances and parents decreed. Some of these, like Robert Maxtone Graham, cut the tie quickly and never looked back. Others reared American families but continued to visit relatives in England, though not usually accompanied by American wife or children. The spouse remained at home to oversee farm operations. After a three-month sojourn in Great Britain, one of these gentleman-settlers returned home to Le Mars, where his "native" wife met him at the depot. In his diary he wrote: "and the first person I saw was Maggie herself in the distance—she looked good to me, the dear old girl."[28]

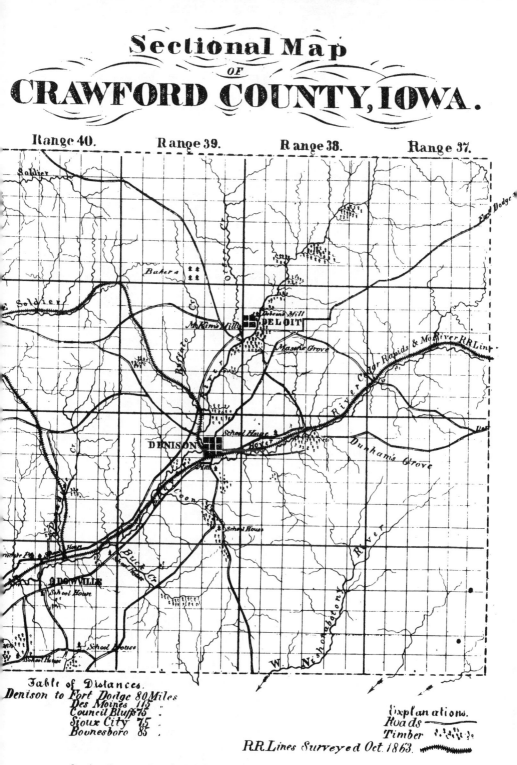

Sectional Map
OF
CRAWFORD COUNTY, IOWA.

Range 40.   Range 39.   Range 38.   Range 37.

Sectional map, Crawford County. Fred and William
Close farm, 1877, located in Range 40 on Soldier Creek.
(*Courtesy of the State Historical Society of Iowa*)

Civic dan...

Carrie Wygant (*extreme left*),
William Close's friend,
Denison, 1877.

Robert Maxtone Graham
(*center*), 1888.

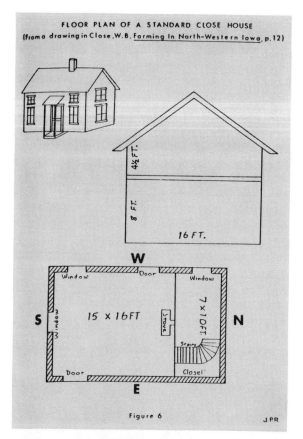

FLOOR PLAN OF A STANDARD CLOSE HOUSE
(From a drawing in Close,W.B. Farming In North-Western Iowa, p.12)

4½ FT.

8 FT.

16 FT.

W

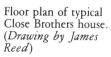

Window   Door   Window

15 X 16FT   Stove   7 X 10 FT.

S   3 pds.   N

Door   Stairs

Closet

E

Figure 6   J.P.R.

Floor plan of typical Close Brothers house. (*Drawing by James Reed*)

(*below*) Barlow hall. (*Sioux City Journal*)

(*above*) Dromore Farm (Capt. Reynolds Moreton), Le Mars, as it appeared in 1953.

(*left*) Capt. Reynolds Moreton's house, reduced from seventeen rooms, as it appeared in 1953.

T. J. Maxwell, groom of Fred Close, as he appeared in 1953.

Barn built by Col. James Fenton near Remsen, as it appeared in 1953.

COLONISING IN IOWA, U.S.

(A Hint to the Younger Sons of our Aristocracy, and eke to the Daughters thereof.)

Lady Maria. "How LATE YOU ARE, BOYS! YOUR BATHS ARE READY, AND I'VE MENDED YOUR DRESS TROUSERS, JACK. SO LOOK SHARP AND CLEAN YOURSELVES, AND THEN YOU CAN LAY THE CLOTH, AND KEEP AN EYE ON THE MUTTON WHILE EMILY AND I ARE DRESSING FOR DINNER."

Lord John. "ALL RIGHT. HOW MANY ARE WE TO LAY FOR?"

Lady Emily. "EIGHT. THE TALBOTS ARE COMING, AND MAJOR CECIL IS GOING TO BRING THE DUKE OF STILTON, WHO'S STOP- PING WITH HIM."

"Colonising in Iowa, U.S." (*Punch*, 12 Nov. 1881)

"Agricultural Depression—And How To Meet It." (*Punch*, 15 Oct. 1881)

(*right*) Le Mars Opera House. (*Courtesy of the State Historical Society of Iowa*)

(*below*) Le Mars, Dent bank corner. (*Courtesy of the State Historical Society of Iowa*)

Prairie Club interior. (*Courtesy of the State Historical Society of Iowa*)

House of Lords Cup, won by Fred B. Close.

How the Game Was Played

URING the winter of 1880–1881, William Close in England learned of the duke of Sutherland's proposed railroad tour of western United States scheduled for the following spring. Not only was the duke an intimate friend of the Prince of Wales and therefore a desirable personage to connect with the Iowa colony, he was also the biggest landowner in Great Britain, holding title to 1,358,000 acres.[1] Close persuaded the Sutherland touring party to route the trip from Chicago to Omaha by going north to St. Paul first. In St. Paul he would meet the duke and his entourage and escort them as far as Sioux City, passing through Sibley, Le Mars, and other points along the way.

The duke of Sutherland loved trains. On the 1876 goodwill trip to India with the Prince of Wales, he frequently replaced the locomotive engineer, taking over the controls and emerging dirty but happy after a good stretch of track had been traversed. Queen Victoria, however, had never been pleased about his friendship with her son and was once heard to remark, "he does not live as *a duke ought*."[2] He was too often implicated in scandalous incidents, many of which also involved the Prince of Wales. He, too, had made love to the beautiful rich courtesan, Giulia Barucci, the "greatest whore in the world," as she called herself, and when the letters Sutherland had written her were made public he said he had hardly ever read "more innocent or worse written" letters.[3] The Prince of Wales stuck with the cronies he liked, and Sutherland remained a favorite. At the time of his trip to the American West, the duke was fifty-three, more interested in Yankee railroads than in purchasing still more land, although William hoped to persuade him to buy, once he saw the fertile prairie.

W. H. "Bull Run" Russell, the correspondent who had achieved fame reporting the American Civil War and the Crimean campaign, was in the ducal party. They were met in St. Paul by Gen. Henry H. Sibley and other dignitaries, including land agent Henry Drake of the Sioux City and St. Paul Railroad, and of course, William Close. General Sibley entertained the visitors with vivid tales of his campaigns against the Sioux Indians in 1862, "in which he destroyed the invaders and broke their power for ever," wrote Russell later, a little confused as to which side was the "invaders." Russell found it hard to realize that Indian fighting had taken place there only nineteen years before.[4]

Early on 25 May, when the special train was due to depart from St. Paul, Russell asked Close where he might purchase candlesticks; the gaslights or petroleum lamps in hotel bedrooms were too dim for good reading. Together they set out to find an ironmonger's shop. " 'Don't lose your way,' said the good-natured landlord as we left the hotel," Russell wrote, "No danger of that! Was I not in the hands of a local expert?" They entered a shop, found what they wanted, and leisurely strolled to the station. "We walked down to the platform and inquired for the special. The porter, pointing with his finger to a bridge far away across the river down below, said slowly, 'I guess she'll be about there. She went off five minutes ago.' Mr. Close tackled the occasion at once— the station master was hunted down, the telegraph set to work, an engine and a carriage were prepared, and amid much abjuration from our friends, connected with imaginary dangers from collision, etc., we were delivered over to the conductor, who had never missed us, or thought we were in the train." In this way William, whom Russell describes as "our very arch guide," did not let the duke of Sutherland get away from him.

The maps spread out before the visitors showed squares belonging to the railroad and now for sale. Russell described the terrain as "undulating plain covered invariably with thick, coarse grass and seamed with deep water-courses, which in England, indeed, would be called rivers, by the sides of which grew trees and dense vegetation. The houses and stations were of wood, and I do not think that I saw a stone or brick building for many miles." They drew to a halt in Sibley, where, Russell reported, the Closes owned 42,000 acres that they planned to carve up into one hundred farms with buildings. The reason they were inspecting this particular part of the prairie was to "gratify the desire expressed by the Duke...to see a country of such great natural fertility and resources, in the process of turning the virgin soil." The visitors stepped off the train, climbed into waiting carriages, "and drove to one of the farms, Le Mars...which was inspected with great interest by the Duke and his agriculture friends, as the plough was then turning soil that never had yet been touched by the hand of man." Distracted by his almost prurient interest in the coulter's ravishment of the virgin soil, the duke (or perhaps only Russell) failed to understand that Le Mars was the name of a town, not the Closes' farm.[5]

Back on board, William presented figures on profits accruing from buying this land cheap and selling it dear: "we heard of persons coming from districts in Ireland, Scotland, or England, who had associated together for mutual help and support...." Mr. Drake spoke of the millions of acres "of unsurpassed farming and stock lands...at the disposal of the 'wide, wide world,' if it has money in its pockets, with the certainty of a magnificent fortune out of that investment." But soon the facts and figures jumbled together in their heads and according to Russell the visitors tired of instruction. The train passed through Le Mars without stopping, much to the disappointment of many colonists there, who had been tipped off by Close Brothers. The town of Sutherland, Iowa, remains as a commemoration of that brief visit.

BEFORE leaving London, William had organized a new firm, the Iowa Land Company, Limited, capitalized at £500,000 ($2,500,000) put up by seven London businessmen. William needed more money to take advantage of the imminent, great land-buying opportunities, made possible by his special arrangements with the Sioux City and St. Paul Railroad. Although capital in Close Brothers had increased greatly in a short time, helped also by Benson's contribution as partner, much of their cash was already invested in land. The stipulated aim of the Iowa Land Company echoed the activities of Close Brothers: to purchase acreages in Iowa and elsewhere in the United States and Canada, manage farms for investors, improve these farms and lease them, provide mortgages, and oversee large-scale stock feeding operations. Moneylending of various sorts would dominate Close Brothers activities in future years, just as it would with the Iowa Land Company. Once the cheap land was gone these companies became banking firms primarily, dealing in land mortgages.[6]

In 1881 the two Close-controlled firms purchased 74,300 acres in northwest Iowa and sold 24,100 acres, most of the land acquired from the railroad with a single purchase of 40,630 acres in July at the attractive figure of $6.50 per acre. The Iowa Land Company with its huge capital resources was fully in place at the time of the duke of Sutherland's visit. If the duke didn't want more land for himself, Close hoped he at least would become a major investor in the company. However, "the Duke of Sutherland did not back the Iowa Land Company," Close wrote years later. "We fully expected him to do so, but I think somebody else on his journeys got him to invest elsewhere."[7] Nevertheless, the Iowa Land Company by the following year had nearly doubled in value and with its stock selling on the London exchange at a premium of 25 percent, it was believed to be the biggest foreign company operating in the United States.[8]

More than a thousand farms were created by the Closes in those years, 1880–1881, and already they were moving into southwestern Minnesota, buying 2,100 acres in Rock and Nobles counties in 1881. The subsidiary businesses generated by this activity, the services provided by rapidly growing towns, and the wages paid laborers of all kinds, though incalculable in dollar terms or even in numbers of persons involved, was obviously enormous. These fertile lands would have been developed in due time by other means and under the guidance of other capitalists, if not the Closes, but by doing well what could be accomplished on a massive scale, they settled this last frontier of the Middle West with astonishing rapidity. The "go" in the Closes' operation infected everyone in the region with a surge of confidence in the future. The *St. Paul Pioneer Press,* once so critical of the Closes for their emphasis on gentlemen immigrants, now headlined their accomplishments:

THE CLOSE BROTHERS
Their Astonishing Growth in Wealth
One of the Wonders of the West[9]

The deployment of the individual Closes to handle the business details effectively is no better illustrated than in the spring of 1881. William remained in England very late to guide the Iowa Land Company through its formation and to oversee the London end of Close Brothers. He and Mary did not arrive in America until 16 May, only ten days before he met the duke of Sutherland in St. Paul. Mary did not accompany him; her father had died suddenly in a Dubuque hotel, 7 April, perhaps while on a return trip from visiting his sons Ed and Henry near Cherokee.[10]

JOHN CLOSE, who up to now had remained in the background, went with his friend Richard Sykes to Iowa in April. After a stay at Syke's "Larchwood," John spent time with James in Le Mars and Sibley, getting an intimate glimpse of the business, and with Fred at Quorn, gaining a better understanding about farming before returning to Manchester in early summer. It was his only Iowa excursion, but the knowledge he gained through even such a brief experience with the country sharpened his questions. He knew himself to be a sound, careful, prudent businessman, but he retained toward his younger brother, William, a certain suspicion that accounts were not always kept accurately, that he allowed too many slipshod negotiations. The talent of a successful salesman and promoter might not be matched with wise attention to the letter — all the details that constitute sound business practices. In May 1882 John wrote William in anger regarding the accounting of investments he had received.

> You will have to admit when you see them that either they are d____d bad or there must be some mistake. Unless you can give me some very good reasons backed by facts and not opinion, I shall clear out of farming. Buying land is another thing, but breaking and letting farms on your terms won't do. Compare your estimate given to me in 1879 with the actual figures.... Your saying...that we must not blame you if the farms don't pay won't wash. You have done just what you like with my money (even to using it) and the gross result is a loss.

JAMES, with his easily dispensable bachelor digs in Le Mars, perhaps gave the most of himself to Close Brothers, for he could go on short notice to wherever his services were needed. He searched for new lands across the northern Iowa border in Minnesota in April 1881. With reliable help in the Le Mars office and another Briton in Rock Rapids, James moved his location to Sibley, where the chief activities were now taking place. Constantine Benson joined him there.

From his offices in the Sibley Hotel, James issued a call in May for breakers to work the prairie. He also helped plan a new brick building for Close Brothers in Sibley. Contracts were issued for the construction of sixty farmhouses with brick foundations and chimneys. Not all the rooms would be plastered, however; instead, "Ceilinged inside with matched lumber. . . . The land broken this season will be back-set next fall, and thus made ready for seeding in the spring." Furthermore, hay would be put up on all the farms owned so that a renter taking over on 1 March, the usual tenant contract date, would have feed for his cattle and horses before the new spring grass became available.

500 RENTERS WANTED

This summer we have opened upwards to 300 new farms, sinking a well, building a convenient house and roomy barn, and breaking from 60 to 100 acres on each farm. These farms are to be let on terms that no industrious man can fail to make profitable.[11]

"And as James B. Close will have charge of the business," the *Sibley Gazette* reports, "the relations. . . will be pleasant," for "those who have had dealings with Close Bros. in the way of contracts for breaking, find them to be honorable gentlemen and always ready to do what is right."[12]

SINCE James remained mostly in Sibley, an hour's train ride north from Le Mars, Fred spent more time in the Le Mars office in addition to managing the farms on the West Fork. This put him in the center of the colony when plans were underway for the June Derby, a racing event the British hoped to make as important as the celebrated meets at Rochester and Saratoga Springs. Fifty horses were in training. Fred arranged special fares on the railroads, so that spectators could come from Chicago, St. Paul, Omaha, and points along these routes. The cost of a round-trip ticket from St. Paul was one-way plus one-fifth. A large grandstand had been erected on the southwest edge of Le Mars, costing $1,000, and the hotel keepers in Le Mars were busily "getting out their extra cots, and looking up their surplus china." Horse talk was everywhere, "on the street corners and the corridors of our hotels." The British would come together for this "grand equestrian tournament" and all who participated would have a sense of the vitality of the colony. No better paradigm of life could be held up: playing the game for all it was worth.[13]

On the morning of the Derby, "Red caps and blue caps, green caps and yellow, could be seen filing through the crowds, noise and confusion. . .and Le Mars looked very like a city of the first class rather than the third," a newspaper-man commented. A thousand people jammed the streets on the way to the race grounds. The scene was described as "brilliant in the extreme, the throng of people, the vehicles of all kinds, the brilliant costumes of the ladies, the driving, the riding, the music, the fighting, the gambling, the drink, the mounted police, the unmounted, ditto; the jockeys, the 'let-her-roll' of the man at the wheel (you were not forbidden to speak to this one), all made up a lively panorama that only Le Mars and the English Races can produce. You could back your fancy to any figure you pleased, and the book-makers called the odds in the most approved race-course fashion."[14]

"The weather was warm. . .but there was a fair breeze," and the "race course was in most excellent condition—firm as a rock, smooth as a floor and dustless as my lady's boudoir." The finishing touches to the grandstand had been completed the previous day; shortly before the 1:00 P.M. starting time, leading off with the West Fork Plate, the stands began to fill. On the track spectators saw "gentlemen riders in their gay and unsullied colors and their grooms unswathing bandages, lightening girths, or restraining the impatience of the highly trained and noble animals that seemed conscious of and eager for the coming struggle." Meanwhile, "Scores of elegant turnouts were driving leisurely across and around the park. . . .Lemonade stands, refreshment booths, and the inevitable hazard tables were surrounded by throngs anxious to slake their thirst, or make a fortune. Brilliantly costumed riders dashed hither and thither either to test the mettle of their steeds or convey important messages relating to the pending contests. The betting men, with hands filled with greenbacks, pencil and cards, added to the hubbub, by offering to wager in any conceivable way. . . .The ladies, too, English and American, were present in force, their elegant toilets adding picturesqueness to the scene." It all re-sembled Firth's 1858 genre painting, *The Derby Day,* which for years was the most widely known picture in England.[15]

"Are you ready, gentlemen?" the starter called and the flag fell, just as a carriage entered the grounds and partially obstructed the straightaway, but Jack Wakefield avoided it and quickly took the lead, pressed by Fred Close, who came in second. The Hail Columbia Stakes for Americans was entered by horses with such plebian names as Ketchup, Kitchen Maid, or Little Harry.[16]

The most exciting race, the Le Mars Cup, was one and one-half miles over six flights of hurdles, with Americans allowed to enter. The prize of seventy dollars went to Willie Gaskell, the Closes' first cousin, riding an American horse, Sunbeam, which beat out William Close's Petrarch (purchased from Con Benson). Will Farquhar's Speculation unfortunately "flew the track at the third hurdle and threw its rider, but without hurting him much." The year 1881 was conspicuously successful for American race horses: Iroquois won the

Derby, Foxhall the Parisian Grand Prix, and Sunbeam the Le Mars Cup. One Englishman was heard to remark, "A Yankee horse won the Derby in England, a Yankee horse wins the Derby today, and by God, I'm a Yankee!"[17]

In the trotting race with sulkies, Fred Close was an easy first with Kitty. In the International Scurry that followed, the American horse Kitchen Maid defeated Fred Paley's Ned. The good sportsmanship displayed by participants struck an observer as a welcome change from the usual "bickering that has done so much to bring the noble sport into disrepute. . . . If a horse was beaten his owner made no outward sign of grief."

That evening Apollo Hall was draped in American and English flags for the *soirée dansante* hosted by Close Brothers for about sixty couples, most of them British. In one corner a buffet supper with wine and other refreshments was laid out. The ladies wore evening gowns, the gentlemen white ties. A number of American girls, invited as partners to parties such as this, ended up with British husbands. Other unattached ladies like the Humble girls were guests of homesteading brothers and thus became rapidly acquainted in the colony. Some matrimonial matches were arranged in England because of friendships formed among the Iowa colonists. Walter Cowan wrote his mother in March 1884: "Another festive farmer from these parts. . . who used to be Joe's 'fag' at Harrow is expected to return shortly bringing with him a blushing bride, the beautiful Miss Hobart, sister of the future Earl of Buckinghamshire. The said future Earl is going in for breeding thorough-bred swine near Le Mars."[18]

The Le Mars Derby in June of each year developed into the most important single event holding the colony together, a celebration of their common enterprise that attracted almost every Briton in the area. The brilliantly illuminated Apollo Hall filled with handsome, stylish dancers reassured participants that a famous colony did indeed exist. For this sense of community, constantly attended to, Fred Close was chiefly responsible. The races appealed to even such distant colonists as the Cowan brothers, who were friendly with only a small number of British neighbors and seldom appeared at social events. "We are going into Le Mars on Tuesday to be present at the races," James wrote his mother. "I play in a football match the next day and am going to a ball in the evening, so that I am going to have 'quite a day' next week altogether."[19]

The Derby gathering in June 1881 resulted in a sudden determination to establish cricket, as well, in the colony, organized by Fred Paley. Gerald Garnett and the Ellers brothers practiced together in the Broken Kettle creek region west of Le Mars, and other potential players worked out at Quorn. As a courtesy Captain Moreton was named president of the cricket club, but F. R. Price and Paley were actually in charge. Price had achieved national fame as a cricketer while at Queen's College, Oxford. The first cricket game was played on 2 July in a field near the Le Mars brickyard, a match between the Moreton pups and the Le Mars club. Two years later the Le Mars team was good enough to defeat the St. Paul team and afterwards were entertained by their St. Paul hosts in the best restaurant in the city. It was the first week of August, the very height of the farm harvest, but they were far removed from the threshing machine and bundle racks. On the one hand there were the demands of the land and the rhythms of the seasons; on the other, the life to which they had always been accustomed and which they intended to continue.

Fred Close recognized the role of sports in keeping up morale and set many of the contests. Some of them were spur-of-the-moment affairs, such as the paper chases on horseback across the fields, with Fred acting as "hare," spreading tattered paper from a large bag to mark a sporadic trail. After a ten-minute lapse the "hounds" would start in pursuit.

Another meeting of the English Jockey Club in September coincided with the agricultural fair. This brought sports and good farming together in the same event. The Plymouth County Agricultural Association had been formed in 1872, but under the firm leadership of Captain Moreton and the Closes, the event developed into a major annual affair. In 1881 a Floral Hall forty by sixty feet, a Vegetable Hall, and stock pens and sheds were built on the 40-acre fairgrounds, where the track and grandstand were also located. (A tornado destroyed the buildings the following year, but the facilities were partially rebuilt through donations from the British.) Premiums amounting to $1,000 were posted; the association and prominent colonists added another $1,000. Close Brothers, for instance, put up $50 for the best 5-acres of wheat grown in the immediate four-county area. "Let the farmers of these counties take pains to verify the yield per acre...and be in a position to present to the proper officers, properly authenticated evidence...."[20]

The fair's star animal attraction was William Close's thoroughbred stallion Elsham, supposedly valued at $25,000, which arrived in July to a flurry of newspaper acclaim. A bay of large size and big-boned, he came from Lord Falmouth's stable and was listed in the stud book as sired by Knowsley (by Stockwell, out of General Peel's dam), "which are points horsemen will appreciate," the *Sioux City Journal* reported with the same nod toward lineage given the blooded gentry who were settling the region. Elsham's readiness to stand at stud was announced in regular newspaper advertisements. The Close brothers swept the honors in horse flesh.[21]

Captain Moreton and James Fenton divided the cows and bulls prizes while James Close won every category concerning sheep. In the vegetable, grains, and floral departments many Americans competed successfully. The September gala included track and field events, even a race for men over thirty in which Moreton, Cooper, and James Close participated. Eleven men ran the 120-yard hurdle race over ten flights of hurdles; four athletes tried to outdo each other in throwing a cricket ball; six ran the mile; and a horde of seventeen stumbled along in the sack race, every man furnishing his own sack.[22]

Entertaining though these contests were, the serious attention focused on horse racing, especially the hurdle competition for the Barrow Cup, "an elegant $200 affair" promoted and funded by Fred Barrow, proprietor of the House of Lords. Barrow had emigrated to the States in 1864, settling first in eastern Iowa and then the Dakota territory. He moved to Le Mars in 1880 with the advent of the British colony and opened his public house, which soon became a favorite haunt of the pups. In the race Fred Close took the lead but when his horse came up to the first barrier it backed away, refusing to jump. When Fred forced another run, horse and rider fell, and many in the crowd thought he had been killed or terribly injured. Yet he recovered quickly and brought the horse back into the race and actually won—to loud cheering— beating out his brother William's Petrarch. Horse-racing fever even got to James Close, who bought a horse that had won the Great Metropolitan Stakes at Jerome Park.[23]

The following year, a month before the June Derby, Willie Gaskell, the Closes' cousin, begged William to sell him Lady-in-Waiting. "I think you might let me down with £100 [$500] and not £150 [$750], as it is a long price & I know what you gave for her." Willie got his horse and rode her in the Missouri Stakes, where she seemed about to come in second when the horse ahead fell dead, much to the owner's distress, for it was his chief asset. Gaskell gave him the stakes and helped take up a collection, which finally amounted to $80. The star of the Derby was Jack Wakefield, particularly impressive on Fay Templeton, named for a singing actress who had appeared at the opera house a few months earlier.

After the 1882 Derby came the July footraces and cricket matches, which were even more enthusiastically subscribed to than the year before. One sports-minded pup, who was also private secretary to Captain Moreton, left in late summer for Virginia to take a spa cure because, the press reported, he "has applied himself so continuously to his business that he must rest."[24]

In the colony atmosphere of robust health, there was no place for those of weak physical or mental makeup. But sickness and death occasionally claimed a member, especially those men who had been sent out because the fresh air of Iowa was expected to improve their health. Percy Atkinson, an Oxford man, had been married only a few months before his death in August 1881. Another, a pup on Constantine Benson's brother's farm, died following a shooting expedition to Minnesota during which he caught cold. In the winter of 1881–1882 Hugh Hornby, twenty-three, the son of Sir Edward Hornby of Sussex, died of pneumonia; another young man, thirty-one, died of diphtheria. A colony country newspaper published a memorial poem for these last two:

> Two of our countrymen have passed
> Beyond the veil, far to that unknown land;
> 'Tis only short week ago we saw them last
> And now they're missing from our little band

Later stanzas placed a final faith in God, who must know why these things happen. In the midst of a lush Iowa summer, such bleak moments lay far behind. Strenuous sports contests proved one's bodily health, making it seem unlikely that illness could strike a deathblow.[25]

Lawn tennis, which began in earnest the summer of 1882, was played alternate Saturdays on the same turf used by the cricket club. Although a form of tennis had been played in France since the Middle Ages, official lawn tennis in Great Britain had only come into existence seven years before. In America, lawn tennis had begun the previous year, so the Le Mars tennis club was one of the earliest in the nation. By the next year Le Mars was participating in matches with St. Paul and other large cities.[26]

The game of golf with its Scottish origins may actually have been first played in the United States on the Nicholson pastures south of Le Mars in the mid-1880s. The first permanent golf course established in the States, the St. Andrews course at Yonkers, New York, dates only from 1888. Gutta-percha balls had been knocked about pastures at various locations in the East, however, and if the Le Mars Scottish golfers knew they were the first to import the game, they made nothing of it in the local press.[27]

The same could not be said for polo. Fred Close believed himself to be the first polo player in the United States. When he emigrated to Virginia in 1874, he already possessed a knowledge of the game, which he learned from army friends who played in India. The usual official date of polo's entry into America is 1875, when James Gordon Bennett, Jr., who had witnessed polo matches at the Hurlingham Club in England, brought back polo mallets and balls to New York and induced friends to join him in creating American polo. Cow ponies from Texas were trained and several matches played in 1876.[28]

The polo ponies in the Close Colony were also Indian — quick, smart, and easily trained. They seemed to catch onto the game and were adept at reversing the field with little guidance. The official date of the beginning of Le Mars polo is 1885, with the formation of the Northwestern Polo League, including clubs at Omaha, Blair, Yankton, and Sioux Falls. In 1887 the Le Mars Polo Club put on a demonstration game in St. Louis and helped that city's polo players organize, while at the same time the Le Mars Cricket Club was competing against Minneapolis. After the Le Mars polo team had triumphed in Sportsman's Park at a subsequent contest, one player was heard to remark that his pony "is even aware of the distinction between on and off side." Wearing uniforms from England, the Le Mars polo team was a major attraction at county fairs throughout the Middle West and a featured event at the St. Louis Exposition of 1893.[29]

Ice hockey, which the colonists called "polo," became a favorite winter sport, with players dressed in calico shirts and pantaloons. As fans developed for the hockey club games, a subscription was taken to buy navy blue uniforms. Coaching or tally-ho riding was also a popular pastime, the ladies along, especially in the early days of the colony when four-in-hands would parade through Le Mars and proceed to the open country. "Lost between Merrill and Le Mars, an English Coach Horn," read one newspaper notice.[30]

The most punishing sport on a player's body was English football, which to an American spectator looked like "an Arkansas rough-and-tumble free fight. But they love it." Broken collarbones, dislocated joints, fractures were often the price; this aspect of sports seriously interfered with the farming business. A pup named Thomson was a particularly ardent rugby player. He was the son of the archbishop of York, the third-ranking peer in the realm after the royal family, and it may have been about him that William Close commented, years later: "A Bishop's son was the worst among them!"[31]

Throughout the year, but especially in fall and winter, hunting expeditions pursued wild animals and birds. Some parties returned with hundreds of bagged fowl or other game, but occasionally the shooting was very poor. To hedge against the possibility of coming back empty-handed and being jeered by friends, a group of English hunters in a prankster mood stole the fresh-killed wild ducks from a peg outside Dietrick's meat-and-game shop in Le Mars and stowed them away. The hunt was a failure, but after they'd shown their bogus ducks to friends, they walked into the butcher's and resold the birds to the unsuspecting proprietor.[32]

On winter weekends elaborate hunting parties sometimes amused the locals, who generally hunted for meat, not sport. "Sunday hunters—a number of gentlemen on foot or on horses—and ten hounds with pedigrees, caught a rabbit, and it wasn't a good day for hunting, either." Another day a wolf-hunting party set off across the snowy fields, the dogs apparently hot on the trail. But the scent turned out to be from the muskrat coat of one of the huntsmen, who, according to the press, "narrowly escaped from being torn to pieces by the infuriated pack."[33]

AFTER sports, the next most important feature of colony extracurricular life was the Prairie Club, modeled after a gentleman's club in England. It had come into existence at Captain Moreton's, then moved to rooms over a downtown Le Mars store. When the *Field's* man visited in 1881 he reported: "The club at Le Mars is as yet the weakest and worst attended of any British one in America; but with new rooms and increased numbers this will probably cure itself." By December of that year a grand opening of new quarters in a brick building took place. The *Field's* observer maintained that in spite of the criticism that clubs in colonial situations had a demoralizing effect, they were in fact quite the opposite in their function: "Nothing so keeps up the *esprit de corps* of Englishmen as a club of their own." Club life exercised "a moral control over the actions of new arrivals" and the opinion of fellow club members was not likely to be ignored, even by the most obstreperous newcomer. Social drinking in a club of gentlemen resulted in less alcoholic abuse. "In a western town these arguments possess ten times the weight that they would at home." The Le Mars club might be improved, he thought, by having membership open to all colonists. The selection committee in fact seemed to have admitted most of the gentlemen-class Britons who wished to join, but some who lived at great distances did not bother.

The new club quarters in the center of Le Mars had a cloakroom attended by an obsequious porter and large, well-lit rooms attractively furnished in masculine club style. Folding doors separated the chambers as needed; one room was devoted to reading and letter writing, with desks, easy chairs, books, magazines, and newspapers. A fully equipped kitchen served fairly elaborate meals.[34]

The *conversazione* held at the Prairie Club's new home on 17 December 1881 offered a musical program of English ballads sung by fellow colonists, a violin solo, a lady playing the piano, a duet for violin and piano, but most of the entertainment involved sipping coffee and conversing. Among the hundred people present were Iowa's Senator A. H. Lawrence, Lord Hobart, the mayor of the town, and most of the prominent colonists, including such resident leaders as Captain Moreton and James Close (both Fred and William were in Europe) and some prospective new leaders, including Captain Frederick Robinson. He and his wife were in charge of the pups on the Close farms at Quorn. Robinson was one the mature settlers William sought to stabilize the community; with his military background he would exercise discipline in keeping the pups in line, plus setting them a proper model to emulate. Robinson's father had been vicar of the same Warwickshire parish for forty-two years. His son Frederick chose the gentlemanly profession of the army, joining at nineteen and serving for seven years. In the winter of 1873 he shipped out to America and settled on a sheep ranch in California. After six years of ranching experience, he heard of the Close Colony and decided to move to Iowa.[35]

Also present at the Prairie Club opening were Alfred G. Lascelles, second son of the Hon. George E. Lascelles of Sion Hill, Yorkshire, whose mother was the daughter of the earl of Mansfield. An Oxford graduate, Alfred had sailed to the States aboard the *Celtic* with William and Mary Close in April 1881. He proved to be good at several sports but was an indifferent farmer and soon returned to England, where he was called to the bar of the Inner Temple. Later he occupied several distinguished posts abroad, principally that of chief justice of Ceylon. His great friend in Iowa was an Oxford classmate, the son of Sir Matthew Dodsworth of Thornton Watlass, Yorkshire. Whereas Lascelles soon tired of the prairies, Dodsworth, who possessed considerable sums for investment, became a partner of Close Brothers for a time in their Sibley, Iowa, branch. But the old pull of the class system drew Dodsworth back to England. Not only his father but his older brother died, and in 1891 he fell heir to the title and Dodsworth lands in Yorkshire.[36]

At the time of the Prairie Club opening, another mature colonist present was Arthur Gee of Rectory Farm, Cambridge, who had experienced great difficulties getting settled in Iowa. He purchased land near Sioux City in 1879, then chose a stock farm near Le Mars, where he and his wife might enjoy the society of the colony more easily. He began his colonial experiment with five hundred sheep while his house was being built and went into cattle raising as well. With land prices steadily rising, early settlers were tempted to reap their profits and move farther West, and this was why Gee was able to buy his neighbor's farm in 1882. But the old neighbor kept sneaking back to remove items, including the boards of outbuildings, until finally Gee summoned the sheriff to have him arrested. The neighbor was hauled before a judge and fined. But in the free-wheeling style of the times, such a settlement became a laughing matter and did not settle much—though the thievery did stop.[37] Fred Close caught the frontier spirit more adroitly upon learning that someone was stealing wheat from his bins on the Quorn farm. "All hands and the cook kept a lookout but they couldn't catch on. Fred determined to hire a detective. Did he send to Chicago? Nixy. He set Dick Hynes to work. Dick soon got a pointer, and in a very few days he had a colony of thieves bagged. All quietly. No fuss."[38]

During Gee's brief, elaborate colony stay, he and his family returned to England several times for long visits. He also began a joint stock-raising venture with another colonist but that partnership was dissolved in November 1883. Nothing much in his Iowa life worked out satisfactorily for Gee. Once he lost a fine span of horses while fording a small river. And his property continued to get stolen: "The man who picked up my black satchel will please leave it at Dent bank at once," read a personal notice in the newspaper. Finally: "Arthur Gee and his family, after giving Iowa two trials. . . took permanent leave."

For two decades the Prairie Club served as the inner sanctum of the colony; lucky Americans entertained there relished the atmosphere, "a paradise of luxury, ease and comfort," as one editor said, and when he met a direct descendant of General Banastre Tarleton of the Revolutionary War, he noted in the youth "a marked resemblance to that warrior."[39]

A COLONIST'S physical health was bolstered by sports and games, and his social life was nourished by the Prairie Club. The third ingredient for a well-rounded existence was the spiritual, as Captain Moreton from the beginning recognized. For one's business aims to work out satisfactorily, a balanced attention to the next world—as well as this one— usually seemed appropriate. This practical use of religious activity was fundamental to the Victorian scheme of well-being.

The colonists were mostly High Church, and even though Moreton was the brother of an earl, the chapel evangelicalism he favored was not their usual brand of religion. James Close, Captain Moreton, and other colony leaders met in 1881 to establish a proper Anglican church. Episcopal Grace Mission had been in existence some years, but the building was too small and not fashionable. Many colonists were sons of clergymen and had deep, early memories of beautiful country churches. During the initial organizational meetings the local Episcopal clergyman from Grace Mission had to remind the British that if a new church were formed "it would be a part of the American Episcopal Church, under the authority of the Episcopal Bishop of Iowa," not the archbishop of Canterbury — as some by their attitude seemed to imagine. In their eagerness to anglicize the church as well as the countryside, they had forgotten where they were. "Captain Moreton said that he was not strictly an Episcopalian, but he was ready to do all he could to furtherance of the work." One of the colonists possessed architectural skills and undertook plans for the building and vicarage. Construction was expected to cost $7,000, but after completion the total came to merely $3,200, most of it contributed from England, since the church was deemed a foreign mission.[40]

The new vicar arrived in midsummer 1881, just in time to bury colonist Percy Atkinson. The Reverend Mr. Cunningham was thirty, born in Hampshire, attended Oxford, and after his ordination he conducted services in Staffordshire, Oxfordshire, and his native Hampshire before emigrating to Le Mars. He was appraised in the press as "a young man of pleasing address...and said to be...of great learning." In addition to the Le Mars church, he held services in various parts of the colony, including the home of William Close at Quorn.[41]

In early January, after six months in his new parish, the Reverend Mr. Cunningham boarded the East-bound express. In Philadelphia he stayed with the bishop of Pennsylvania while awaiting the arrival of his fiancée, the daughter of the vicar of St. Edmunds, Dudley. Mrs. Cunningham became a lively addition to the church activities, helped organize fund-raising events by holding musicales, selling her own watercolor plaques, and leading the ladies of the congregation in charitable causes. A son was born shortly before her first year in Iowa was over.

The idea of an Anglican church existing at the center of the colony was almost as important as the institution itself. The very look of the *Book of Common Prayer* and hymnals reminded worshipping immigrants of their earliest family years. But in practice St. George's was mostly a Le Mars religious entity. For settlers living at some distance, it could not become an intimate part of their lives. James Cowan wrote home from his ranch on the Big Sioux River, some twenty-five miles from Le Mars: "In your last you ask about Church. There is no Church here nearer than Le Mars, and of course we can't manage to get in without starting at about 9:30, in which case we would need to be up at about 6 A.M. to get thro' 'chaws' etc. in time....On Sunday we do 'chaws' late...."[42]

St. George's still stands, a wooden replica of an English stone country church, its tower diminished by some fierce Iowa storm that happened in the last hundred years. The parishioners are a mix of many nationalities, though a high percentage are descendants of early British settlers, many of whom were yeomen employed by the gentlemen — but such class distinctions have long since blurred completely. St. George's is now on the National Register of Historic Places.

CHAPTER ELEVEN

Colony Concepts, Personal Destinies

 HE frequent, reliable, and comfortable trains nationwide meant that British settlers in various parts of the country could look up one another and compare experiences. At the invitation of the British Association of Kansas, a Close Colony delegation of eight (headed by Montague J. Chapman) journeyed to Florence, Kansas, for a dinner party Christmas Eve, 1881. After toasting the queen and the president of the United States, the speakers emphasized the necessity for pluck, perseverance, and energy for success in settling and lamented the too-prevalent notion among gentlemen that prosperity in America was there for the asking. Failure could come, even though one arrived with capital, native intelligence, and social credentials. After the convention, the Le Mars party continued by rail to New Mexico, where they had been invited by other British friends. They accepted an engagement to return the following summer for a fishing expedition, disregarding for the moment the likelihood of harvest demands.[1]

Iowa colonists traveling to Rugby, Tennessee, found the colony numbered about 400, with sixty-five Victorian Gothic wooden buildings. It seemed a markedly different atmosphere, partly because of the wooded mountain setting. Rugby's location had appealed to Hughes on two scores: the climate was mild; and unlike Iowa or Kansas, which had richer land, Tennessee was not plagued by periods of drought, flies and grasshoppers, or drainage problems.[2]

The South seemed a natural home for transplanted Englishmen, given the large proportion of Southerners who were English in origin, though Hughes had personally deplored their cause in the Civil War. He thought his colony might aid the postwar recovery, with England sending "our best blood into the United States." This infusion should also nullify the risk of future hostilities between England and the United States. Rugby would play a peacemaker's role in binding together again the states North and South, thereby strengthening the country and furthering international tranquility. Hughes had been criticized at home because he had failed to start the venture under the British flag; so these reasons were put forth by way of justification. But exactly how the colony would function economically was only vaguely addressed.

After the war a group of Bostonians hoped to relocate unemployed workers from depressed factory areas of New England in this part of Tennessee, a sort of post-Civil War "carpetbag" scheme with benevolent intent. But the plan never developed and Hughes was able to purchase the area under the aegis of his Board of Aid to Land Ownership. The board sold lots and acreages to the incoming British settlers, and American artisans erected most of the buildings. Hughes said a colonist might choose any number of occupations such as livestock raising, vegetable or fruit culture, or, following the lead of the local farmers he might raise corn and other cereal crops—or he might become a beekeeper, go into the lumber business, or raise poultry. These vague suggestions were for the edification of the very young men who were expected to apprentice themselves initially to persons engaged in these occupations. Although Hughes tried to sound knowledgeable about a prospective colonist's gear—whether particular tools, a gun, or special clothing should be brought along or purchased in America—and his advice in general was to travel light, his comments carried none of the authority William Close's had, for he lacked the practical experience necessary to advise. Hughes urged the emigrant to always remember that "he is going to try an experiment which *may not* succeed."

This frank expression of doubt was in strong contrast to statements from the Close Colony leaders, who had some qualms but seldom voiced them. Instead of emphasizing the young man's chance to make a fortune, Hughes advised him to take little cash along for it would only get him into trouble. He depicted Rugby as a society where one's wants were simple and easily satisfied. A little money would be needed because the newcomer would be obliged to join the supply association—a cooperative store—since facilities for shopping were limited. He would be required to pay the entrance fee for the colony club "(which controls the lawn tennis ground and the musical gatherings, and otherwise caters for the social life of the settlement), and to support the vestry or the choir."

American critics of Rugby, particularly the press, found Hughes's sentiments dilettantish, confirming the weakest and worst features of the gentleman class as they became immigrants in American rural regions. Who would do the work, how would they get their food? Lawn tennis was all very well for spare time, but who would accomplish the daily tasks of life? The Tabard Inn, the colony's hotel as well as headquarters for the board, served food and provided clean rooms for vacationers who came for the salubrious mountain air, and the miles of hiking trails and bridle paths. But did it serve serious settlers or merely British upper class tourists? Even Hughes's stipulation regarding the prohibition of alcoholic spirits was mocked by the press, which claimed that drink-minded colonists would seek out moonshiners who kept supplies hidden in hollow trees near Rugby and say: "Beg pardon, sir, I would like to loan you a dollar," and thus the transactions would be made.[3]

In the summer of 1881 Rugby suffered a disaster. Two guests at the Tabard

Inn and five colonists died of typhoid fever. A polluted cistern, too near the Inn's cesspool, was believed to have been the cause. An immediate exodus of colonists ensued as did much adverse international publicity, for Thomas Hughes was one of England's best-known writers and any news about him or his project made good copy. One of the dead was Philip Nairn, from a well-placed Scottish wool-merchants and banking family. Nairn had formerly been a pup in the Close Colony. One relative who journeyed to Tennessee in the wake of her brother's death "found the key of his cottage hung on a nail at the door, and with all of his things intact and in order. Hotels and stores were all closed, and all wore a most forlorn aspect. Some young men of that kind whose return would be a terror to their families remain there, living on doles from home, supplemented by what they get by sport...."[4] The *Chicago Tribune,* in its account, attributed the collapse to the laziness of the inhabitants, who seemed to regard their stay at Rugby "as a pleasant picnic, in which fishing, botanical excursions, literary pursuits, and lawn-tennis were the prime entertainments." Mr. Hughes was no doubt honest but woefully naive, and once the problems of the real world had to be faced, the colony folded. And this "once more proved how visionary are all schemes based upon literature, esthetics, and a lively imagination," for these sentiments had nothing whatever to do with the hard facts of life.[5]

Hughes's eighty-three-year-old mother, who arrived in April with much fanfare as a grand gesture of faith in her son, stayed on, though she was in poor health. Hughes himself came less and less. Meanwhile, the Rugby Canning Company opened in 1882 with no fruit or vegetables available for canning. Nobody seemed to be running Rugby.

The *Le Mars Sentinel,* gathering its information from recent visitors to Rugby, in March 1883 reported that only two hundred colonists remained, "the majority of whom spend their time in hunting and playing billiards," and although they owned thousands of acres, "only 50...are in cultivation! What a vivid contrast Rugby presents to our own rushing, pushing, thriving, bustling Plymouth County!"[6] Commercialism, not idealism, was the proper prescription for colonists. In the Close Colony the oddness of exuberant sports played on the frontier was offset by the fact that many leading sportsmen were also serious, successful farmers.

The Tabard Inn was reopened and attracted cash customers by 1884, when it was destroyed by fire; although a new hotel was built, it did not flourish, for Rugby itself continued to decline. When Mrs. Hughes died in 1887, the last family connection was gone; Hughes was too ill and discouraged to attempt to carry it further. Some of the land was sold to the state of Tennessee for back taxes. With the Board of Aid unable to muster sufficient capital to continue, the colony was on the verge of collapse. A phrase from *Tom Brown's School-*

days might have served as epitaph: "Nevertheless, play your games and do your work manfully—see only that that be done, and let the remembrance of it take care of itself."[7]

THE frankly commercial nature of the Close Colony resulted in easier assimilation, but one Iowa feature threatened to scuttle the whole enterprise: the Prohibitionists were becoming very strong. Fred Barrow, proprietor of the House of Lords, was actually sued by a woman for serving liquor to her husband, who could not handle it. Although she didn't win her $1,000 court action, the idea that a wife could employ such measures was unsettling for the twenty-two saloon keepers in Le Mars.[8] One favorite pub of the English, Windsor Castle, had already been converted into Deacon Gilbert's Harness Shop. Should the Prohibitionists succeed in passing laws against the sale of liquor in Iowa, it would seriously affect immigration to the state. Not only the British were accustomed to alcoholic beverages as part of normal life, so were the Germans, Scandinavians, Hollanders, and other European settlers who were arriving in great numbers. The *Sentinel* deplored "the goody-good people who want to transmogrify our State into a grand, perennial Sunday-school...."[9]

Support for the impending amendment to the state's constitution continued to mount. At a temperance picnic held in a grove near Quorn, about four hundred assembled to sing songs and listen to speeches one moonlit night in June 1882, then rode home through fields of grain, marvelling over the magnificent British barns along the way, without a thought that what they espoused might uproot the colony in which they took such pride.[10] Few of the Prohibitionists were members of the Prairie Club or gentlemen of that ilk. Fred Close was quoted in the *St. Paul Pioneer Press* as saying that the English would leave Iowa if the amendment passed and became law. When asked by the *Sentinel* for a further comment, Fred replied that since business would be interfered with, the Close Brothers would probably move elsewhere.[11]

Fred and William in their Denison days had encountered the temperance movement. In the summer of 1878 they were merely new settlers and so they could be amused by "the Temperance wave" that washed over Denison and lasted three weeks—all sympathizers wearing blue ribbons in their lapels. "The ribbon does not always wear well," William wrote in his Journal, "still I am told one or two habitual drunkards have sworn off and have been sober since the movement started, so in this case it has done some good."[12]

The Denison temperance people had hoped to hire "the famous Mr. Drew," until they found out his fee was $100 plus all expenses; it was then they reconsidered and decided a Mr. Dart at a more reasonable salary would do just as well. Later in Des Moines William met Drew and attended one of his mesmerizing lectures; since he was "making money fast at this business," no doubt if the Denison people had really bargained they could have gotten him for less.

"I attended one of the temperance meetings held here by torchlight under the Courthouse trees," William reported from Denison. "The audience was largely composed of women and children," and the speeches alternated with songs. "It was a proud time for the habitual toper of whom there were three or four in regular attendance, and I was told they made the same speeches every night. 'Give us your experience,' was the universal wish, and these fellows would mount the platform and relate how and when and where they took to drinking, and describing all their past lives—teaching, in my opinion, the young idea how to shoot [paraphrasing poet Edward Young]. . . and scarcely elevating the morals of the numerous children around." After the speeches the audience was urged to sign the pledge. " 'Come up,' says the chairman, 'come up and sign.' Not a stir. Then the ladies on the committee went round, and I was presented by each in turn, being fresh to the meeting. I soon wished I had adopted Fred's plan of tying a bit of blue ribbon to his coat and passing for a *signer* instead of being the *sinner*, as all who did not sign were considered, by the knot of pious citizens who superintended the meeting."

On the Denison courthouse lawn, the temperance ladies found few sinners ready to become teetotalers, "but their efforts were at last rewarded when an old woman of some 70 years hobbled up and put her mark on the paper, and soon after a youth of 15 showed a brave front and signed the pledge. They were both vociferously cheered, and the meeting was then adjourned." The poor showing of converts may have reflected the fact that the entire town had been canvassed, "and the two who signed were only visitors who happened to be by. Still, the results weren't very grand for so much oratory of the gutter style. All went home satisfied, and resolved to meet again soon and have another 'good time.' "

Four years later in June 1882, the Prohibition amendment actually passed in Iowa, but whether it would be enforced was another matter. "Le Mars has grown weary of too much temperance discussion," wrote one commentator. But the camp meetings continued, with hymn singing and antiliquor speechifying. Now another sort of outing took place almost as often: secret binges in out-of-the-way country spots with illegal liquor. One observer noted the contrast between the two kinds of gatherings: the attendance at the righteous conclave was often more numerous, but no more enthusiastic than those attending the other kind of gathering. "The exercises, too, were of a different character from those usually held at orthodox camp meetings. There was singing, it is true, and that was according to Hoyle. Experiences were related, and that was regular. There was a sort of commingling together of 'spirits,' and that is generally considered a proper thing. There was an abundance of beer and any number of cigars, and in this respect camp meeting No. 2 differed from camp meeting No. 1."[13]

The Prairie Club with its stock of wines, whiskies, and ale became even more important to the colonists during this restrictive period—which did not last long. In October the district court in Davenport pronounced the Prohibition amendment unconstitutional, a decision upheld by the Iowa Supreme Court three months later. Normal life returned, at least for a time. In 1884 another Prohibition statute passed, but this one remained in force. Although some saloons ignored the ban, a few, such as the House of Lords, did not escape notice and were fined. By midsummer 1886 antagonism between the Prohibitionists and the "wets" had reached such a pitch that the Revere House was burned down because its owner was against liquor; a few weeks later a Sioux City Methodist minister was shot dead for his antialcohol views. By this time the British colony had sufficiently merged with the locals so that their generally more tolerant opinion on the liquor question did not arouse antagonism toward them as a group.

ALTHOUGH the British life-style in Iowa was frequently at odds with local custom, the colony leaders were adroit in public relations, the most persuasive argument being that the success of the colony meant monetary gain for everyone in the region. In the early years Fred Close's presence and charismatic appeal went beyond words or official Close Brothers statements. His marriage to Margaret Humble in October 1881 carried symbolic significance for the entire colony: this commitment in private life suggested a long-time involvement with the project underway, a move toward permanence, a building toward the future. Now the dashing colony head had a worthy consort. They were a lively, good-looking pair and well-suited in lineage, interests, and energy. Margaret was an accomplished equestrienne and later won prizes in competitions. She had grown up with a taste for sports, outdoor life, and country-house living. She had the breeding to move on any social level with ease; in a few years she would be presented at Court and named lady-in-waiting to Queen Alexandra, but her later life would bring enormous trials which only someone of remarkable independence and toughness of character could have endured.

The wedding celebration in Le Mars began on the eve of the nuptials with a grand ball given by the mother of the bride and Mrs. William Close, with 150 guests in attendance. Wedding gifts were heaped in an impressive pile on a table at one end of the hall, a few of the larger silver pieces jointly presented, with the names of the donors engraved in the metal. Who gave what, and what all the presents looked like was reported in the press. An unexpected, famous guest at the wedding was John Walter, "The Thunderer," proprietor of the

Times of London, who was on an inspection tour of American agriculture. Fred, hearing about Walter's trip, invited him to attend. The occasion impressed Walter deeply, and upon his return to England he frequently mentioned the Iowa colony in glowing terms; later, some of his kin emigrated there. Before the Abingdon Agricultural Society, Walter proclaimed that Englishmen going out who possessed some sense, who were industrious, and who didn't mind the rigorous climate, would be so successful in agriculture that they could retire by age fifty.[14] His prophesy proved to be true. Partly because of the enormous increase in land values, early homesteaders frequently retired to cottages in rural towns before they were even that old.

The wedding vows were exchanged in the Congregational church (Margaret's preference), although the Anglican vicar officiated. After the celebratory breakfast, the pair departed for Chicago and Europe, where they visited the country homes of family and friends, stayed at the Close home in Antibes for a time, and met still more relatives in Italy. Margaret and Fred did not return to Iowa until the following spring. By now the colony, Fred's farm operation, and Close Brothers were flourishing nicely and his absence for a long period could be afforded. During these four years of Iowa residence he had become a rich man. Prior to his marriage, Fred divested himself of property held jointly with his brother James, a portion that came to $150,000. Considering his holdings in Close Brothers, his land, and stock investments, he was worth about one-half million dollars.

Since the start of the Close Colony in late 1879 (and partly due to it), Le Mars had doubled in size in just a couple of years, with new additions added to the city limits. The gas-lit streets had stone gutters and crosswalks. Two roller mills produced 150 barrels of flour a day, with thirty employed, making the town the most important milling center between Minneapolis and Kansas City.[15] Two new hotels opened in 1882: the Richards House, a three-storey brick structure with a central court covered by a skylight, and the forty-five-room Revere House, where diners enjoyed oyster soup in season, turkey, and a variety of excellent cakes. Other facilities for transients included the Petry Bath Rooms, equipped with steam cabinets in which George King, an English patron, once found himself during a boiler explosion. His companion climbed the walls "dressed like Adam before the fall and yelling like a Comanche Indian," while King "promptly put his head in the 'sweat box,' where he remained till the storm was over."[16]

The best city grocer could provide 60-pound lambs for Christmas and strawberries in late April. Two Britons put up 1,000 pounds of ice to keep until summer, when they sold it to thirsty customers. Lee Sam ran one of the laundries, with a directory of San Francisco tacked to his wall; the other was the Shirley Lodge Laundry, operated by an English woman. Both had wagons making the rounds for pickups and deliveries, even going into the country to

Captain Moreton's. Le Mars was up to date in taxi service, with the carriage stand situated in front of the Post Office. The patrons at the Revere House had a direct phone line connecting them with the livery run by an Englishman and his Scottish partner. A bookseller offered current English and German language books; a steamship agent opened a travel booking office; a dealer in musical instruments and sheet music imported two Broadwood pianos directly from England. At about the time outlaw Jesse James was shot in St. Joseph, Missouri, an "English lady" advertised: "experienced in teaching, is prepared to give music and singing lessons at the residence of pupils." And a painter who had studied with an "Art Master of Leeds, England," planned to be in Le Mars and offered to give lessons. The usual mix of the frontier prevailed.[17]

The British did not have a monopoly on opulent living, as the rich land promoter T. L. Bowman proved when he invited the local top society to a housewarming on an appropriate day — the Fourth of July 1882. Mrs. Bowman had helped design the "Swiss Cottage" house, an eclectic mixture of Gothic and rustic styles. Chinese lanterns outlined the wide porch, and visitors were received by a Negro butler in a swallowtail coat and kid gloves. The front parlor walls were papered in satin gilt, Brussels carpet to match, and heavy raw silk drapes covered the windows. The fireplaces throughout were dark marble, elaborately carved, and there was a good deal of expensive furniture, including a Decker Upright Grand piano. Bowman admitted spending $7,000 on the house, $5,000 to furnish it — a lavish outlay considering that much local land sold for $15 an acre.[18]

With the British so strongly present in Le Mars, "culture" became rampant. Several times a year a *conversazione* with musical performances took place at the Prairie Club. The Philharmonic Society with 65 members met Monday evenings for rehearsals. Hoyt's Opera House, completed in 1884, seated 1,200 and was equipped with modern backstage dressing areas, a good deal of scenery, a hot-air furnace, and gas lights. All sorts of troupes came through Le Mars, from opera societies to dramatic players. The Whiteley Company performed *The Hidden Hand,* with "the bewitching Nora Vernon," who "fairly captivated the audience, and broke our English boys all up." George C. Milne appeared in *Othello,* and *Iolanthe* was hailed in the press. The best central seats were often cordoned off for the British, who would sometimes arrive on horseback from great distances just before curtain time. Should the performance be bad, singers and actors might be hooted off the stage. If the theatrical piece were Gilbert and Sullivan or some other well-known vehicle, the young men might jump to the stage and put on the show themselves, doing it "right" (though frequently somewhat drunkenly). The imperious manner of the British both startled and amused (when it did not annoy) local residents. One day in a butcher shop a native listened to Mrs. Dalton, an English matron, instruct the butcher on how he should trim the meat she'd ordered — cut off that end, remove the fat, pare down the outer flesh—until finally only the center remained. After she left the shop, the butcher asked what kind of meat he wanted, and the local replied: "I'll take the Dalton cut, too."[19]

On his American tour Oscar Wilde lectured in Sioux City, and a large contingent of the Close Colony went to hear him. The *Sentinel* editor condemned those in the audience who had hissed and booed, for Wilde was to be admired for taking unpopular stands and speaking for his convictions. A Le Mars florist promised to introduce the Oscar Wilde sunflower for the summer of 1882.

Lillie Langtry didn't arrive in the region until 1887, when she appeared as Galatea in Council Bluffs. Although the temperature that night in mid-August was said to be 103° (certainly an exaggeration), Lillie Langtry wore a Mother Hubbard costume, and the spectators were disappointed not to have a chance to glimpse her famous figure.[20]

The Le Mars Amateur Dramatic Club staged performances locally and in Sibley, Iowa, where a substantial new English colony was developing, due to the Close Brothers office there. After the final curtain the British would enjoy a social hour before they heard the train whistle—the last evening locomotive from St. Paul—and they would rush to the station and board the train for the fifty-mile trip to Le Mars.

THE Close brothers themselves often reappeared in Le Mars at crucial moments for the well-being of the colony. In early May 1882, after Fred and Margaret returned from their honeymoon, Fred immediately set about the construction of their Le Mars home near the courthouse. When it was completed in July, Mrs. Humble joined the household. The convenience of living in Le Mars instead of the West Fork residence was obviously appealing to both Margaret and her mother. Will Humble, the brother who had started the family's involvement with the Closes when he became a pup, remained in the colony three years, then moved to Dakota Territory and became a grain buyer.[21]

William and Mary, however, were less frequently visible in the colony than William would have wished. A dozen years later in divorce proceedings, Mary was questioned in court as to where she had resided in the course of her marriage, and her testimony reveals some of her bewilderment regarding their many moves:

"We went to London first," she said. "For a number of months...I think nearly a year."

"And after that?"

"We came to America, to Le Mars."

" For how long?"

"Several months."

"Then where did you go?"

"To Lake Minnetonka."

"What state?"

"Minnesota."

"How long did you live there?"

"Several months."

"Then where did you go?"

"I think we returned to England."

"How long did you remain in England?"

"I don't remember...a year or so I think."

"Then where did you go?"

"We went sometimes to the south of France."

"Did you return to this country?"

"Yes, we returned to America again."

"When?"

"I could not tell you. I don't remember."

"After returning to America did you go back again to Europe?"

"Yes."

"What part of America did you go to when you came back?"

"I don't think we did return to England at that time at all; I cannot remember. I am very bad about dates. I am not sure that I did not start on with my maid to America and Mr. Close joined me. I am not sure that he did not join me at that time in Chicago, and now I think he did. I am not sure whether we returned to England again or not. I would not be able to tell without referring to letters."

"Can you state whether during the principal part of the time since you have been married you have lived abroad or in this country?"

"Sometimes in England, sometimes in the south of France, and sometimes in America."[22]

TO a stable banker like John Close, his brother William's constant movement might indicate not enough attention paid to the business in which he had placed money. He hectored William about procedures and seldom got the reassurance he sought. "The reason I am discontented is that as an investor I cannot get my accounts in," he wrote William in March 1882. "I know there is difficulty in dividing the crops with the farmers but I understand most of the crops are threshed in the autumn and winter, and that being the case, there should be some rent coming in by Xmas. You see we are in March already and I have not the slightest idea what I am to get for 1881." What John did not understand was that not all the grain was threshed. Some might be held for storage until the market price improved, after the initial glut of commodities in the fall. The Sibley railroad grain elevator, which Close Brothers owned, held 4,000 bushels of wheat and 8,000 of flax at that very time.[23]

> Then my next complaint is that though I hear from you all that lands have increased tremendously, I have a sum of about £2,000 [$10,000] which has never been invested & I have missed the price.
>
> Third, I cannot get this vexed question of interest settled. Take last year alone from January to June. You had £4,000 [$20,000] of mine lying idle in New York. Now I ought to have whatever interest you get on that amount from your bankers. But can you honestly say your firm has not used that money for its own purposes? I know something of your past financial arrangements. . . . Thus if you have made use of this money you should pay a liberal interest for it. . . .
>
> James wrote in July to say he had sold some land of mine at a good profit, but from that day to this I have not heard a word about it. I am reduced to think he was inventing when he wrote. No, I won't sell yet, but I want my accounts sent in & my interest received by you from the bankers paid.

Answers to these nagging inquiries could only come from Iowa, where James was fully occupied with land sales and plans to lure a railroad through the newly acquired lands (a scheme that never materialized). By the end of 1882 Close Brothers had bought for their company, other individuals, and the Iowa Land Company they controlled a grand total of 135,000 acres in Iowa and southwestern Minnesota, with some additional holdings in states farther west. At any given moment it was difficult for the Closes themselves to know how much land they owned. Management men ran the separate Close Brothers land offices; stewards were in charge of about forty tenant farms each. Fred Close told the *Le Mars Liberal* that the Closes had exclusive control of half a million acres, which they were offering to incoming settlers. Immigrants were arriving in America in great numbers; 75,000 landed in New York in April alone.[24]

Fred and James increasingly became the official spokesmen for Close Brothers; William made little effort to conceal his withdrawal from the Iowa scene. In early October 1882 he sold 720 acres that he and Roylance Court farmed on the West Fork for fifteen dollars an acre. There was also a temporary falling out among the Close brothers at about this time, with William and John in England ranged against James and Fred, a consequence of intricate business negotiations in which all four were financially involved.

The trouble began over the Iowa Land Company's purchase of large tracts from the Sioux City and St. Paul Railroad—at least 27,000 acres in addition to the initial purchases of 1881—most of these in the northern Iowa counties and southwest Minnesota. The Milwaukee Road claimed the Sioux City and St. Paul lands belonged to *them,* and with the title now uncertain, the newly purchased acres could not readily be resold to settlers. The question involved whether the U.S. Congress through the State of Iowa had actually granted these "primary and lieu" lands to the Milwaukee Road first, since the tracks of that line crossed with the Sioux City and St. Paul at Sheldon in O'Brien County. Both railways had been given the primary right to all odd sections of land lying within ten miles on both sides of the track and up to twenty miles in "lieu" land rights (to compensate for acreages already in the hands of settlers). Therefore, a forty-mile-square section where the tracks met at Sheldon was involved in the dispute. Since neither side could agree, $160,653 was put in escrow by the Iowa Land Company. As a consequence, land buying by this company in a crucial region was effectively curtailed at this time.[25]

A reasonable explanation for the formation of the Western Land Company, 17 October 1882, with a declared capital stock of one million dollars, was to circumvent this block and get back into land buying from the Milwaukee Road through the creation of a totally new company. The six partners were James and Fred Close; Constantine Benson; Attorney Charles Ball, the Close's early legal advisor; Judge J. H. Swan of Sioux City; and another employee, the Bohemian Francis Marek. According to the articles of incorporation, the objectives of the Western Land Company were similar to those of the other Close companies, but with greater emphasis on mortgage and loan transactions.[26]

As it developed, the Western Land Company in its first year bought only 3,500 acres, and that from partners Marek and Swan. The following year the volume was fairly light—only 5,760 acres.[27] The headquarters of the company was Sibley, Iowa, with James Close in charge. An explanation as to why William was not involved in this firm would seem to be that his connection with the Iowa Land Company and its special relationship with the Sioux City and St. Paul rendered him ineligible for land-sale dealings with the Milwaukee Road at this litigious moment. There is too little evidence to be certain that the Western Land Company was formed without his knowledge or consent, but letters from John at this time revealed a strong irritation with James, although that could have been caused by James's habitual tardiness in sending along accounts and paying rents and interest due. John ended a letter written to William on 4 July 1883: "All I say is D them at Sibley, D D D *D*." The title dispute was settled in December 1886, at which point the Western Land Company purchased 38,000 acres from the Milwaukee Road, the last major acquisition of railroad land involving the Closes. At that late date there was very little cheap, undeveloped prairie left in Iowa.

The founders of the colony on the prairie were fully occupied attending to business elsewhere, and the colony, if it had taken hold, would thrive or die in accordance with its own validity.

CHAPTER TWELVE

Two Colonials

WO young Britons, Walter and James Cowan, exactly fit William Close's notions regarding recruits for his colony. Their letters home, most of them now in the special collection of the London School of Economics library, constitute the largest and most complete record of what it was like to be a gentleman settler in Iowa. The Cowans were grain merchants of Edinburgh. Richard, the boys' father, was not only a director of the Bank of Scotland but justice of the peace for Midlothian before he retired to the south of England, hence to become a keen follower of his sons' pioneering ventures. Their mother came from a genteel family of painters and line engravers.[1]

The four Cowan sons were educated at Winchester, the eldest receiving a commission in the army and serving in India, eventually as a major. The second son shipped out to New Zealand with the intention of settling there but died by drowning. Walter, the third son, failed to receive an army commission; so in the spring of 1882 he traveled to Canada to see about locating there or in Iowa. His schoolmate, Gerald Garnett, was already happily residing in the Close Colony. In Toronto Walter met the captain of the Winnipeg cricket team, once a navy officer but now in farming, who warned Walter against being swindled into buying the wrong sort of land. After a brief look at Manitoba and a few weeks in the Close Colony on the Garnett farm, he returned home. The following year Walter, age twenty-four, and his brother James, nineteen (who also failed to get an army commission), emigrated to the States. Walter knew too much about the pup system to consign himself and James blindly to such a procedure. Instead, they hoped to make private tutorial arrangements with a landholder, with the help of Garnett.[2]

On 10 April 1883 Walter wrote his mother from the Prairie Club in Le Mars:

> We drove out to Garnett's farm, which is 25 miles off, and I am very proud of having been able to find my way across the tractless waste, as I had only been over the ground once before. We took our bearings by the sun and struck N. West till we reached him. He was very glad to see us and made us very comfortable, Jem [James Cowan] quite enjoying his first experience of farm life. Garnett has got some very nice pupils now and with them and some other friend of his we made quite a merry party. . . .[3]

No single British farmer had pupil openings for both brothers, however. In the long run Walter figured this might be an advantage, since the experience each would gain would vary. James apprenticed himself under H. J. Price, a former master at Cheltenham, and Walter went to James Watson, who enjoyed the luck of having his old nanny serve as housekeeper. The Watson farm was only three miles from Garnett's, the Price establishment a few miles beyond that. Walter felt deeply indebted to Garnett for what he had done for them. "Our great advantage is having no Americans on either farm. We both of us have good homes, good food, and English gentlemen to associate with, and 'what could you wish for more?' Both Price and Watson have taken us as *extra* hands and this being so and considering the comfort we are to enjoy, I am quite willing to agree to Gerry G.'s arrangement and pay for our board." The charge would be three or four dollars per week. "I hope that. . .when we have proved ourselves good hands they will knock this off, but I do not grudge paying for comfort when I know that I get my money's worth. It is a very different matter to paying a large premium in advance, and we are much more independent."

In response to a query from their father as to whether California might not be a more suitable place to locate, Walter replied on 13 May 1883:

> My present impression is that Jem and I could not do better than go in for raising pigs in this part of the country. Jem when at home seemed to have rather a prejudice against the porkers, but I fancy he has changed his mind rather since he has seen more of them. I cannot understand why more fellows don't go in for them on a large scale. Everybody keeps from 25 to 100 and all agree that nothing pays so well, but no one about here devotes himself entirely to them, and I cannot help feeling that where there is such a demand for them, a regular pig farm would be a real paying concern, far more so than cattle, as of course they multiply so much more rapidly.

After one month in Iowa, Walter tried to sound mature and knowledgeable; he had absorbed local hearsay about farming. But nobody seemed yet to have told him that a cholera epidemic could wipe out an entire herd in a matter of days. For that reason no farmer went solely into pig farming on a large scale.

Some of the zest felt by the young Britons when they found themselves well settled among congenial friends shines through Walter's ingenuous remarks: "Health brings happiness and as I never was healthier in my life than I am now, it follows that I never was happier." Crops were late being planted as there had been too much rain, but he had been out harrowing. The ground was heavy and it was hard work for both himself and the horses. On the day he was writing they encountered a hail storm so severe the horses refused to leave the stable and had to be watered by buckets brought in to them. "My face is very tender from hail stones in spite of the veil which I wore. The poor cattle look miserable, but we cannot help them, poor brutes. Gerry Garnett has had 8 acres of barley sowed on the side of a hill washed clean away, hardly a seed remaining. . . ." This was a foretaste of the disasters and setbacks the Cowans themselves would come to endure.

Watson's renovated house was long under construction, and Walter didn't unpack or settle in for weeks. On Sundays he saw his brother James and the other days he was up early and working late, since all the farm work was two weeks behind schedule. On 3 June Walter reported: "Yesterday was the day fixed for the spring meeting of the Le Mars Races. . . ." Instead of attending, he stayed home and helped in a housecleaning, since the plasterers had finished Watson's upper story. "I scrubbed till I nearly broke my back, but those dirty Yankees leave traces behind them which no scrubbing will take out and our poor housekeeper is at her wits ends how to obliterate the distressing remembrances of the dirty brutes. All Yankees paint their floors brown, but I never realized till I tried my hand at scrubbing what the reason was."

The Cowan parents inquired about their sons' companions, since both boys were fairly young and unsophisticated. Tales abounded of wildness and drunken sprees among the young men sent "out." John Hope, a former Close colonist, wrote in *Blackwood's* magazine of the need these young men felt for cutting loose: "Being utterly sick of the monotony of the snowed-up prairies, and glad to be once more in the congenial society of fellow countrymen, they determine to make a night of it, and have a 'real good time.' " What happened was very similar to "a breaking-up supper at school, or a farewell wine at the 'varsity,' only with this difference, that the gambling-table and the 'cooler' take no part in these typical festivities." Hope explained that the "cooler" was the "lock-up" — "a kind of caged den into which young gentlemen playing football with an empty pickle-jar at 1 A.M. are liable to be placed." One young Iowa Englishman "amused himself on one occasion by playing a number of games at billiards with the saloon-keeper for an equivalent number of bottles of champagne." Since everyone in England recognized that a certain amount of "spree-ing" went on among young men at school and university, when these individuals were 5,000 miles from home, was it any wonder similar revelry occurred? Of course, some became drunkards, "and if the death registers of that part of America were searched, several Englishmen's names would appear. . . ." Died of the DTs.[4]

Walter told his parents not to worry. "I fancy Jem is older than most fellows of his years and has more sense than to 'pal' with any of the wrong sort. There are plenty of the right sort out here who would always give a word in season if it was wanted. . . . Indeed, in a place like this it is very difficult to form any friendships at all except fellows on one's own farm; one hardly ever sees anyone else, and though one makes acquaintances in town, they are merely acquaintances and nothing more. It may be a whole year before you happen to meet the same fellow again. It is a very different thing to school, where you are constantly in companionship with so many fellows."

The distance the Cowans lived from Le Mars and the lack of time for social activities accounted for this isolation, which wasn't the case with Captain Moreton's pups and others near Le Mars. Courteously, Walter thanked his mother for sending a supply of calling cards, tangible evidence of how far indeed he was removed from the world of English social life. "The supply, however, exceeds the demand at present and the goods are arriving to a very flat market. My stocks will be sufficient for some time to come, I expect, and you may cease shipping till further orders."

In early June after two months as a pupil of farming, James wrote his father that he felt he should be working for wages instead of paying room and board as an apprentice. A salaried hired hand at Garnett's advised him either to get paid for his labor or buy a farm and begin stock raising. "Just grow sufficient corn and grain to feed your animals on, and put up good buildings as soon as possible; don't buy land on a thickly settled part but where one can get lots of pasture for cattle...." Hogs could return a farmer 30 to 35 percent. To sound businesslike, he calculated the cost of a sample swine production setup. "I would like to settle at once, whether or not we are going to stop about here, and if so look out for a farm *at once.*" The reason for haste: "Land is rising so rapidly now that if we wait a year we will have to pay probably from five to ten dollars an acre more for it than now...."

The two primary mistakes young Britons generally made if they had command of their own money was to buy land with insufficient capital and acquire stock without having sufficient food to feed them. It was much easier to buy land than to get rid of it if things didn't turn out as expected—which the Cowans learned to their regret. With the price per acre constantly rising, anxious newcomers to the scene were strongly tempted to get into the game as quickly as possible.[5]

One reason for the escalating price of land was the discovery of coal on Captain Moreton's farm in mid-October 1882. The serendipitous find occurred while well diggers were sinking a bore. Dromore Farm, high on a roll of land overlooking Le Mars and the Floyd River valley, lacked sufficient water for the large livestock operation under way. Hoping to create an artesian well, Moreton ordered the drill sunk very deep, and at 225 feet a vein of coal was struck. Moreton tried to squelch the rumors that immediately began circulating, thinking the coal might have only been a pocket. Further down another 3-foot vein was discovered, and upon laboratory analysis its percentage of carbon proved higher than in any coal thus far discovered in Iowa.[6]

Geological surveys had given no indication of coal in northwest Iowa. The need for fuel was so acute—no wood, even—that this factor had been a drawback to early settlement of the prairies. Although railroads partially solved the problem by hauling in coal, the supervisors of Plymouth County kept a standing offer of a cash award ($1,000 in 1875, $5,000 by 1884) for anyone discovering a workable coal mine in the county.

On the strength of scattered reports regarding coal on Dromore Farm, land speculation became feverish. Mineral rights on 1,720 acres of farmland in the vicinity were sold at once. Captain Moreton ordered an expensive diamond drill that could encapsulate a core of earth for more accurate study. For the next three months, during the worst winter weather, Moreton and his coal advisor worked to verify their findings. On 1 March 1883 the *Sentinel* announced the richest bituminous coal ever found in Iowa was on Dromore Farm; the newspaper also issued a special supplement intended to lure prospective mine-fever settlers. Prices for land in close proximity to the mine rose to $100 and in some cases $300 an acre. No wonder James Cowan wrote his father that they ought to buy a farm at once! "Captain Moreton's coal is almost a certainty now," he added.

A coal mine in this part of the world still struck many people as an impossibility; some believed lumps of coal had been dropped down the hole. To stop this slander, Moreton published a log of his prospecting. The newspapers supported his move to verify the coal discovery, hailing him as a "plucky Englishman" who had solved the fuel problem "by John Bull grit and $5,000. . . ." Another group, the Plymouth Coal Company, capitalized at $10,000, began prospecting in the western part of the county. The only colonist involved, Frank Sugden, treasurer, sold out quickly "for a handsome sum." All of which indicated that the coal-mining craze was partly speculative, and those who took advantage of credulous investors and got out in time made tidy profits.

Captain Moreton, however, proclaimed his integrity and continued to back his coal hunt with money from his own pocket. He formed the North-Western Coal and Mining Company in June, with himself, his son, and other stalwarts in the British community on the board of directors. However, mining did not commence at once, perhaps because Moreton and his associates lacked the capital to undertake the expensive operation. Other prospectors reported coal discoveries, among them the mayor of Le Mars. Moreton kept the coal interest alive by publishing in January 1884 a second log of his test diggings, following it with a subscription appeal aimed at securing $5,000 to sink the first shaft. "I trust that your confidence in myself personally, and in my discovery may not be misplaced," he said in the local press. "God has greatly blessed this county and country by giving wealth for man to develop. May it be ours to acknowledge him always, and help to enrich one another." The Victorian Christian credo could not have been more succinctly stated.

James Cowan wrote his father in January 1884: "It will also be a great thing if this coal business turns out a success, which I hope it will do, as we will get our coal much cheaper and it will, I hope, raise the value of our land. I don't know whether it will make Akron (or Portlandville) grow at all. . . if it does, it will be a grand thing for us."

Digging for coal began during the chilly weather of January and February 1884. When the miners reached 80 feet they started pumping water; by

August the drilling had attained a depth of 100 feet. Subscribers to the shaft fund held a meeting, but not enough were in favor of continuing. They learned that an experienced coal miner had tested the coal and discovered it to be worthless lignite, not bituminous. This expert, hired by Captain Moreton, departed the region as a consequence of his findings. The coal boom came to bust.

Many investors bitterly accused Captain Moreton of promoting the coal boom to inflate land prices, then profit personally from the collapse. Such charges greatly upset the dignified leader of the colony, and he replied that he had lost $14,000 in the venture; he had only hoped to benefit the community and help enrich everyone, and like others, he'd suffered from the failure. Furthermore, had not his name and presence in the Close Colony brought in a quarter of a million dollars in capital funds from British settlers—or very much more? An inflow from which everyone benefitted one way or another.

The ugly brouhaha over the aborted coal discovery caused Captain Moreton to lose interest in the colony itself. He left Le Mars the following year, placing his sons in charge of Dromore Farm. By 1885 the pupil system, too, had been largely discredited and few paying boarders were being taken on by anybody, unless privately arranged for. Captain Moreton moved to Dixon, Illinois, where he soon made his influence felt, criticizing the dangerous behavior of boys and girls in sailboats on the Rock River, especially their habit of standing upon the seats while the sails were spread. Many mothers in Dixon, when they read this message from the newcomer who signed himself "Captain in the British Royal Navy" forbade their daughters to board a boat on the river, and the local boys, much angered, awaited their chance to get even with Captain Moreton. When the old seadog himself was out boating a few days later, he was the "first to get spilled into the water by a violation of his own rules," and the local press made much of this deserved dunking—while the Dixon boys cheered.[7]

THE amount of capital the Cowan brothers had at their disposal depended to some extent upon their father's confidence in the wisdom of their choices. Therefore, in letters home they took great pains to explain their thinking, because only if their father was fully informed about their situation would he loosen the pursestrings. They obviously counted on his benevolence, were nurtured by it, almost as if *he* were sharing their adventure—another example of the basic strength derived from the closely knit Victorian family and the sustaining love generated within it. James reported rumors that £10,000 ($50,000) was needed for ranching, for it would "be fatal to anyone starting on a small capital." James knew his father regarded him as inexperienced, having been in Iowa barely two months. "Of course, if we were buying land we would have Gerry [Garnett] with us or get him to do it for us."

They need not put their faith blindly in Close Brothers, having such experienced friends on hand. Furthermore, their brother Henry had written "about what Sir William Robinson told him about the Closes, and I believe there is a good deal of truth in what he says.... I should always be very cautious in buying land through them."

If Walter had never felt healthier or happier, James, too, though inclined to bouts of despondency, was enjoying himself. He relished the cowboy experience of breaking in a three-year-old colt "which had never had a saddle on," and he had been out alone on the Great Plains. "If you can picture me in an old cloth hat, flannel shirt with rolled up sleeves open in front, pair of breeches, thick boots and spurs, with a big stock whip, riding a bay mare and sweeping majestically across the boundless prairie, followed by three faithful hounds, the herd in the distance and no houses within two or three miles, you will have me as I have been for the last three weeks."

The fierceness of the weather struck many newcomers as the most awesome feature of Iowa. Walter Cowan describes a midsummer hailstorm: "To my horror I heard a roaring which I thought must be a cyclone, and my first impulse was to jump out of the buggy, lie flat on the ground, and let the horses take their chance.... Just then, however, a hail stone fell, which warned me of what was coming. I saw one of these hailstorms in Manitoba and I knew I stood a poor chance unless I got under shelter. Nothing for it but to reach Garnett's as soon as possible, only three miles, but a hilly and bad road. The colts wanted no whip.... Mud was flying pretty thick and one of my eyes got bunged up, but mud is nothing when hail was behind.... Coming down one steep hill I could see Garnett's fellows standing under his verandah watching me in the distance. When about one quarter mile from the house the stones fell thicker, and one caught me on my knuckles and made me drop my reins, but I had them again in the other hand and went past his house as if I was racing and just reached his stable as the storm came in real earnest."

As he was unharnessing, three stones struck his hand, which began to bleed, "Another came whack on my knee-cap and lamed me for the while." He abandoned the team, rushed for cover, and the horses sought the stables on their own. "Inside the stable I was safe from the hail, but Garnett's horses were frantic, as the windows were smashed right in their faces and they were kicking and struggling to get loose." By this time Walter noticed that the "fellows standing under the verandah" had all headed for the storm cellar, which increased his anxiety, for he thought they might have seen a tornado "which would, of course, have blown away the house and stable. I accordingly crept out of the stable with my coat over my head and crept under a weighing machine, where my head and shoulders were covered but my legs got it pretty hot."

As soon as the storm was over, five minutes later, Garnett came running from the house with tears in his eyes. Together they located the horses and buggy, some distance away, Watson's pair somewhat bruised, with a bleeding cut over one of the horse's eye. Garnett's losses in grain were total — £1,000 ($5,000) — and he ordered his men to plow up the corn and turn his livestock into the ruined grain fields. "His hay land is also damaged very much but he will have to sell a lot of his cattle, having no corn and not enough hay to winter them on." One hailstone weighed six and three-quarters ounces — they were the size of eggs and potatoes. Eighty panes of glass were smashed in the house and outbuildings. Garnett in his shock quickly adopted the fatalism so characteristic of a midwestern landsman and said to Walter it served him right, since only last Sunday he'd boasted about his crops when writing home.

After this devastating account, Walter blithely queried his father as to "what amount of capital you are prepared to provide us with, and also whether you could send it off on receipt of a telegram." Richard Cowan had told them that provided they were properly advised, he would like to help them with a good land-buying opportunity. It didn't occur to Walter that his striking account of the Iowa weather might cause some doubts at home about the wisdom of locating in such a place. James in his letter at about the same time even speculated that the hailstorm probably ruined some farmers, who would have to sell out, "and we *might* possibly get a chance of buying land cheap shortly."

A few days later Walter received belated birthday greetings from home; he was twenty-five. "So you were all drinking my health at home with bumpers of 'the boy,' while poor little me had only clear spring water with which to return the compliment." The Watson cook baked him a rhubarb tart, "with my initials beautifully engraved upon it!... Poor body, she has been suffering... during the past week from pains in her back and so I have been helping her in the kitchen a good deal and have been doing all the cooking, with her sitting by to watch me.... Never before did I know how to *stew*...I actually made cock-a-leekie one day, (not that you make it by stewing) and it was my 'chef d'oeuvre.' All our dishes are 'a'ecosse,' everything 'a l'Americaine' is teetotally tabooed." But Walter was even prouder of his new skill as a builder of barley stacks, until he was roused out of bed at 5:00 A.M., "told that the top had fallen off my stack, that it looked like rain and that I had better get it fixed before the rain came on." He had constructed the stack properly, "but Watson told me to put another load on, and it was just this extra load that came down again...."

The perils to crops not only descended from the sky but also came from the land. James reported to his father:

> A grand prairie fire has been coming up all day just across the railway on both sides of the river, and this evening after 'chaws' we saw that some hay stacks were being threatened, so we went down armed with pitch forks and wet sacks to try and save them, which we managed to do by burning all round them a wide band. We were only just in time, as the grass was very long and the fire came up very fast. It was a magnificent sight: the

flames leaping up 8 or 10 feet and the fire extending over some miles. At one time we were completely surrounded by fire, standing on the island we had made to protect the stacks.

In spite of the risks involved, Richard Cowan consented to his sons' buying plans. In late summer they put money down on 222 acres lying along the Big Sioux River just beyond the southwest city limits of Akron. It had belonged to a widow who had a $600.00 mortgage on it, from which the Cowans were exempt. They paid her $2,053.50 on 29 September, at the closing. On 13 November they added another 80 acres to the parcel for the price of $1,200.00.[8] "The farm would have been sold long ago if it had had any buildings on it," Walter wrote. "The previous owner lived in town and ran the farm from town, going in and out every day. This plan, however, would not suit a farmer coming in from 'back East.' They like to be able to come in with their goods and chattels and go straight into their new house, and consequently will not buy a farm without buildings." But the Cowans preferred to build their own structures exactly as they wanted them.

While the growing season was still on, they made arrangements to have hay put up, which they would need later for their cattle and horses, and they bargained with carpenters about the construction of their buildings. Beginners though they were, their chances of striking satisfactory business deals with workmen were greater because they acted within the context of the local, settled British community. They decided to engage the same man who had built Watson's house. "He is quite a swell out here, being one of the oldest inhabitants of the town, an elder of the Church, and J.P. for the county!" Another surprise of this egalitarian society was that such a title—justice of the peace—carried none of the significance of honor attached to it in Great Britain. The office usually meant a small side income for a respectable citizen who didn't mind being roused from bed at any hour in case of a hearing or a wedding. "Having one's house built by a real live J.P. seems very grand, but he is a very good workman, and just as honest and impartial in his business capacity as he is when dealing out justice from the bench."

Walter's trust might have been a bit naive. John Hope in his *Blackwood's* article (1884) said that young Britons in America frequently got taken by the natives: "They have to pay through the nose for everything." They also tended to embark on expenses "incommensurate with the profits obtainable from their farms." A similar view was voiced by a later writer in *Blackwood's*: "The English gentleman does not bargain with a tradesman....of the bargaining and scheming which go in actual business, he has not the faintest conception...unless he happens to have seen two Norfolk farmers haggle for hours over the price of a pig."[9]

The Cowans planned to have the granary and barn built before the house, following the procedure of other pioneers; they would live in the granary while the house was under construction, "which will save us paying for our board any more." They also anticipated taking part in the construction and thus saving money. While one brother helped haul lumber from town, the other would assist the carpenter. "We mean to do *all* our painting ourselves, which will be quite a saving."

When the Cowans' parents read a 9 August dispatch in the *Times* of a terrible hailstorm in Iowa passing through three counties, they were naturally alarmed, remembering Walter's vivid description of an earlier storm. But he replied: "We saw nothing of it in this part, although it did a deal of damage North of us in Minnesota." Now that Walter was a landowner his attitude toward the natural forces had changed. Like any other settler who had staked out a life for himself in new quarters, he became a booster. "This has certainly been a terrible year for storms all over the world, and the States have had a full share of them. The State of Iowa, however, has been singularly free of them, and I trust it may long maintain the reputation it has this year received."

While this comment was probably greeted with some astonishment, questions from home were equally disconcerting to Walter and James. In midsummer in response to what must have been his mother's query as to whether the Iowa scenery inspired Walter to write poetry, he replied: "I am sorry to say I was not seized with any poetical inspiration while herding cattle, but I dare say the inspiration will come next year while I am ploughing, and I will publish my first poems in the *19th century:* 'Lines on a Plough share by an Iowa farmer, composed while following the plough through the Alluvial deposit of a valley in the Great North West.' (Oh, oh, and laughter). Your letter has put quite a new idea into my head of how to make money farming."

The house went up so quickly they didn't have to live in the granary after all. They walked to their farm each day from their respective residences. "It is very convenient. . . having Watson's so close that we can live comfortably and yet be on the spot. If the farm had been further away we would have been living in the stable and 'batching' it," James said. By the end of September the roof was on, the windows in place; plastering was to commence shortly and they hoped to move in three weeks. The well digger "put a new point onto the pipe and drove it down again and now we have a constant supply of good cold water."

The fall meeting of the Jockey Club would soon take place in Le Mars, "and Walter and I are going in, partly to ensure our buildings 'in the first class insurances, one against fire, and one against damage from hail' and tornadoes, etc.," but also to have a good time attending the Race Ball in the evening. Their letters mention few such colony social occasions. Perhaps they left out the lighter side to convey an impression of their seriousness.

They did not forget to relate their hardships. In mid-November (1883), "Getting up to cook an early breakfast, washing up dishes, grooming the horses, driving six miles with the thermometer at 3° Fahrt., packing up boxes,

driving back, unloading, doing chaws, trimming lamps, cooking supper, eat-
ing it, and then washing up again hardly puts one in a good mood for writing
letters," or for anything else.

They still did not have an overseer or housekeeper, although an English
couple was expected shortly to serve. "I don't mind the cooking," Walter explained, "but what I hate is having to wash up dishes afterwards. One never
gets a quiet evening, as when the everlasting washing up is over, one has to
bake, and it is generally about midnight before one goes to bed. . . . We have
moved into the house now but, of course, everything is upside down, and it
will be some little while before we get settled. It is most comical how everything gets frozen in this weather; even the very ink which I am writing with
had to be melted on the stove before I could begin writing."

The scarcity of domestic help seemed about to be alleviated when a batch
of prospective hired girls arrived in Council Bluffs from Germany. "Le Mars
needs a large invoice of just such girls," said the newspaper, which the previous
year described "a hired-girl panic." "The dear creatures are offered three dollars
a week in private families, and yet the housewife must serve the hash herself."
A few Negroes seeking domestic work arrived from Kansas in 1881, but they
did not remain long, reportedly discouraged after hearing of the severe winters. During most of these years, European immigrant labor provided what
domestic help there was available.[10]

The Cowans were indeed fortunate to have an English couple — the Taylors — working for them. Mrs. Taylor proved to be "very energetic and. . .clean
in her arrangements, a good cook and I think very economical. Tho' we are a
pretty large household and there is the baby. . .she manages wonderfully well."

Although it was now winter, much work on the farm could still be done.
They cut fir trees along the river for fuel, to save on coal, but putting in fence
posts was out of the question: "The ground is so hard that you can't make any
impression on it with a crow bar even. You might just as well try to put posts
into solid rock." They enjoyed a bit of shooting and hoped soon to buy a
couple of hounds for wolf hunting — not the fancy dogs favored by other British hunters. A biography of Disraeli and *A History of Our Own Times* by
Justin McCarthy constituted their reading matter, part of a packet of cheap
editions the family sent out.

From home, a draft for £580 ($2,900) made it possible for them to close
the deal on the second portion of their land. Their father had actually remitted
more than asked, and James hoped "this may not have put you out at all." This
was their first winter on the prairie, and while their parents were alarmed by
reports of the bitterly cold temperatures, James assured them that it was an
exceptionally mild winter. "You wish to be told *exactly* how we are, and all I
can say is that we are *exactly* as comfortable, happy, fat and jolly as we possibly
could be."

CHAPTER THIRTEEN

Getting On with It

PRING arrived; the crashing of ice breaking up on the Big Sioux River, "reminds one of a tremendous big waterfall, and every now and again there is a report just like a gun," wrote Walter. By mid-June all 70 acres of corn had been planted, as well as the barley, oats, and wheat. Since their father was especially interested in grain, Walter described their first harvest in some detail—how they cut the oats and barley by hand but hired a mechanical binder for the wheat. The machine came out in 1880 when Walter was working in an office, and he remembered how the price of Manila hemp jumped, since binder twine was made of it. Bundles were bound and dropped on a cradle, then dumped at regular intervals so that they could be subsequently "stooked." After that came threshing, "the worst job on a farm," and they were obliged to help the neighbors as well, "to repay the men that help us." Then haying. "After hay there is a quiet time with nothing to do but put up yards and sheds for stock in winter, do some fall ploughing, dig pota-toes, etc. Then comes the frost and...the corn is ready to gather."[1]

By mid-August 1884, after almost one year of farming, the likelihood that Mr. and Mrs. Taylor, the Cowans' valuable couple, would leave to start their own farm alarmed the Cowan brothers. The most offensive aspect about the prospect of Americans working for them, James felt, was their prevailing attitude toward animals.

> A Yankee looks upon a horse or any animal simply as a machine out of which to get as much profit as possible at the smallest possible cost and trouble; and also as something which is meant to be ill-used. The way some of them treat their horses is simply atrocious and makes me so savage sometimes that I can hardly control myself. If we had a Yankee on the place here, I know I would kick him till he could not stand, within a week of his coming, for ill-using something.[2]

The Cowans' thriving hog production was an encouraging sign of their growing success at farming. They sold nine fat hogs, one of them weighing over 500 pounds, for $100. Their Poland-China boar from Wisconsin, "a pedi-gree with him as long as my arm," was surely the best boar around. James believed too little attention was generally paid to having good boars, "and consequently most of the hogs you see are bad." If the class system with its emphasis on bloodlines worked for people, why not for animals?

Cholera was in the neighborhood, but James was optimistic about avoiding it, since their herd had "plenty of grass and fresh water and plenty of shade, which are the three great secrets in hog-raising." So many pigs—it was hard to count them all. "They just swarm in every direction, the little ones, and the big ones are shut up in a big pasture running down to the river." Meanwhile, with threshing well under way, workdays began at 6:00 A.M. and lasted until after 9:00 P.M. "I was in the dust and chaff all the time, and I didn't get the dust out of my lungs for two days."

The other news was that their neighbor and boyhood friend, Gerald Garnett, had sold his farm and gone into a cattle company headed by Captain Moreton. "He no doubt got a good price for it and is still living there and managing the place for them. They have a capital of $125,000, and I expect will make it pay well." The Cowans must have regarded Garnett's departure from farming as a somewhat discouraging sign, casual though James seemed in relating the news: "By the way, did we ever tell you that he had sold his farm?"

James figured Cowan Brothers were worth thirty-five dollars an acre at present, since all the necessary buildings had been erected. "The farm now looks awfully neat and workmanlike to my idea," and the total cost of improvements put the cost per acre at twenty-five dollars, "which would leave us a considerable profit if we wanted to sell." Provided, of course, there were buyers at the gate.

Calamity suddenly befell them—a severe run of cholera in their swine. Walter reported to his father, 28 September 1884: "We moved all that seemed quite well (9 sows and 22 pigs) up to Sinclair's farm, and I only wish we had done so sooner, as none of them have as yet shown any sign of disease. The remainder we enclosed in a yard about ¼ mile away from the buildings, and some of them have died since being moved. But there have been no deaths during the past three days, and I am beginning to hope that the disease is dying out. Up to date, we have buried 63 pigs, 10 more are missing, which have doubtless died either in the corn or down at the river, making 73 dead in all." They still had the valuable boar and 19 pigs on their farm. "It is a heavy loss to us, as we were calculating on our pigs being worth about $10 a head in spring and 73 of them means $730." The corn intended for their feed could be sold, but the market was low, only $0.15 a bushel, and so for their expected 1,000 bushels they would only realize $150. Their high hopes for early profits have been thoroughly dashed.

The killing frost was expected the first week in October, and after that, the corn picking would begin. "The corn has all to be picked by hand; that is, a man goes with a wagon and tears the husk off the ear with his hands, then breaks the ear off the stalk and chucks it into the wagon. It is only after a good frost that the corn will break off at all easily. The process of gathering corn is called husking, and it is a very slow, tedious operation and terribly rough on the hands."

James named their establishment "Riverside Stock Farm," Walter explained, "but no official intimation of the fact has yet been given to the public, and I expect the farm will continue to be spoken of as the 'Cowan boys' place' for some time to come. Farms are always spoken of by the name of the owner, and fellows who christen their places are rather ridiculed." In addition to Moreton's Dromore Farm, there was Prestledge, Gypsy Hill, Troscoed, Garrickdale Farm, Inchinnoch, Carlogie, Carleton Stock Farm, Floyd Valley Farm, and Westbourne. "Watson calls his place 'Snowdon,' which is a constant source of letters and telegrams going astray, the name being taken for the owner and 'not known.' One young Britisher on the road to Le Mars rules supreme over a house and a few sheds called 'Locksley Hall,' much to the amusement of our neighbor Sinclair, who says he must call his place 'Windsor Castle.' "

The Cowans sought a pup to help with the work. James informed his sister: "The 'pup' which Mrs. Close spoke about once has at last been heard of. We got a letter the other day from his respected par-yant, viz, Lt. Col. The Hon. Sir James Fraser, whoever he may be when he's at home. . . . We have not yet answered him but intend to write him an evasive letter at present, as we would much prefer having a 'pup' someone had seen, whom we know, or about whom we know something. . . ." The wrong sort of lad in their household could be disruptive. Wryly, James told his young sister that "the standard required by the firm necessitates his having been at a public school," but he must not have reached any position of prominence, for it likely would have spoiled him. "Home educated gentlemen are strictly excluded. . . ." Since the father of the pup in question, referred to them by Margaret Close, identified himself so pretentiously, they were warned off. But Walter felt they might have to take young Fraser, rather than have nobody at all.[3]

The "perfectness" of the Riverside Stock Farm was described to Mr. and Mrs. Richard Cowan by a young settler who went home for a visit. Walter told his mother that his friend meant to convey "the perfect order and tidiness in which we endeavour to keep everything round the place, and in the perfect *location* of our buildings, rather than in any unnecessary perfectness of design or construction. . . . Yankees as a rule are terribly untidy and seem to have not the smallest sense of neatness; and it is surprising how most English fellows follow their example and leave tools and machinery littered about at random, exposed to weather instead of putting them in their proper place." If he had said the *neatest* farm instead of the most perfect, he would have been more accurate; the farm looked even better after the pastures had been fenced, plus "the erection of the hog pens, hog yard, granary, two corn cribs and garden fence. . . ." John Hope, in his *Blackwood's* article, explained that a typical British settler, unlike the Yankee farmer, spent more on the farm than he could ever get back in profits. "They first improve and enlarge the house and the buildings, buy a large stock of new harness, implements, etc., and try to impart to their houses the ship-shape appearance of a prosperous English farm." And this was what the Cowan brothers did.[4]

By the middle of October the cholera epidemic had passed (a severe frost usually brought an end to it), and those pigs saved by a removal to the Sinclair farm were retrieved. While busy in the weary routine of picking endless rows of corn, exciting news arrived from their friend Joe Jefferson, who had been working for a large cattle company in southern Wyoming. Joe had been enlisted in a posse to catch a ring of dangerous cattle thieves. The lure of Wyoming set in strongly. How romantic and colorful Joe Jefferson's life seemed compared to theirs!

The Cowan brothers decided they would like to stay with Joe next summer in his interesting locale, but such a trip could only come about if the Taylors were persuaded to remain and run the farm in their absence. They were induced to do so by going shares with the Cowans on 1885 crops, as well as on livestock produced.

News of the Wyoming plans unsettled the Cowan parents considerably, and Walter took great pains to explain their reasoning—why they wished to spend next summer in Wyoming instead of tending to business on their Iowa farm. It was not merely the grandeur of the mountain country that attracted them, but "I think we will, according to our arrangements, be able to spend the summer more cheaply in Wyoming than we can here." They expected to earn their keep herding cattle for *wages,* which was the touchy, almost unmentioned fact—a clear departure from the gentleman's role as landowner which they actually did not relish much. *Now* was the chance to try Wyoming cattle-ranch life, because surely the Taylors could only be held onto one more year. "I can place implicit confidence in him, and I know he will look well to everything. He has no knowledge of accounts, but this will not be wanted. There will be nothing for him to *buy* for feed, as we will leave enough on the farm for everything. There may be some hogs to sell, but in that case we can see the weighing ticket and know that we receive cash for the proper weight." No doubt these specific details regarding business arrangements with Taylor were meant to allay the senior Cowans' uneasiness, though surely for them it was not so much the honesty or capability of Taylor that was in question as the signs of restlessness and instability of occupational intent by the Cowan sons.

In the share-rent system, the tenant and landowner had the same interests at stake over crops. "Then as to the livestock: all he has to do is to feed them, and we will leave plenty of corn and oats for this. The cattle will be in the pasture finding their own living before we go away, and so beyond milking one cow, he will have nothing to do with them. The pigs he will have to feed with the corn we leave, but as he has a few pigs of his own running with ours, I know they will be properly fed and get neither too much nor too little." How balanced, mature, and wise Walter attempted to sound. What parent couldn't see the strain to reassure behind these words?

Their father questioned the exposure of the Iowa investment, wondering if they were adequately insured, to which Walter gave a detailed answer. An English insurance agent allowed them coverage beyond the normal two-thirds of value. "I suppose he could trust us not to burn, strike by lightening, or blow away our buildings on purpose." And while on the subject of natural disasters: "One of the great features in favour of Wyoming is the absence of storms. If the wind was to blow there it cannot destroy anything and very likely that is why it does not blow there, but reserves its energies for these regions."[5]

In mid-May 1885, after the small grain had been planted and the corn-fields readied for sowing, they boarded the Union Pacific for Wyoming, leaving the Iowa farm "looking very well." The Taylors had just increased in number: "a dear wee calk putting in her appearance on this earth just in time to wish us goodbye. . . ." Walter regarded Nebraska as "the most dreary, monotonous, desolate country I ever wish to see," but Rawlins, Wyoming, "is a very nice clean little town with plenty of money in it. The people are a deal better class than what we have in Iowa. They are well educated people, refined and wonderfully hospitable." Their friend Joe Jefferson introduced them around. "I only wish I could import a few of them to Akron to teach our neighbours there how to conduct themselves."[6]

James immediately landed a job cowpunching at thirty or thirty-five dollars a month, depending on how much his efforts were worth. Walter did not fancy sleeping outdoors this early in the year, but in mid-July he joined the roundup. He wrote his father 21 July 1885 that he would be going back to Iowa before his brother. James "is very keen to have a shoot before returning, and I think he certainly deserves one, as he has worked hard all summer. I am not particularly keen about a shoot myself and have a kind of desire to get back to the farm again." Already he was wondering what they would do for farm help and asked his father to let everyone know they were looking for a suitable pupil, whom they'd like by the following February.

The Wyoming experience struck the two Cowans quite differently. James told his mother that Walter "is rather sick of the country, which I can understand, as he has not had much to do." Financial prospects seemed better in Wyoming than in Iowa, James believed, provided they were willing to put in two or three years of rough labor. "One thing I am bent on, however, is to get out of Iowa on the first opportunity," but he knew Walter did not agree. "I simply can't put up with these beastly storms, which seem to be getting worse every year."[7]

A June storm in northwest Iowa crushed houses, ripped away groves, destroyed crops. The Le Mars railroad depot was lifted off its foundation and pushed onto the main tracks. The Cobden Block, where the Prairie Club was located, lost much of its brick facade. Hoyt's Opera House was "partially unroofed and half of the front cornice torn off." St. Joseph's Catholic church lost its spire; Captain Moreton's stock sheds were wrecked; the sign of the Albion House disappeared entirely. The front of the Close Brothers stable was taken off, and the skylight in the Richards House was blown out. All the Revere House windows were broken, which "filled the house with wind, rain, and dismay." A travelling salesman "rushed out of the Richards House for a place of safety, found it across the street, where he spent a half hour holding to a post, while the wind churned him up and down on the ground and the rain gave him a thorough drenching, and when he got back to the house he looked like...he had been spending the evening in a mud hole." One settler told the newspapers that he "had enough of the wild western land where the playful cyclone rages and concluded to spend the remainder of his days in the highlands of Scotland."[8]

While such devastating displays of the extremes of Iowa climate convinced James Cowan that he should live elsewhere, some settlers found a heartwarming camaraderie in sharing nature's adversities. The round up of names of those killed (and several were), what property had been destroyed, and what had happened to everyone constituted a kind of reckoning—who they were, what they were doing—which they hadn't considered in the midst of their normal, busy lives. People living close to the land often found that these crescendos of nature helped connect themselves to one another. The bad times served, just as the harvest and feast days did. All the clergymen of Le Mars joined in the official service of thanksgiving. Captain Moreton was in charge of the collection, which became the basis of a relief fund for those most in need.

To his army officer brother, soon to depart for India, James admitted that the hard cowboy life had great appeal because of its simplicity and ruggedness: "Of course, I don't like working for wages, and it would be ten times nicer to have cattle of one's own," but he still preferred ranch life to farming. "If I had to work for wages, 'cow-punching' is the job I would take up." If both he and Walter were salaried cowhands and saved their wages, in three years they would have the capital to start their own cattle ranch, "but Walter does not seem to like this country and prefers farming." Walter envisioned a steady living out of continuous farm work, but James preferred living on the rough, strenuously saving money, to "get back to the old country sooner."[9] This adventure as a colonial he hoped would some day end with repatriation.

That dream was held in reserve by many Close Colony settlers; they had other places to go, if not home. Their families and friends would somehow take them in or help make arrangements in another part of the world. Although Walter was more sanguine about Iowa than James, he was by no means ready to become a naturalized citizen. "The only advantage in becoming a citizen is the privilege of voting, and in return for this a man has to renounce allegiance to all foreign kings, rulers, and potentates, and 'especially Queen Victoria of the British Isles.' This is rather a big thing for a man to swear all at once, who has been born and raised a British subject."[10]

When Walter returned to the farm in early September (he had been delayed a bit—"it was the ladies that kept me so long up there, but I was able to tear myself away from them at last"), he was gratified to find everything "looking first class," from the animals to the buildings and crops. Taylor and his wife had been extraordinarily good stewards. Walter immediately marketed six steers at a 120 percent profit. He sold 26 hogs for "a very poor price" of $3.35 per 100 lbs, but he had to get rid of them because they were "too fat to keep." At an auction he picked up seven calves and two heifers for feeding, since the hay crop had been good though difficult to gather because of the weather. He was back in farming again.[11]

James remained in Wyoming, and his response to his father's entreaty that one or both of them come home for a visit during the winter was: "I don't want to go home until we can pay our own way." Trip expenses would cut seriously into their meager capital, and they didn't think they should leave Taylor alone again so soon, particularly since he spoke of departing the following spring.

The unexpected success of their fledgling cattle business in Iowa struck James as significant. He began to consider more extensive cattle raising, buying yearlings and "turning off three-year-olds every year." By feeding cattle on homegrown hay they would realize maximum profits, and "the steer business would pay even in Iowa, tho' far better here [in Wyoming].... I am quite of the opinion that we should take the first offer that would cover the money we have laid out, and then look out for a new location." He was eager to glimpse Washington Territory and British Columbia, especially the latter, for "if possible I would like to be under the British flag."[12]

The cattle and hog markets turned sharply down soon after Walter had sold. Although swine prices had seemed low when he shipped them, the levels now were "positively ruinous and farmers are saying they never want to see a hog again. Everybody seems to be selling off all their hogs, and those not sold are dying from cholera." With so few pigs left in the lots, Walter was certain prices would go up because of demand, and he wished he had more of them. He soon had additional cash; Richard Cowan had sent his sons another draft— for which Walter thanked him, somewhat uneasily.[13]

Not until mid-November did James finally return to Iowa from Wyoming. Both brothers were somewhat dismayed to learn their neighbor, Watson, was pulling out to join a cattle-feeding firm in Le Mars. They purchased three fine cows in the Watson sales. "It seems a pity for Watson to sell out, as there is no doubt he is doing well; but I daresay he will do better by fattening." It wasn't that Watson had become discouraged about farming itself. He started with "big capital and got good cows...and having always had good luck, he has now about 150 head of the best cattle in this part of the country." Why, then? More certain money could be made in other business pursuits.

Already restricted in their Iowa social life, Watson's departure created further isolation. "When he is gone we will have only one Englishman within any reasonable distance of us," Walter wrote his sister, "and that is Sinclair, who is quite close. He is a married man and the proud father of a daughter about two months old. His Mother-in-law and sister-ditto- are going to pass the winter with him. It will be a change for them, as they generally winter in Italy. We go up there sometimes to spend the evening, but though the sister-in-law is very attractive, we are neither of us 'entangled' yet. The whole party, baby included, came here the other day for afternoon tea and appeared to enjoy themselves."[14]

Earlier, Walter had written his father that "a fellow wants a wife in a country like this." But he and James were insufficiently settled to contemplate matrimony. When their friend Joe Jefferson became engaged—to an American at that—they were bemused, envious, and forced to reflect upon their bleak bachelorhoods. Walter "could not bear the idea of his marrying a Yankee," but when he met her he changed his mind. Jefferson enlisted Walter's aid to break the news to his mother, for the family would be upset "that he had chosen a girl for his bride in such an out of the way place as Wyoming; the land, as people at home think, of nothing but lawlessness, revolvers and bowie knives." The Jeffersons made no objections, aside from their concern that Joe should wait until he could afford to marry, applauding "the additional incentive to him to *work*," as if he had been slacking. "Poor Joe. I am afraid no amount of work on his part can either make cows more prolific or better the price of beef, but he must wait now with a light heart and hope for the beef market to go up."[15]

THE new year seemed a natural time to appraise their welfare and prospects, and James concluded in a letter to his father in January 1886 that the only people who succeeded in farming were those who had large amounts of capital or else very little. Many Close colonists invested not only in land and stock but in town lots, livestock companies, and small-town collateral businesses such as real estate or insurance, and by this diversification managed to profit from the development of the entire area. They were not in danger of being wiped out by a dip in the cattle market or an epidemic of hog cholera. The other kind of pioneer, as James correctly observed, simply had no choices: the entire family resources had been sunk into making the venture succeed, long hours of unremunerative work were expected, years of commitment. With wife and children as the work force, these families remained afloat despite all vicissitudes. They were capable of "living on bacon and flour, and as they are always married, they have no expense in the way of wages."

The Cowans, although willing to do physical hard labor and possessing some capital, "slip between the two stools." Not rich enough, nor yet so desperate, or of the peasant class. Surely the only way to escape would be removal to Wyoming, where they could "either buy a ranch...or take up one by declaring your intention of becoming an American citizen. In this way you need not actually take out your papers for five years...plenty of time to sell or do anything you like if you don't want to take out your papers; but in the meantime the land is yours." James was quite willing to go along with these stipulations, for he was certain he would not become a citizen. It would cost them only about $200 a year to live, since they would shoot their meat and required few groceries.[16]

Cash to purchase a Wyoming ranch would have to come from the sale of the Iowa farm — *that* was the stickler. James feared they would not be able to get $35 per acre, since land prices had stagnated. If they sold the farm at $30, as Walter suggested, which they could probably get, it would mean their three years of living expenses had cost them $3,000, with no profit for their labor. This would be bitter to take. In short, since they could not dispose of the Iowa farm easily, they had better plan to keep it going, even if both were working in Wyoming. Last summer the Taylors had made absentee farming possible, but since they were ready to take a farm of their own, the Cowans had to make other arrangements.[17]

They hired a new housekeeper surprisingly easily. James wrote his sister in March: "She seems very tidy and a great 'rustler,' which being translated means one who is very energetic. She is very 'high toned' for a housekeeper, being the daughter of a well to do English farmer and is apparently quite eligible, so there are new dangers of getting entangled you see looming up in the new future — she is nearer suited to Walter than to me, however, in point of age, though not very well to either of us." Her brother had worked for Watson. "They are a better class than the ordinary run of tenant farmers in England. Indeed, most fellows mistake the one at Watson's for a 'pupil.' "[18]

In matters of class standards, Walter and James still told the family what it wanted to hear: that the boys were negotiating the free, easy American society and sticking to measurements of who would do and who would not. So long as their English steward, Taylor, looked after the farm and his wife kept house, they could pride themselves on having managed to cling to gentlemanly life. But they were quite aware how fragile their hold upon the genteel stance really was. Their stints of long labor in the harvests, though good for their health (and character, making them tougher), was somewhat tarnished by the fact that they *had* to do it. Constant physical drudgery spoiled their hoped for illusion of being gentlemen settlers — taming the new land to fit *their* image, not having the experience totally shape *them*.

"There is one thing we have been pretty lucky with and that is our horses, which are the animals I care most about, and I rather flatter myself we have a better stable than most people out here," James reported. Cattle raising required too much capital; their pig herd was subject to costly cholera epidemics. One area of animal husbandry remained promising — horses, to be raised for market either in Iowa or Wyoming. It was an idea the Cowans would pursue and develop, until horse handling became their major enterprise in the last years of the decade.

James persistently cited the Iowa weather as his chief reason for wanting to leave. If ever he needed evidence for his complaint, the winter of 1885–1886 provided it. "We had the most frightful storm for cold I have ever seen, about two weeks ago. Lots of people had cattle and hogs frozen to death. The thermometer went down to nearly 40° below zero, and a regular hurricane was blowing for three days. I never saw anything like it."[19]

For weeks the Cowans received no mail. James wrote of "two or three trains temporarily abandoned in the middle of a snow drift, not being able to move either way." Added to their problems, they experienced a sudden run of bad luck with their animals: "A favorite cow got unwell and died....the most valuable mare in the stable died after a 6 hour illness, of cholic." Walter and their houseguest, Joe Jefferson, had gone to Le Mars for a three-day weekend holiday, leaving James to cope; "another cow became seriously unwell," but not with the same ailment as the first. When another mare took sick, James telegraphed a veterinarian in Sioux City, who did not, however, arrive at the Cowans' until 10:00 P.M. — and stayed all the next day with the sick horse. To "put a final 'flumaxer' onto me," Joe Jefferson's dog disappeared. Walter and Joe returned to find an exhausted James, who "hardly had any sleep for three days and was rapidly sinking," as he could now humorously put it. The mare died, for the veterinarian attending her "did not understand the case from the beginning." In response to his father's query about what to tell a parent who had six sons he hoped to ship to Iowa to become pupils, James suggested that all six be sent "to be instructed in farming to us...we will allow him a large reduction in premiums and have some extra stalls put up in the barn to accommodate them."[20]

It finally occurred to the Cowans that since loyal Taylor was only planning to *rent* a nearby farm, not strike out as a homesteader himself (he still did not have the capital), they might hang onto him if they asked him to become *their* renter, going shares in an equitable fashion, more or less as they had arranged it last summer while they sojourned in Wyoming. This would allow them time to concentrate on some new direction that might grant greater use of their intelligence and ingenuity. They couldn't see the point of expending more brute, physical energy when there was such a slim chance of profit.

They persuaded Taylor and his wife to stay on and disengaged the new housekeeper. With their course now set, they had only to justify it to their father, whose cash involvement and loving concern made him a virtual partner. "Our idea is to go out to Wyoming again," James wrote. Although younger than Walter by five years, James often appeared the stronger in resolute action, more extreme in opinions, prickly in temperament. Easy-going Walter found the ladies of Wyoming an extra inducement, and his friendship with Joe Jefferson, employed by a cattle syndicate, made the Rawlins scene appealing. Probably the wedding would take place soon.

They were also drawn toward Wyoming because in Iowa they had become such recluses. Watson's departure made a serious difference, further isolating them. Only Sinclair's warm, festive, British household nurtured their sense of still belonging to the civilized world. James wrote his sister (18 March 1886): "Sinclair is going to have his baby christened on Monday & we are invited to the ceremony, where we are to meet two more eligible young ladies who have the reputation of being very pretty. Neither of us have yet made their acquaintance but both being suitable in every respect, I think it seems a good chance, as two sisters are not so liable to fight, living in the same house, as two of the gentler sex who are not so nearly related." This double matrimonial idea came to nothing, although the slim possibility of it, confided to Lillias, suggested how desperate they were beginning to feel.[21]

James made no bones about it. "We don't intermix much with the Yankees in this country. I wish the people round here were like the Wyoming lot." The Cowans made little effort to involve themselves extensively in colony get-togethers. Perhaps James's early distaste for Iowa prevented him from joining in. He seemed to prefer privacy and had a low tolerance for fools. However, he misstated their situation when he told his sister that "the only Englishman anywhere near us now is Sinclair, which is rather a nuisance...." Actually, society of his class, background, and tastes was immediately available in the area, but he made few overtures toward these people.

In the seven years the Cowans owned and intermittently lived on their farm, their neighbor across the Big Sioux River (a stream less than fifty-feet wide) was F. P. Baker, an Oxford graduate, son of a Worcestershire clergyman. His mother's family was solid in the county aristocracy. It would seem Baker possessed the social qualifications the Cowans sought for their company, but they never mention knowing him. Why? Perhaps because Baker had an American wife.

Baker first visited "the great North-West" in 1879 but did not emigrate until the spring of 1883, the same year the Cowans arrived. After serving time as a pup, he bought a large tract on the Dakota side of the Big Sioux, then married a Wisconsin girl who had come west by prairie schooner. They settled down to domestic life in a small frame house almost exactly the dimensions of a Close Brothers' farmhouse—and may have been one. Two sons were born, Lionel and Rolle. Alvira Baker was the kind of sturdy helpmeet a pioneer needed; her background in rural Wisconsin prepared her for the even rougher country conditions of Dakota.

Baker was nicknamed "Pasha" by family and friends, after Valentin Baker, the army officer who, following scandal and imprisonment, was posted in Turkey, and became commander-in-chief of the Khedive's army, hence his sobriquet. In no way except surname did Baker resemble Pasha Baker. He lived a quiet, fairly cramped life in the small farmhouse and had little to do with the Close Colony, though he did belong to the Prairie Club. Baker made frequent trips to England to visit relatives but never in the company of his American wife, who remained on the farm, keeping an eye on its operation. Baker employed a capable overseer and seldom dirtied his hands with physical work on the farm; he was always splendidly dressed. *Cornhill* magazine, the *London Illustrated News,* and other newspapers and periodicals from home arrived in his mail, and he had the leisure to pursue his hobby of painting competent watercolors—English churchyard scenes, fens, and moors.

When his son Rolle became old enough and showed an interest in farming, Baker let him handle affairs. Rolle could set a cultivator better than anyone around, neighbors still report. Baker bought one of the first cars available, a Winton, which he had shipped from Chicago. He never cared to drive it himself, but Rolle did, with Baker riding grandly in the back seat, dressed in what the locals refer to as a "top hat" but which may have been a British bowler. Altogether, he seems to have lived at an even greater distance from his American neighbors than James and Walter Cowan. Occasionally he made himself known by letter to the Akron newspaper on some abstruse subject, in which he always displayed a remarkable amount of knowledge. One such letter concerned mathematical conundrums. Which number, 194 or 186, is closest to 190?

> I think it must be admitted that 194 and 186 are equally close to or distant from 190....As all mathematicians know, much juggling may be done with figures, and there are many well known paradoxes on allied lines in which it is sometimes difficult to detect the misleading figure or figures. The fact that 4 is the error of both parties, and therefore equalizes the error of both, is of course incorrect, as may readily be seen by supposing a different case as follows....

Baker proceeded to draw an elaborate example, dazzling in complexity, quite the sort of letter one might read in the *Times*. It would be hard to imagine many of his local American readers understanding any of it.

Baker remained a true British colonial in the United States, living out his life with very little accommodation to his back-of-beyond surroundings. His handsome sisters sent photographs of themselves taken by a Cheltenham studio photographer, and a cousin dressed in Indian Dragoon uniform had his portrait snapped in Malta. These family mementoes ended up in the library of the Baker mansion, a mile from Akron, Iowa. His wife "Vira" rooted Baker to his new land, and his American children would thrive and accomplish the distance he himself could never put between his background and life's new circumstances in America.

For one hundred years the Bakers remained where F. P. settled. The small prairie house where the family first lived is still there, now a caretaker's cottage for the grand Baker mansion subsequently erected. He persisted in his plan to establish himself as an aristocratic country squire in terms familiar to the world of late-Victorian England, even though by the time he was able to indulge his dream fully, there was hardly anyone left of the Anglo social set who might have understood what he had in mind.

Family documents indicate that in 1911 Baker inherited an estate left by a bishop — a relative — property that included the usual mix: stock in a Bombay railroad, the "living" from several farms, and other income-producing sources. Baker engaged a Sioux City architect to excecute construction of a house that he largely designed, apparently remembering English country houses he had admired. Baker owned draftsman instruments — neat rulers, calipers, sextons (all housed in a beautiful box), but he relied upon the skills of the professional architect. The house was to be set in a park with a winding drive sweeping around to the front, which faced south. Trees lining the road would make a proper alley.

The Baker edifice was situated on a slight rise above the floodplain and overlooked the lonely, somewhat barren environs of the Big Sioux River. Of the fifteen rooms, eight were originally bedrooms. Downstairs was dominated by a typical great hall with an enormous tiled fireplace. The six-foot-wide stained birch staircase leading upstairs featured a handsomely tooled banister. The ceilings throughout were twelve or more feet high. In the art nouveau library (sets of leather-bound classics), the wainscoting had been stained dark green. Cast-bronze hinges, doorknobs, and window hardware were clearly the best procurable. Thick, beveled plate-glass doors led to terraces on the first and second floors. The reinforced concrete structure, an early example of its kind, possessed a stucco quality, while the beams and natural wood details gave the flavor of English Tudor. The wrap-around second floor terrace suggested that compelling views would constantly entice one outside. Indeed, the vistas were impressive, though somewhat empty and melancholy, perhaps because the elaborateness of the house failed to mix with the simplicity of the prairie surrounding it. Plans for a tennis court and large garden never materialized, nor did the rifle range.[22]

The kitchen with its huge tiled stove area provided ample workspace for the four girls in service. And on the top floor was the ballroom with a hardwood floor, but it was seldom if ever used for dancing. The billiard room, also planned for the third floor, was never completed. A smoke bin in the attic was designed for the curing of hams, and the cellar provided a proper space for wine storage.

All details of the building's construction were meticulously watched over by Baker. The plaster specifications give some notion of the quality he sought: "a scratch coat made of goat or cattle hair, the hair to be well-beaten and soaked in water." This coat remained on the walls three or four days before the "brown coat" was applied — it contained cement plus hair and lime and was to stand two weeks before the final coat, plaster of Paris, was laid on.

By the time the mansion was finished, Baker was almost done for, too; he lived only about ten years in his splendid house, much of that time as an invalid, confined by a stroke to a bedroom on the first floor, just off the great hall.

One of the present-day Baker clan, reflecting on the family past, reported that there used to be a saying among them that if Pasha Baker had remained in England "he could have been titled, since he was of royal blood. Now you know that's not true! *Is* it?"

No, not exactly. The description had gotten a little out of alignment in its American transplantation. Baker's father, mother, and a host of cousins, some with five and six surnames linked by hyphens, were listed in *County Families* and similar blueblood reference books. The Baker pride in family pedigrees was perfectly consistent with land ownership, for the person who owned the soil was lord and master. His power and wealth exuded from the earth itself and the fruits thereof, not from dependence on one's fellowmen — engagement in lowly acts of industry or demeaning business activity. The landowner had a relationship to the Almighty which in the medieval mind bred the notion of feudal aristocracy. In the great chain of being the relationship of a man-of-the-soil to God was a paradigm of the kingdom itself: the sovereign and his subjects.

Baker with his impeccable lineage, living in his grand house in South Dakota, embodied in his days a surviving remnant of feudal ideas. And yet the gist of what he had been up to seems rather hard to perceive as one stands on the steps of the Baker veranda and looks across the brown, fallow fields toward the muddy Big Sioux River — now and then a tumbleweed slowly wheeling into view.

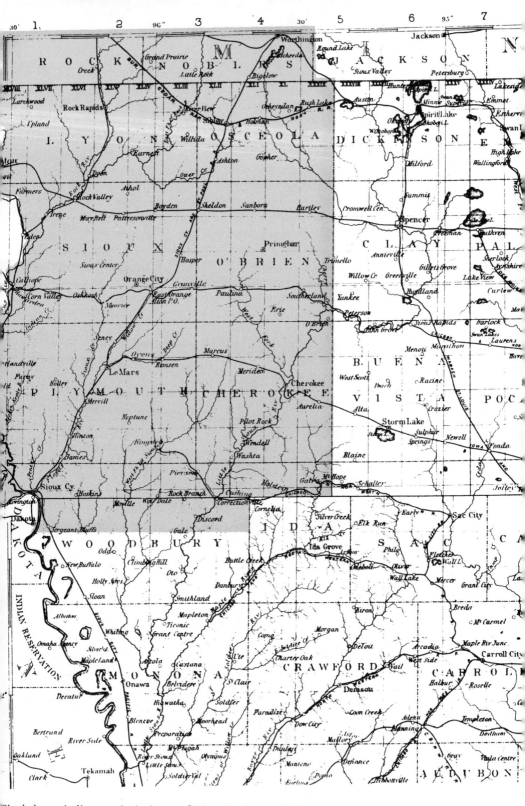

Shaded area indicates principal area of Close Brothers activities, 1879–1884.
(*Courtesy of the State Historical Society of Iowa*)

Heacock Mill, Kingsley (Quorn). (*Courtesy of E. V. Heacock*)

Randolph Payne, Englishman and pharmacist, Kingsley.
(*Courtesy of E. V. Heacock*)

HIS GRACE THE DUKE OF SUTHERLAND, K.G.

THE IRON (RAIL) DUKE FINISHING HIS GREAT AMERICAN RIDE OF
TWENTY THOUSAND MILES, AND RETURNING "AS FRESH A
WHEN HE STARTED."

The Duke of Sutherland. (*Punch*)

Carlogie, the Farquhar
farm, Brunsville, as it
appeared in 1978.

Judge's stand and grandstand, Le Mars Fairgrounds, 1880s. (*Courtesy of the State Historical Society of Iowa*)

Polo mallets. (*Courtesy of the State Historical Society of Iowa*)

Close Brothers land office, Quorn, restored (1976).

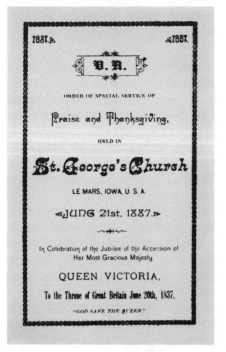

V. R.

ORDER OF SPECIAL SERVICE OF

Praise and Thanksgiving,

HELD IN

St. George's Church

LE MARS, IOWA, U. S. A.

JUNE 21st, 1887.

In Celebration of the Jubilee of the Accession of
Her Most Gracious Majesty

QUEEN VICTORIA,

To the Throne of Great Britain June 20th, 1837.

"GOD SAVE THE QUEEN."

Golden Jubilee program,
St. George's Church, 1887.

(*below*) F. P. Baker home, West
Akron, South Dakota.

Walter Cowan
(*Courtesy of J. O. C. Willson*)

George Hotham.
(*Photo by Dick Koerselman*)

CHAPTER FOURTEEN

The State of the Colony

Y 1883, the year the Cowan brothers arrived in Iowa, some of the earlier settlers had already tired of the adventure and in decamping bad-mouthed the country, much to the ire of the locals. "It is not what it is represented to be, they say," reported one newspaper. "Its re-sources are exaggerated, its climate misrepresented.... Tilling the soil and tending the cattle is such very hard work.... It is no place for a gentleman to live. Consequently, they are returning home and filling the small space ac-corded them in the drawing rooms with the result of their acute observations and wails of disappointment.... There is no sadness in the Northwest over their flight. In leaving they sundered no ties which will bleed at their depar-ture.... The idea of caste, of an American aristocracy, is unknown to the brawny-armed settlers...."[1]

What befell the Closes' town, Quorn, seemed to portend the waning of British presence and influence. The Chicago and North Western Railroad, building grades and laying tracks from the east, finally neared Quorn in the spring of 1883. On 22 June landowner and railroad-builder John I. Blair, whose firm, Blair Town and Lot Company, brought into being some eighty towns, purchased for $1,000 the site of present day Kingsley, one mile east of Quorn. The platting of towns expected to be served by railroads was one of the chief speculative ventures in the settling of the West: some became rich by having a town successfully burst into being; others saw their nebulous villages wither and die as the transportation system bypassed their cherished spot. Blair employed a Vermonter, N. P. Kingsley, to lay out the new town, which, instead of Quorn, would be served by the railroad.[2]

When news of the creation of Kingsley became known, Quorn citizens pretended to be calm, although all businesses quickly crossed the West Fork and settled near the railroad. "Those travelling between here and Kingsley in the night should carry a headlight, otherwise they might run against some of the numerous buildings now on the road," the *Quorn Lynx* noted. Some in Quorn thought the old town would remain as the residential section, but when the Post Office and all other town identification was transferred to Kingsley, the village of Quorn was doomed. Observers speculated that the development of Kingsley at the expense of Quorn was a reaction against Close Brothers, who had been too assertive in trying to induce the railroad to come to Quorn. It seems more likely that the Closes were simply not watching developments carefully enough; nor was the survival of Quorn of vital interest to them any longer. By the time William Close returned to Iowa in November for his only visit in 1883, the removal of businesses to Kingsley had been largely accomplished.[3]

Ironically, while the Closes were losing their town, the Paullins were succeeding with theirs. Paullina, platted in 1882, was served by another spur line of the Chicago and North Western, the same road that shunned Quorn. With the help of a steady supply of pups, Henry and Edward were busily establishing their wheat, flax, and stock farms. Although in April 1883 newspapers reported the Paullin brothers "temporarily embarrassed," they were soon "again all right, and doing a more extensive business than ever."[4]

The search for cheap, available tracts led Close Brothers north to Minnesota, which like northwest Iowa was a pocket of sparse settlement. Railroads were just beginning to penetrate the region, thereby providing sound transportation for agricultural products. As early as 1879 James had been scouting in Pipestone; by 1883, southwestern Minnesota had become a major interest of the firm. An agreement was worked out with the city of Pipestone in April 1883 whereby in exchange for ninety-nine town lots and a half interest in 200 acres north of the city limits, the firm agreed to establish an office in Pipestone; exert influence to promote more railroad building to the town; give priority to developing land nearby; and erect a good hotel to cost not less than $11,000, which had to be finished by January 1884.[5]

The hotel was completed on schedule, and Fred and Margaret Close moved to Pipestone in February 1884, settling with Mrs. Humble in an apartment above the company office. Fred revealed plans to start a major horse-breeding establishment and built a large barn, mostly to accommodate his brother James's increased holdings in thoroughbreds. William and Mary Close also bought a house in Pipestone at about this time. Other prominent Close colonists, such as Almeric Paget and Ronald Jervis, took up residence. Some of the newcomers seemed quite eccentric. A Pipestone reporter said that one settler "has but recently returned from Florida, where he has been fishing all winter for alligators, one of which he succeeded in capturing alive and is making a household pet of it at his home. . . ."[6]

The removal to Pipestone did not mean that the Fred Closes were gone entirely from Le Mars. On the eve of Lent (1884) a masked ball was held in Apollo Hall, with Margaret dressed as gypsy, Fred as clown. One Mardi Gras reveler came in black and white satin as dominoes; Constantine Benson wore Calcutta evening dress, his sister was "a Greek Lady"; Ronald Jervis appeared in an Indian costume; another as an Australian officer, and an American guest got himself up as an Episcopal clergyman.[7]

To promote Pipestone, Fred started a novel advertising campaign which fitted neatly into Close Brothers' need for lumber shipments from the East. Since all this new wood on railroad cars would be passing through hundreds of miles of farms and towns, why not tell onlookers where it was going and why? Cloth banners were strung along the cars bearing the inscription: "Dakota is Busted. This entire load of lumber is bound for the Great Pipestone Country, for Close Bros & Co. . .from the Eau Claire Lumber Company, Eau Claire, Wisconsin." Upon arrival, the boards were stacked on the lots next to the Close Brothers office, and much of downtown Pipestone seemed to have become "one vast lumber yard." This sort of splashy hucksterism was just what the town fathers had hoped for. An estimated eight tons of Pipestone promotional material was distributed throughout the United States and Great Britain in 1884.

As a result of the hoopla, one railroad, the Burlington, laid tracks into Pipestone from Luverne, Minnesota, in 1884. Five years later the *Pipestone Star's* assessment of the Closes' contribution to the Pipestone boom concluded that the thousands of dollars spent on advertising had made their community "famous the country over," and "a steady stream of immigration is now flowing into the country; homes are being created and the wilderness of a few years ago 'blossoms like a rose.' "[8]

But actual farm settlement was not accomplished so easily. In 1921 William looked back on this period of Close Brothers' investments: "there had been rain for three years before we bought these lands [in southwestern Minnesota] and we sold most of them off at double the price within a year; but unfortunately a period of drought set in and the lands, being sold on time, reverted to our Company."[9]

The British venture in Pipestone was depicted in a 1937 romantic novel by Minnesotans, Maud and Delos Lovelace, *Gentlemen from England.*[10] William Close appeared as a shrewd New Englander who swindled gullible Britons into buying land for twenty-five dollars an acre, which the railroad would happily have sold for five dollars. His offer to "locate your son in a home of comfort and refinement where under ideal conditions he can learn the art of American farming" was also a "sell." The young apprentice farmers found themselves indentured servants and most of them rebelled. The British immigrants to Pipestone (called "Rainbow") included black sheep and those with dishonorable pasts. The despair and loneliness of many of them comes through — "He's the son of an admiral, they say. He'll never see England again." The hero won colony approval by successfully hunting Three Toes, a famous local wolf — an episode closely modeled on Fred Close's extraordinary wolf hunt in February 1885. Fred and his companions, including Ronald Jervis, rode horseback from Pipestone on a hunt one Sunday morning, their hounds soon starting up a wolf. They chased him over the hills and flats of prairie, hour after hour, twenty-nine miles before they had to give up. It was 6:30 P.M. and too dark to continue. All the riders had experienced "one or more falls...some of them quite hard," said a reporter. "The hounds kept on the chase and have not returned. Any party sending Mr. Close information as to their whereabouts will confer a great favor."[11]

The Lovelaces's characters in *Gentlemen from England* endured hardships and some of them died, but no roots were put down. They were "not really adopting the new home." Their role was to make this part of Minnesota livable for others. "Our dollars got nothing much for ourselves. But what else fed the Americans through the grasshopper plagues, and what else paid for the good houses and barns, and for breaking up the virgin prairies!...The cash we paid out has made a backlog that will last longer than we have."[12]

THE British "invasion" of the United States seemed more than merely amusing to some observers, who were especially alarmed by the scope of the pound sterling outlay involved. When a bill was introduced in Congress in 1884 to stop these "Leviathan squatters" from grabbing even more of the country, two Congressmen spoke of 21 million acres held by noncitizens. A journalist totaled the acres held by nine Englishmen and it amounted to a territory equal in size to New Hampshire, Massachusetts, and Rhode Island combined.[13]

Although no U.S. law was passed to stop this foreign investment surge, a number of British critics warned their countrymen about the vast amount of capital flowing out, estimated to be "about £17,000,000 [$85,000,000] in one year." Perhaps an even greater loss to England was the vital resource of its bright, educated young men who were emigrating at an astonishing rate; England was being stripped of "a large amount of our inventive talent."[14]

By writing letters to the London *Times,* William Close tried to stop rumors that those who owned land in the United States had to become citizens to enjoy their full privileges of ownership. Even the U.S. Consul in London backed him, noting that only mining claims had to be accompanied by citizenship papers, since these were essentially gifts from the government.[15]

The farm-pupil system came under increasing public attack in Britain. Early on, the *Field* had given a favorable report on the Close Colony pup scheme, but the reporter made no mention of those unfortunates who happened to be assigned to ignoble farmsteads with poor, boorish farmers as tutors. The most scathing account appeared in *Blackwood*'s written by a former Close colonist, John Hope.[16] He mockingly described a typical eighteen- or nineteen-year-old youth, who "probably recently left some large school, where his success at cricket has been more noticeable than his progress in the sciences." Since he had no profession, his parents seized upon the opportunity of an opening in western America, "found in some newspaper...and which further goes on to state, that certain benevolent persons will receive young men into their homes and 'teach them farming.' " All sorts of visions of country lanes, a bountiful earth, great hunting and fishing, and eventual proprietorship of a vast tract of land constituted the "pretty fiction."

After buying passage, travelling 5,000 miles, and arriving in late winter, as he had been advised to do, what did he find? A huge white expanse, "nothing to break the monotony but one or two thickets of small young trees at long intervals." These so-called groves were but a couple of lines of ten-foot high trees set against the north and west winds. "Behind this a small white wooden house, near which is a wooden stable and other buildings, and a yard enclosed by posts, boards, and 'barbed' wire. In one corner of this, a rough, hay-roofed, tumble-down-looking shed affords shelter to some eight or nine head of stock; and a big heap of straw provides a warm bed to a large number of hogs. . . ."

Machinery was buried in snowbanks, some of the drifts ten and fifteen feet high, and around the house were curious mounds near the foundation. "They are caused by stable-manure being heaped to the height of two and a half feet, and several feet in width, in order to keep the wind from penetrating under the house." Since it had been twenty-degrees below zero for the last month, the windows were closed over with frost, and the frozen rope could hardly be lowered into the well for water. The farmer and his sons pulled on felt socks and odd snowboots to do "chaws," feed the animals maize, and then return to consume their own food, which was salt pork, fried potatoes, and pancakes. The cooking was done by the housewife in a room fifteen by twelve feet, the chief chamber of the house; in addition to the stove it contained a cupboard, table, shelves, a few chairs. The only other room on the ground floor was a tiny bedroom used by the farmer and his wife, heated when the door was left open to the main room. Upstairs the children slept under the low, sloping roof, meagre warmth coming from the stove pipe that went through the room. Blizzards had recently swept the region, and if by unlucky chance you were away from shelter, the "biting wind penetrating to the very bones, and a blinding snow dashing over the face" could easily result in your death—perhaps only a few yards from the house door.

On this typical 160-acre farm, the fields in April were prepared for planting; a modest crop would result, and only a little money. Had advertisers such as Close Brothers "spoken of peasant proprietors and peasant holdings, not one-tenth of the young fellows who either are at this moment or have been in the Western States, would ever have gone." If the aim of the "great foundations"—the public schools—was to produce peasants for the American frontier, then instead of studying classics and mathematics, the schoolboys had better be given picks and shovels and assigned to road repair, for at least it would tone up their muscles and be more in keeping with their future occupation. The class of men operating ordinary American farms corresponded to the English laborer in a wayside cottage. Hardly a fit scene for a gentleman's son. Why was it taking so long for word to get around?

For one thing, the land purchased did usually go for a higher rate later on when the young immigrant sold out. Since no money had been lost and in some cases an actual gain was posted, the true nature of the situation was still not understood in Great Britain, Hope said. He considered the case of a gentleman emigrant who bought a farm "at the instigation of a well-known firm of land-agents," while in his premium year as a pup. "By the end of that time two things had occurred. Firstly, the 'pup'. . . did not fancy farming and returned to England. Secondly, the land, which had cost only ten dollars per acre, realised exactly double that sum throughout. However, this result had not in any measure been produced by the agricultural training of the 'pup,' while his premium was merely an unnecessary deduction from the profits of the land speculation."

However, most inexperienced youths, such as Hope described, would never have had the opportunity to profit from land sales, had they not been on the frontier, receiving expert advice from men like the Closes and their associates. Hope was no doubt sarcastic and bitter because of his own miserable experience as a pup—not on a farm of an English gentleman, as advertised, but in a mundane American settler's household, where he clearly must have felt totally out of place and cheated.

Disparagement of the farm-pupil concept suddenly became proportionately as vehement and widespread as praise and enthusiasm had been only a few years earlier. Hugh Davies-Cooke, outward bound from Great Britain to New York, on his way to Wyoming, wrote his parents in April 1883: "Some of the fellows on board have been out to Morton [*sic*] and Close at Le Mars and are all of the opinion there is nothing to be learnt there and no work done, Close and Morton feather their own nest well and that's all. The advice I get from all is 'the farther you keep away from them [the] better for you.' They have a lot of young fellows there who do nothing else but smoke, drink and gamble; they form a deck to themselves and are continually at war with the Americans around and hated by all: Morton may be a very good fellow, and everyone says he is, but as to having any power over his pupils, it is a farce. . . ."[17]

The strongest case *for* the pupil idea was made several years later in *Macmillan's*, where it was pointed out that a young man going out really had only two choices, either work and board with people of his own class where he would have "the same comforts and refinements he would have at home," or hire out as a regular working farm hand where he would have none of these. Some parents seemed to think the company of their educated son would be sought for its own sake, whereas the truth was, gentlemen immigrants "as a class have not. . . a very good name. . . never done a day's work in their lives, have not the remotest notion of how to set about a single farming operation...." True, the pupil worked for no wages, but that labor amounted to very little; often there was a real risk of damage to animals and machinery by inexperienced hands. The work of training these newcomers needed some compensation, and the apprentice idea was a sound one.[18]

As the Close Colony matured, the pupil system became a less noticeable feature, particularly when Close Brothers abandoned sponsorship of the plan (which seems to have begun in 1882). From then on it became largely an individual matter; when the colony began to number over 500, as it did just two years after it began, personal contacts (such as the Cowan brothers had with Gerald Garnett) usually served to make the intermediary arrangements for a young man wishing to go out.

The de-emphasis of the role of pups in the viability of the colony coincided with a softening of British exclusiveness. It began to seem less important to many Britons that they keep removed from the Americans, particularly among those colonists who were married and raising families. While the Prairie Club membership was still limited to bona fide Britons, holding oneself aloof ceased to be the encouraged style. An aristocracy based on money and position no matter what the individual's national origin began to take the place of Anglo exclusiveness. Overtures of friendship of a formal sort had been characteristic of the colony since the beginning, with the Prairie Club *conversaziones* open to a few of "our American cousins" and honorary memberships extended to high-placed locals, though only for one year. Before long the polo team was over half American and many non-British had learned cricket. Several marriages brought the two countries closer—even Captain Moreton's son married a Le Mars native.

However, the June Derby in 1885 remained very much an English affair, though the weather was typically Iowa—hot and steamy. The races were interrupted by downpours, but the crowd's enthusiasm was scarcely dampened. In the Grand National Steeple Chase, Fred Close's John Campbell, the favorite, came in third after a spill, but the next year this horse won the House of Lords trophy permanently for Fred (a three-time winner); the silver trophy stayed in the family and is now in the Des Moines home of Margaret Close's great niece. For the sixth race, another steeplechase, Fred mounted John Campbell himself, but "he could not get him over the sod hurdle and water jump and was thrown in his effort to make the animal leap."[19]

Fred's reappearances in the colony were as much dictated by athletic zeal as business calculation. Margaret shared his equestrian interests. In the winter of 1884 at the Le Mars St. James Catholic church fair, she received 219 votes as the best lady on sidesaddle, though she lost out to a local American. While the Fred Closes seemed still to be part of colony life, they were primarily involved elsewhere. Even during the month of the 1885 Derby, Fred was busy laying out a town in Cottonwood County, Minnesota. But his connection to the colony remained active—especially through sports. In December 1886 the press reported: "Fred Close has established a toboggan slide at Sibley, which he has named the 'White Bear.' He would like for Le Mars friends to come up and have some fun."[20]

During the mid-eighties, James Close appeared in Le Mars less often, for he was fully occupied with the Minnesota land development. In 1884 a Close Brothers office opened in Chicago, and the following year they sold their major properties in Le Mars—a hotel, barn, and nearby cottage—to a Chicago investor who had probably been induced into the purchase by James. As cheap land ceased to be available, the firm increased its involvement in mortgages and debentures. They sold "City Improvement Warrants" for street, sewer, and water-main projects in Chicago and its suburbs, Tulsa, St. Louis, Kansas City, and St. Joseph. James and his wife, Susan Humble, and William and Mary lived for a time in the lakeshore village, Highland Park. The Chicago branch of Close Brothers began to be phased out in 1909; it had assets of over $1 million. When World War I began, according to the oldest living employee of Close Brothers, R. W. P. King, the British government curtailed financial involvements abroad; "the American business was disposed of so far at least as English investors were concerned and the proceeds remitted to England, shortly before I enlisted in the Army in 1915."[21]

While the Closes moved farther away from the colony they founded, those who still participated in the venture prided themselves on having accomplished the settling. Fulfillment of the colony dream meant gradual disappearance of the very qualities of specialness that had made emigration to Iowa appealing. The Jubilee of Queen Victoria's fifty years on the throne was a celebration in Le Mars not so much in defiance of the alien land in which colonists now lived but an occasion to take stock of accomplishments—and in some ways to sing the swan song of the colony itself. One great, glorious British celebration; after that they would settle down to minimizing differences, would actually become Americans themselves, since after all most Yankees hailed from elsewhere.

The Le Mars committee on Jubilee preparations met "every fifteen minutes for days and days past," as one weary Englishman put it. The weather had been rainy, but on 21 June 1887 the day was bright, the temperature delightful. In England, too, the sky was cloudless and crowds began to swell outside Buckingham Palace. At 11:30 A.M. the Queen, her daughter, and daughter-in-law, Alexandra, climbed into the golden landau and were driven to Westminster Abbey, with the Prince of Wales and various dukes of the realm as outriders in the procession.

In Le Mars that June morning, St. George's was filled with both English and American worshippers. The chancel was decorated with the stars-and-stripes and Union Jack; over the altar hung a banner with the inscription, V.R.—1837–1887. The vicar, after cataloguing the Queen's virtues, stated that emigration had served to propagate faith in Her Majesty and all she stood for. "If, this morning, I have revived your patriotism, it is but to make you love your adopted country the better." He noted that many native Americans in the congregation had profound love, respect, and sympathy for the queen. The people of the two nations had in common a sense of duty, observation of the Sabbath, and love of liberty—the bonds were deep and abiding. "I will now close my sermon by applying my text to Her Majesty, Queen Victoria: 'She who ruleth over Great Britain is just, ruling in the fear of God.' God Save the Queen!" The organist pulled out all the stops and the congregation burst into song. At the end of the services the treasurer, on behalf of dozens of contributors, presented the church with $550 in gold to liquidate the debt.[22]

On Wednesday, the second day of the Jubilee, two thousand spectators gathered for the June Meet of the Jockey Club. Some of the ladies were driven to the fair grounds "in queer little carts," according to one witness, "or if on foot, they invariably carry canes and are followed by a parcel of dogs, generally small greyhounds. The English flag floats everywhere, English airs are tooted and drummed in all directions, and the English accent is heard on every hand."[23]

That evening a Jubilee *conversazione* was held in the Opera House, the stage festooned with English and American flags. The vicar again officiated, but there was less sermonizing and more musical and dramatic offerings: a tenor solo, "The Boys of the Old Brigade," and the St. George's Glee Club in "Hail Smiling Morn." But the most stirring moment was "Marching Through Georgia," the chorus made up of fifty English boys, who repeated a verse behind the scenes after they'd left the stage. In this theatrical blend of the British and American, the vicar found an appropriate message: social and commercial interests which had built the city possessed strong ties in common, which eased relations between "the different nationalities constituting our population." After another rousing "God Save the Queen," three cheers were shouted for the queen and the president, and everyone left in a high mood.

On the following day field events took place at the fair grounds, with a tug-of-war between England and Ireland. This encouragement of national rivalry may have seemed a return to emphasizing the divisions between people rather than their sameness. The afternoon spun on with races, jumps, throws, and other tests of human athletic skills, followed by a grand ball in Apollo Hall, where dancing continued until 2:00 A.M.

By now the colony was eight years old and a sorting out had taken place. While some continued to feel part of "the picnic," others like the Cowans found themselves increasingly removed. In a cricket match against Winnipeg in September 1887 the Le Mars team consisted of the Cowan brothers' closest friends—Garnett, Watson, Sinclair, and Will Farquhar. Perhaps if Walter and James had had the time, inclination, and talent for such sports, they might have felt differently about living in Iowa. But while their friends were playing cricket in Canada, they were tending to their horse ranch in Wyoming and trying desperately to figure out some way to rid themselves of the unwanted piece of the Close Colony that they still owned.

The great influx of pups earlier in the decade had fallen to a very few. There had been a number of takers and many returnees; a settling in or a moving on. The moment of participation as pioneers building up the country had passed. Plenty of land was still available, such as the Cowans' farm, but at prices that no longer seemed attractive. It was all "developed," the virgin soil plowed and planted.

FOR the British, the subject of naturalization became ever more pressing. If the options of a young man—freedom to move toward the best opportunity, wherever it presented itself—were no longer really viable for a colonist, then acceptance of one's Americanness seemed inevitable, at least to Charles Dacres, editor of the *Globe,* who was the colony's self-appointed chronicler from the time of his arrival in 1881 to the end of that decade.

The results of the November 1887 election in Le Mars showed an upsurge in Democrat voters, which Dacres attributed to the naturalization of increasing numbers of Britons. (The Republicans were identified as the "Yankee" party, hence most Britons allied themselves with the Democrats.) Hitherto, Englishmen had been reluctant to renounce allegiance to their homeland—it had seemed like repudiating one's parentage. But naturalization needn't mean that love for England had diminished, Dacres said, and asked the question: "What is the main intention of the English settler here? Is it to remain a short time, make money and return as soon as possible to the Mother country? Or is it, as in the majority of cases, to cast his lot with the common weal?"[24] For James Cowan the answer was the former; but Walter was still not sure.

If permanent settlement was the aim, then Dacres asked: "Do we not owe duties where we receive benefits? Should not representation be coincident with taxation?" (A neat turn on the rallying cry of the American Revolution.) "Since we are all taxed, ought we not, in self-defense, to have something to say as to the rate of taxation? Is it not to our interest that we should participate in a government which gives us protection and deals with our affairs?" He then demonstrated the power of a few votes in making crucial laws that affected the lives of hundreds of Englishmen, powerless because of their lack of franchise. "With children born upon the soil of the United States, with house and land and cattle and the tenderest home ties about them here, will not the hesitancy to enter that citizenship...appear as unwise as inexcusable? For these and other reasons every Englishman should be a citizen."

By the time Charles Dacres wrote this call for naturalization, he had married and become a citizen himself. However, his American career from the start had been marked by difficulties. He longed to be the heart and voice of the Close Colony but somehow, he always seemed a little on the outside of everything. This might have been due to his somewhat unstable personality, which put people off and eventually caused them to suspect him of being an arsonist (which the record suggests he probably was).

Charles was the son of Sir Sydney Colpoys Dacres, Lord of the Admiralty, one-time Commander of the Channel Squadron and also of the Mediterranean Fleet. That so many colonists had navy connections was largely because of Captain Moreton. Charles Dacres, whose sire was middle-aged when he was born, served in the navy, where he had some journalistic experience, then settled as a pup on a farm north of Akron, Iowa, in an area known as Indian Creek. He soon published a newspaper, the *Indian Creek Gazette,* with articles about colonists, illustrated and written by members.

In early 1882 Dacres moved to Le Mars with his newspaper, changing its name to the *Colony Sketch,* and began to seek advertisers and subscribers. The first issue in late May was studiously parochial in concerns and was expected to circulate chiefly among the colonists, to amuse and interest them. Dacres soon realized the colony itself was an historic event that needed to be put into perspective. With the aid of a friend he began working on "a history of the English colony in and near Le Mars," but perhaps he failed to get enough subscriptions for his project. If the monograph ever appeared, no copy is known to have survived.[25]

Meanwhile the *Sketch,* instead of sticking to British business, began to comment on the community as a whole, arousing the ire of rival newspaper editors. Particularly galling was Dacres's editorial, "How Shall We Invest Our Money?" — irritating because it emphasized the power of British capital to bestow or withhold favors and sounded a beware signal about sharp Yankees. Dacres widened his range of concerns, even including commentary on the dismal state of Le Mars alleys. In quick response the *Sentinel* mocked Dacres's criticism: "Go easy, Mr. Sketch. Speak reverently of the local powers that be — for they are all 'reform.' " But the *Sketch* continued on its weekly investigative course, number thirteen issued the last week of August, "bright and newsy as ever."[26]

From the earliest period of Dacres's sojourn in the colony, a certain insta-bility colored his activities. When a friend from Chicago visited Dacres in the *Sketch* office in mid-August 1882, "an inebriated granger dropped" by, "picked up an empty gun and pointed it...." Why the gun was thus casually at hand for anyone to pick up is not explained, but the Chicagoan "quietly but firmly caught the i.g. [inebriated granger] by the nape of the neck and the slack of the overalls and pitched him earthwards to the victim's evident discom-fort.... These unloaded guns are usually dangerous...."[27]

Dacres, like many other playacting, gunslinging western Britons, liked to have weapons around. His love of gunfire might have been corollary to his secret love of fires. The first identifiable arson incident occurred in mid-October 1882, when a meat market burned to the ground—"a well greased bait for the greedy fiend." Then in February the fire bug struck twice in one week. A beginning blaze was discovered just in time in a rear shed of the House of Lords tavern. The second occurred when Reverend Cunningham's barn caught fire, destroying saddles, carpets, books, a buggy, and most of the personal effects of an English woman who had recently arrived to be nursemaid for the new Cunningham baby. Her "large trunk containing all her fine clothing, jewelry, and mementoes. . . were consumed," and none of those affected carried insurance.[28]

The *Sketch* transmogrified into the *Le Mars Truth* and continued its high-toned muckraking way. Dacres insisted upon the importance of his presence in the colony, but he wasn't the hail-fellow sort who became a natural leader, perhaps because he didn't participate in the fellowship of the playing fields. A sideliner in such crucial encounters wouldn't in itself doom Dacres to an outsider's role; but he didn't display interest in any of the artistic or religious activities that helped give those not athletically endowed a secure role in the colony. He could ride a horse, however, and joined in on a paper chase at least once.

Since nobody offered to throw a birthday party for him when he turned twenty-six in July 1883, he gave one himself, inviting a lot of people to dine and dance until long after midnight. How quiet the house must have seemed after they'd all gone. Some of his loneliness may have been the result of poor health, which kept him apart. But he refused to give up membership in "The Wide Awake Hose Company," which was the volunteer outfit frequently roused to put out some new fire. Once while fighting a blaze he slipped off a roof and suffered injuries severe enough to keep him in bed for a while. Upon recovery he started up the *Le Mars World* and the *Mirror.*[29]

One of the grandest fires involved the destruction of the Plymouth Roller Mill in June 1884, which at first was believed to have been set by a rival business faction resenting the mill's monopoly. Later, while Dacres edited the *Globe,* rumors and suspicions about his possible firebug activities finally reached the point where he was indicted for arson and tried. There had been thirty-one Le Mars fires in the last two years, over $100,000 in losses. Nobody had actually witnessed Dacres setting a blaze, but immediately afterward he was always on the scene. However, circumstantial evidence was too flimsy to convict him. Some disgruntled citizens felt the British had put pressure on the jury to get Dacres off. Most felt the young man had learned his lesson—if he *was* guilty—and since he'd recently married, would probably settle down.[30]

Newspapers remained in business by stirring up excitement, and Dacres of the *Globe* became a vulnerable target for the *Sentinel,* which cited him for being a defender of "theft and rascality as well as bummerism." Dacres responded with a libel suit for $5,000, which was subsequently dropped, but not until the *Sentinel* had continued to thrust and parry (and sell newspapers) at "the pure and spotless Dacres." There were even insinuations published about Mrs. Dacres by still another newspaper, much to Charles's ire. Rumors circulated that Dacres had "done a little fresco work over the editor's eyes," but the *Sentinel* denied the reports. "Charley admits that he has been wild in his time but claims that his wife has stood by him with a loyalty commanding admiration and has always been an influence with him for good."[31]

During the Jubilee, with all this behind him, Dacres published a special issue and acted like a responsible member of the community. Now a U.S. citizen, he began to participate in political affairs and was a delegate from Le Mars to the Knights of Labor state convention in Des Moines. Perhaps to lay to rest all lingering suspicions that he was an arsonist, the Dacres home itself went up in flames in August 1887. It was situated near the Corkery Livery stables, the prime target. Having had practice in these matters, the rescue of the Dacres's household goods was accomplished with dispatch. "Mrs. Dacres superintended the moving of her furniture like an experienced salvage officer. Charlie was helping out with the horses in the livery barn." After it was over, Mr. and Mrs. Charles Dacres inserted a card of thanks in the *Globe* to all who had assisted them at the time of the blaze.[32]

Somebody's compulsion to set fires continued, and two days later a coal shed burst into flame. When another hotel fire occurred in the fall, the talk about Charles Dacres, arsonist, was again rampant. From his editor's chair at the *Globe,* Dacres answered back: "Those people who are talking about a certain gentleman's absence from Le Mars and connecting his absence, with certain losses sustained at a well known hotel in this city are warned to keep quiet. The party was out of town... on business connected with this office, and such duties were satisfactorily performed, as a call on the proprietor of this paper may prove."[33]

The wildness of Charles Dacres sometimes took the form of innocent *folie de grandeur*—he claimed intimacy with leading figures in England, though some of these he may have known through Admiral Dacres. When the notorious Valentin "Pasha" Baker died, Dacres recounted the scandal that had ruined Baker's career. [He was accused of having kissed a girl against her will on a train in 1875—conduct unbecoming an officer—and was cashiered out of the army. A member of Parliament called Baker's act one of the most atrocious crimes ever committed.] "The writer was well acquainted with the colonel and has always believed him innocent of the charge." This attempt to pass himself off as being familiar with people in the news made his *Globe* more important and helped puff himself up a bit—which he probably needed, given his actual rather scruffy life circumstances. It hardly seems likely that Dacres was even remotely connected with Valentin Baker and the Prince of Wales's set, though he may have met Baker on some occasion. Dacres had been in the colony six years, newspaperman five years of that time. His illustrious father died at age eighty in 1884. Charles, with an American wife and infant son, was a stranded Englishman trying to keep certain illusions about himself keenly in the foreground, in order to keep going at all.[34]

He continued to be sensitive to the gossip and taunting remarks. On 1 February 1888 he published an open letter on his supposed "record" of disrepute. "As far as the record business is concerned, there is not a man, woman or child in this city that can point to a single crime that we have committed. If it is a crime to be arrested on a charge, which after a careful but tedious trial resulted in an honorable acquittal, then the writer is a first-class criminal. But in spite of the pressure brought to bear upon the justice who presided, by men sworn to support law and order, etc., and others we could mention, 'our flag is still there,' and we have nailed it to the mast and many of our enemies *then* are our friends today." He even made the gestures of these friends public: just before Christmas he'd been presented with a pair of dressed Aylesbury ducks weighing ten pounds, and he issued a paragraph of thanks to the donor and his wife.[35]

By the end of the decade, the *Globe* had a new editor and the Dacres family moved a little farther West, where many of the old problems were repeated in a new setting. Violence continued to hover—and finally Charles Dacres was shot to death in Yankton, South Dakota, though the circumstances regarding the fatal shooting have never been clear. Perhaps it happened as suddenly and casually as earlier incidents: a loaded gun on the editor's desk, and an inebriated granger coming into the newspaper office.[36]

CHAPTER   FIFTEEN

A Bit of a Struggle

INCE the Cowans could not sell their Iowa farm, they fitted the place into their scheme of becoming horse breeders, importers, and traders. They hoped to raise some cash through another mortgage and move to Wyoming with horses, machinery, furniture, and household essentials, thereby avoiding further outlays setting up their Wyoming ranch. By renting the Iowa land to Taylor, their overall investment would be in good hands and they might make about 5 percent which, with mortgage payments and taxes deducted, would net them close to 1½ percent in actual profit. James told his father that in Wyoming "I can get $40 a month wages at anything in the summer 'cow punching'. . . until we are able to put in some cattle after the sale of the farm" — which he expected, once the "stand-still" in land sales ended.[1]

"The great mistake we made here [in Iowa] was in putting too much money into land and not nearly enough into cattle." James regarded himself as wiser, more mature, but his horse-business plans actually indicated a repetition of the same pattern; he was going into it because he did not know any good reason why he shouldn't. The economic value of horses to local agriculture and why Americans should recognize the need for quality horses such as Clydesdales or Percherons were unanswered questions. Breeding was often cited as a factor in getting premium beef prices or the delivery of more pounds of milk a month in a dairy; pedigreed hogs might be more disease resistant or gain weight faster; similar favorable points might be raised concerning thorough-bred sheep. But what James failed to consider was whether good draft horse-flesh would fulfill a local need and justify the cost.

He apologized for not informing his father of the horse venture in time for a comment by return mail. "I am afraid you will think we are rushing blindly into new schemes: but we have given a great deal of thought to the matter. . . I know you think I am rather impetuous, but Walter will tell you that he is more sanguine about a good result than I am." James knew his older brother carried more weight at home, being the stable, reliable, steady one.

In mid-June 1886 the Cowans undertook the three-day journey from Akron, Iowa, to Wyoming with a carload of their goods and actually accompanied the horses in their cars. In Wyoming James reported to his mother that the horses created a sensation. "They came pretty near being the best team anywhere round us in Iowa, but out here they hold undisputed master."[2] They were easily worth $500 a team, though they had paid only $380 for their best pair. By emphasizing his growing reputation and skill as a horseman, James no doubt hoped to raise confidence at home. Although they initially rented the 320 acre ranch in the Medicine Bow Mountains, they soon purchased it. Walter outfitted the ranch house with curtains, carpets, pictures — all brought from Iowa.

Once again they enjoyed congenial society, and all the mother-country references came alive. On New Year's Eve 1886 Joe Jefferson had composed a poem about a transplanted young blood who dreamt of old hunting days in England:

> . . . .
> My eyes are soon closed, my memory passes
> Through the days that have gone long ago
> First school days surround me, then Cumberland lasses
> Then a home which p'raps some of you know.
>
> The foxhounds at Isel, the Harriers at Dean,
> And an invite to shoot, from the Squire
> But hunting's my sport, my breeches are clean
> So I'll hunt to my heart's own desire.
>
> What a glorious run! How I rode in the van!
> 'Twas the cream of the country they said,
> How I "pounded" the Master & field to a man
> But remember 'twas all done in bed.
>
> In the evening I danced at the County Hunt ball
> Where the men all wore scarlet or pink
> How we talked of the run, how a friend got a fall
> While to hunting & 'chasing we drink.
>
> But the evening has come, I open my eyes,
> Half awake, half asleep, after rest,
> "Where am I?" I wonder, then echo replies
> "You're at home on your ranche in the West"[3]

The marriage date for Joe Jefferson and his fiancée had still to be set. "I shall be very glad when he does marry," Walter admitted, "as we will then have one more lady among our circle of acquaintances." But for the present she was a schoolmarm in Laramie, some distance away. Both Cowans officially declared their intention of becoming naturalized U.S. citizens, but only to qualify for land ownership under special terms stipulated by law, which enabled them to enlarge their ranch. "Never-the-less, I should prefer to select my bride from among my own people, if I can find one of the right sort. Seriously, I wish we could manage to get home next winter."[4] But it didn't seem likely; so his speculation about finding a suitable British bride was rather futile. He was relegated to gazing upon Joe and Miss Smith enviously, imagining their future happiness; but in doing so he became more deeply involved with Miss Smith emotionally, and she with him.

James returned to Great Britain during the winter and arranged to have the first shipment of Clydesdales transported. He talked over business plans with his father, who agreed to supply additional capital.

"We still have that beastly farm in Iowa on our hands," James wrote his brother Herbert from Wyoming the following January (1888). "That was Chapter I in the lesson of plunging." Walter was home investigating loco weed with the Pharmaceutical Society of London, trying to determine the plant's chemical properties and to choose the right antidote. The Iowa farm, faithful Taylor in charge, became an auxiliary horse ranch, renamed the Sioux Valley Stud Farm. James had purchased a supply of range horses in Oregon, hoping to offer a practical line of sturdy native horses in addition to imported breeds. "I am utterly sickened at the idea of going back to the farm," James wrote his sister from Wyoming, "but Loco is complete master of the field here—about 80% of the mares have got it now, but I think if we get them right away from it that they may get over it." Perhaps it had been unwise of them to carry on horse raising in an area almost exclusively devoted to sheep ranching, though James didn't voice this regret.[5]

Numerous snags delayed the shipment of horses from England, and James was soon out of patience with his English partner. "He is just like all the rest of these people who sit in England and are interested in the stock business out here," James complained to his father in June from Wyoming. "If they find they can't carry out some pet scheme at once, or from low prices don't get their dividend for a year, they at once flare up and talk as if they knew everything, whereas they know next to nothing about the condition of things in this country."[6]

While James oversaw the horse ranch in Wyoming, Walter, upon his return to America from his long winter visit home, settled down to Iowa farming. He had no time for reading or letter writing and could scarcely manage to keep his accounts up to date. "I don't think this part of the world will ever produce an author, unless he treats of insect life and writes his book in the winter....I am writing in the day time now...while the mercury stands at 98° [21 July 1888] and the horse fly disports himself on all exposed parts of my body....Fresh dips of ink are required after every three words...which adds materially to the physical exertion...but helps to drive the flies off. They gather thick on the right hand while it is guiding the pen, but quickly seek refuge in the hair when the hand goes after ink." He was spinning no American tall yarn when he claimed to have swept up five quarts of dead flies from two rooms that had window screens. "We have one variety of fly that attacks cattle and horses and is big enough to frighten a man. Young Tucker was with me when he saw his first specimen, and I found it difficult to restrain his desire to run and get a gun and 'shoot 'un on the wing.' The body of the brute is about the size and shape of the first joint on a man's thumb, so shooting them on the wing would come within the range of practical politics, and I have no doubt they would afford good sport."[7]

Iowa flies were annoying, but the loco weed problem in Wyoming was so terrible James considered quitting the horse business altogether. "I have come to the conclusion that unless a man has unlimited capital he had better leave livestock of all kind alone."[8] He summoned Walter to join him in November; the two rounded up the horse herd and proceeded with them to Iowa. "We left the ranch on Saturday in a pretty bad snow storm, driving our seventy head," Walter wrote, ". . . as Jem aptly remarked, it was like Napoleon's retreat from Moscow."[9]

The horses were loaded onto railroad cars in Wyoming and shipped east, with a pause in North Platte, Nebraska, for the animals to feed and rest. "North Platte is famous as being the residence of the great Buffalo Bill, and as Jem and I were sunning ourselves in front of the hotel, we were privileged to get a fine view of this great celebrity driving around town doing his shopping."

The train run from North Platte to Sioux City with rest stops took twenty-four hours. They arrived at their hotel begrimed and without a change of clothes, since their Gladstone bag had not yet been transferred from the baggage carrier. Both Cowans remained sequestered in their upstairs hotel room until their luggage arrived. "At last it turned up and we were able to come down to breakfast like gentlemen and assume the role of *owner*, as distinguished from man in charge of horses." The social difference remained important to them, although they saw the humorous side of it. Then the Cowans drove their horses the thirty miles to their farm. "The good people of Sioux City seemed not a little surprised at seventy loose horses parading their streets. It is quite an unusual sight. . . ."[10] Walter returned to Wyoming after a fortnight, where he planned to remain with the rest of the horses until February, then haul them to Iowa.

James continued to press the sale of the Akron farm but without success, and their father remitted £1,200 ($6,000) to help them keep going; "our aim must be to get into the importing business as quickly as we can." The Sioux Valley Stud Farm should become famous for European horses, "and an importer is a very big man in this country." If the enterprise succeeded, the Cowans could count on "half-yearly importations and consequent trips across" the Atlantic. In this reading of the future, although their income would derive from an operation in an obscure, distant place, they would still be on the homescene frequently enough to feel part of things. James longed to strengthen his home connections. "One relief to my mind in leaving Wyoming is that there is no necessity now to take out naturalization papers, and I will still be able to say *Civis Brittanicus sum*."[11]

But the horse-trade business turned out no better than their other business ventures. One of their most valuable imports, Lord Devon, kicked a man in Chicago while in transport, and a lawsuit ensued. The market for English Shire and Clydesdale horses seemed weak or nonexistent when the horses arrived in Iowa. Summer drouth burned their crops. "These hot days it takes us all our time to keep these great fat horses cool, while we are dying of heat. It is the most beastly country on the face of the earth." To his brother Henry, James made an even more sweeping confession: "I hate it more every day I stay here—the people and the climate and everything to do with it—it is not fit for civilized people to live in." Also, "It is all right people saying it is so nice being your own master...but I would give anything if someone would take this in hand and just tell me what I had to do...."[12]

Taylor remained the rock, the one dependable factor in the Cowans' life; but even *he* might leave them at any moment, should something more attractive come along. "He does not want to go himself at all," James told Henry, "but his wife is not up to the work anymore." The next year they would be able to keep Taylor only by building him a house and paying $40 a month in wages, in addition to going shares on the farm. It would still be worth it. "After having as good a man as he is with one for seven years, one does not like parting with him. He is thoroughly honest and dependable and never for a minute forgets his place, which nine of ten Englishmen do out here...." The local people assumed that Taylor would side against his young masters, "as being in a subordinate position, they all think he will help them out," but Taylor "is able to give us a wink now and then" to tip them off to a potentially disadvantageous situation, and "none of them have ever got very much the better of us yet, I think...."

"You can trust none of them out of your sight and not one fourth of them in it. All they seem to think about is making a dollar out of you if they can. You have no idea how I despise them. I do not mean this for all Americans, as I have met some very nice fellows in the East, but the ordinary middle class and all these Western Yanks I despise worse than dogs, and yet one has to be civil to them." The weather oppressed as much as the people. "The dust and perpetual howling of the wind is enough to drive anyone crazy."[13]

But hope still rode on their best horses. Walter and Taylor transported Lord Devon and Loyal Tom for exhibit at the Iowa State Fair in Des Moines on 30 August 1889. Lord Devon won a blue ribbon, and the Cowans offered him for sale at $2,500. No takers. He was also shown at autumn county fairs in the Dakota Territory and they planned to enter him in the November American Horse Show in Chicago. James hoped to settle the lawsuit then. But not until the following year did he finally end the legal difficulty with a $300 settlement out of court. He did not want to risk a jury trial. "I am always a little disinclined to trust my fortunes, as an Englishman, to the mercies of the American lower classes."

Alas, few American buyers wanted their stock of imported horses. "The only man that has ever attempted to come to the point and raised my spirits for a day or two turned out to be a rogue." And in horse-trading, scoundrels seemed legion. James remained on the Iowa farm that winter, and Walter returned to Great Britain, partly on business. During the long winter days, James enjoyed the unaccustomed experience of once again reading current literature; he found *Romola* "a new sensation, as reading more than the papers is usually out of the question."[14] Walter need not hurry back—could stay in London until June if he felt like it.

James acknowledged his feelings of guilt—he should have been out hustling horses, traveling from town to town, but the market was so bad the effort hardly seemed worth it. He expected their Oregon-bred horses would average only about $60 a head when brought to sale. Still, to his astonishment, Bradstreet's rated the Cowan brothers' business as worth $20,000 to $40,000. It seemed ironic, for to their minds they were complete failures.

Richard Cowan's health worsened; one of the brothers was needed at home to aid their mother. "If only one knew what to do," James wrote Henry, 10 December 1889. "I am getting terribly sick of this country anyhow." Added to their economic reversals, "as far as we are concerned... the most unsatisfactory part of the whole thing is living in such a beastly country surrounded by more beastly people." Their father's illness might be just the turn of fate needed to call an end to the American effort: "Here we have been for seven years and not only have not made a dollar but have lost ground." With unlimited capital he was sure they could still make a success of it, but as things stood, "I feel very doubtful whether the game is worth playing.... At the same time, I can't help regretting that we ever came to America at all, and I get more homesick every year."

CHAPTER SIXTEEN

Dramatic Endings

HE ordinary course of events in Fred and Margaret Close's lives presaged nothing of the tumultuous change about to occur. Fred was his usual dashing, sportsman self, still setting a young man's pace. They moved from Pipestone, Minnesota, to Sibley, Iowa, in 1888; their firm, now Close and Dodsworth, specialized in "Banking, Real Estate and Loans." Constantine Benson, no longer officially a partner, still helped handle the Close interests there. By mid-1888 the Lyon County *Reporter*'s usual front-page notice about available Close Brothers' land proclaimed in boldface: **"YOUR LAST CHANCE!"** After that summer, no more advertisements of this sort appeared.[1]

From Sibley on 9 May 1888 Fred wrote William in London regarding monetary matters involving Cunliffe Brooks and Company and the sale of part of their Antibes property. He briefly mentioned personal news: "Margaret has taken to riding again. I gave her 'Proposal'—'Leap Year's' daughter by 'Elsham'—a beauty, stands 15.2 and very bloodlike. I refused $300 for her last week. I am glad to hear that Mary is getting better at Antibes. Love to Mary and Ada when next you write." The separation of William and Mary for long periods was still conveniently referred to as a matter of health.

Fred and Margaret lived in Sibley just a few months, for during the winter of 1889–1890 they enjoyed a long stay in England. Some time was spent at Barkly Hall, Leicestershire, with Fred's aunt and uncle, the Sir William Cunliffe Brooks's. "I have been having some capital sport, but unfortunately have already lamed one of my two horses, but in hopes she will be alright in a week. Uncle mounted me yesterday on a hired horse from Leicester. Unfortunately, it was a brute and could not jump a bit. We went bang through everything, smashed clear thru post and rails, and he came on his nose twice. I did not have a fall, which was a wonder, but balanced myself on the brute's ears for a second or two, which was anything but pleasant. I am today going into Leicester to have a row with the man."[2]

Fred also devoted some time to business. He succeeded in raising $3 million in capital to form the Free Land Mortgage Company, scheduled to become officially incorporated under Iowa law in June 1890, with headquarters in Sioux City. Margaret and Fred expected to move to Sioux City upon their return from abroad. In a bad spill while hunting, Fred broke his arm, shortly before taking passage to America. He had his picture snapped by a portrait photographer, arm in a sling, an amused look in his eyes.

Fred had only limited use of that arm when he participated in a polo match between Le Mars and Sioux City on 18 June 1890 in Crescent Park, the Sioux City polo field. Fred's team had scored three goals, and during a pause between chukkers he congratulated his men on how well they were doing. As play resumed, Jack Watson of the Le Mars team "was making a splendid run down the field, when for some unaccountable reason, Fred attempted to cross in front of him, and to the spectators it was evident that the two would cannon." Just before the horses collided, Fred swayed in his saddle. When the horses hit, he was thrown, falling under his mount, which rolled on top of him. As Fred's horse struggled to regain its footing, Watson's went down and also rolled over Fred. Watson was thrown clear and escaped all injury but Fred was completely knocked out.

In the past ten years audiences had frequently seen Fred take a bad fall, but he always got up and laughed it off. Reckless though he was in horseman-ship, he was aware of some of the physical dangers involved. His groom, T. J. Maxwell, said: "Fred was always expecting it. He was always saying to me, 'If I get it, Jack, you tend to the mare.' "[3]

A young Norwegian doctor in the crowd of polo spectators came on the field and attempted to revive Fred. The physician did succeed in restoring circulation, but couldn't bring him back to consciousness. Margaret, although she repeatedly tried to reach her husband, was kept from him. Two additional doctors were summoned by telephone. When they arrived and examined Fred they discovered his right clavicle had been fractured in three places, with the upper part of the chest completely caved in. Worst of all, the concussion was so severe his brain had been damaged, "and there were unmistakable indications of cerebral hemorrhage."

The attending physicians decided against moving Fred from the playing field; instead, they sent for a tent, mattresses, bed clothes, water, and other necessities. The tent was erected over the spot where Fred lay at eight o'clock. During this time Margaret was repeatedly denied access to Fred's side. The physicians and aides confined her to the clubhouse and gave her a powerful sedative, which enabled her to get through the long hours of waiting.

The doctors could do nothing to save Fred, and yet he showed an enor-mous vitality; for three hours his condition did not change. "The breathing was labored, and impeded as it was by the injuries to the chest and hemorrhage of mucus about the bronchial tubes, caused a rattling in the throat that was horrible to hear." By 11:00 P.M. his pulse had grown weaker and more irregular, breathing more strained. At 12:45 A.M. all life signs ceased and the doctors pronounced him dead.[4]

Fred Close's accomplishments in his thirty-five years of life were already legendary—victories in farming, business, and all manner of sports. He had helped launch the largest British colony of its kind in North America in the latter part of the nineteenth century. But such was his zest, energy, and intelligence that had he lived, new worlds would surely have been found to conquer. Citizens of the region were stunned by the news of his fatal accident. Many believed his career was just "entering upon the larger usefulness and responsibilities of life." His closest acquaintances felt that had he been given the choice in manner of death he would have accepted his lot. To die in the midst of a polo match was almost like falling in battle — the final emphasis bound to be placed on his courage, strength, and manliness.

During the eight and one-half years of her marriage to Fred, Margaret had kept a high-mettled pace, apparently enjoying their peripatetic life. They had no children. Fred's reference to Margaret's return to horseback riding after a lapse of time suggests a possible miscarriage or illness. But now her life, in its own way, had come to an abrupt halt. Fred had determined almost every aspect of their daily existence; without him, her situation — even her residency in America — would be completely altered or open to consideration. She was still young — about thirty — and one of the wealthiest young widows in British society, more beautiful than ever. She returned to England and lived with members of her family and Close relatives.

The following year, Margaret was presented at Court. After the mourning period her company was eagerly sought, particularly by impecunious noblemen, who were dazzled by her fortune and beauty. Her successful suitor, Christian Frederick Gordon (known as Eric Gordon and scion of one of the oldest Scottish families), she had known for some time, since he was related to Fred. Eric Gordon, whom she married in 1894, was the grandson of the ninth Marquis of Huntly. With this union Margaret remained somewhat within the orbit of the Closes, but her subsequent life bore little resemblance to those days in Le Mars when she participated in contests to determine the best lady rider on sidesaddle.

Both Fred and William, particularly after their American business successes, had moved easily in the upper levels of British society. Family anecdotes, filtering down through the years, place William on a familiar basis with the Prince of Wales, a connection that may have come about through the prince's crony, the duke of Sutherland. When the prince became Edward VII, William's London residence is said to have been used occasionally by the king for his romantic assignations.

The truth about Margaret's private life became public knowledge eventually. When she married Eric Gordon, she was involved with a lover. Her new husband's understanding that his wife's relations with her lover would continue as before was the most shocking aspect of the scandal that rocked Britain and received wide coverage in the newspapers. In the trial for custody of her child, Margaret's forthright statements about her domestic life caused a sensation. "In bold-faced avowal of her immorality there is scarcely a parallel. Here she is now known as 'the woman who is not ashamed,' " wrote a Hearst reporter.

Sometime in 1892 or 1893, Margaret began a love affair with Lord Granville Gordon, son of the tenth Marquis of Huntly. In the trial he testified his wife was so unhappy about his liaison with Margaret that to deflect his spouse's anxieties Margaret married his cousin, Eric Gordon. In the witness box Margaret corroborated this account: "I really married Eric Gordon to calm the dreadful jealousy of the first Lady Granville Gordon. She would not give the poor fellow a moment's peace. When I got married she seemed to be quieted for a time, but she soon grew as cantankerous as ever."[5]

When the unhappy first Mrs. Granville Gordon finally died ("of a broken heart," according to the tabloids), Margaret insisted that Eric Gordon sue her for divorce so that she could be free to marry her lover. In the custody trial Lord Granville Gordon admitted having relations with Margaret prior to her marriage to Eric but said that his cousin had never objected. Their love affair continued after the marriage, since the ceremony had really been a matter of convenience. Eric denied this version. He claimed he hadn't the least idea of his wife's relations with his cousin until, after the first Lady Granville Gordon died, Margaret and the new widower "ran away," absconding with the child Cicely, whom he claimed to be his. The lovers fled to France and set up a household together. Eric Gordon brought suit for divorce, naming as corespondent his cousin Granville.

At the custody trial, Margaret "was very cool in the witness box," wrote the Hearst reporter. "She said that her former husband was so well aware of the relations existing between herself and Lord Granville Gordon that he told her at one time, when she was going to a certain country house, that he could not accompany her, and that his cousin Granville had a better right. When she left Eric Gordon she had no idea that he would claim paternity of the child."

Margaret on the stand exclaimed: "Look at the child. Anybody can see that she is Granville's."

In July 1902 she had written Eric, from whom she would soon be divorced: "Don't keep me out of the country to prevent me from marrying Granville. You don't know what trouble you are causing me. I swear the baby is Granville's child. For God's sake have mercy on me. Before you ruin two miserable lives think awhile. I swear she is not your child. It was impossible."

According to Margaret, the divorce action had come about only upon her insistence, wanting to be free to marry Granville. Eric had not wished it. She explained that there was a verbal agreement between them. Eric would not claim Cicely, merely sue for divorce. Later, when Margaret brought her daughter back to England because of the girl's illness (an English doctor being preferred), Eric seized the opportunity to file suit for custody of "his" child. "He is a low, contemptible blackguard," Margaret said in the witness box.

When the divorce decree came through in 1902, Margaret immediately married Granville at Dieppe. The child Cicely continued to live with them, "a beautiful little girl who is now six years old," noted a reporter. There followed long entreaties and bickerings over custody of Cicely, with Eric Gordon finally going to court to recover his legal daughter.

"He has no right whatsoever to the child," Margaret told the packed courtroom, "for she is not his. She is Lord Granville Gordon's child. He was my lover before I married Mr. Gordon, but he could not marry me because his wife was then alive. I married Mr. Gordon with the full understanding that my relations with Lord Granville would not be changed. Mr. Gordon consented to the arrangement. My husband and I virtually lived apart. Lord Granville came to visit us immediately after we returned from our honeymoon."

Although sworn to tell the whole truth, by so doing Margaret broke a cardinal rule of society, which allowed any kind of behavior behind closed doors, provided nothing became public. Acknowledged immorality, however, could not be permitted and must be punished by arbiters both secular and religious. Queen Alexandra in particular deemed her role to be that of protector of the rules of moral behavior. The *London Gazette,* "the publication which records all Government decisions, has printed a notice that Lady Granville Gordon will not be received at court on account of the disgraceful exposé of her character in the suit her divorced husband is now bringing against her to obtain possession of their child." Her presentation to Queen Victoria in 1891 would now be stricken from the record. The notice appeared in the section of the *Gazette* reserved for court matters and directly under the supervision of the king and queen. Therefore, the order was believed to have originated from the queen, though it was officially issued through the lord chamberlain.

"This issue of a decree formally, fully, and literally branding Lady Granville Gordon, a woman of the highest rank and title, as an outcast from society is an extraordinary proceeding," according to the Hearst account. It had not been done in over fifty years. In 1837 the new queen, Victoria, banished a lady involved in a sexual scandal. Since then "aristocratic society has become most cynically indifferent to the behaviour of its members," and so the queen's action signalled a campaign to censure those members who were becoming too loose in their conduct. Had the queen merely intended never to see Margaret again, that could easily and quietly have been made known; the formal banishment, however, was viewed by the Hearst press as "a warning to all women with a past and damaged reputations to keep away from court." It also meant that no one in society would speak to Margaret from then on. "If they remained (in England) they could only fraternize with the dregs of society. Everybody of rank, wealth, position, cultivation, education, refinement, would cut them."

The courtroom was filled with "a brilliant throng" who seemed to regard the trial "as they would a Pinero problem play. At each new and startling revelation they seemed to murmur approval, as if they were considering it merely from the viewpoint of dramatic interest. Their lovely picture hats quivered with emotion."

As the case neared conclusion, Margaret's counsel told her that no matter what might be decided on the question of Cicely's paternity, the girl would be taken from her mother, since the judge would consider her to be an unfit person for custody. The judge had already commented unfavorably on Margaret's character. Faced with the prospect of losing her child forever, Margaret donned a disguise, dressed Cicely as a boy, and the two of them fled England for France.

Did the royal decree apply to Lord Granville Gordon as well? Surely in intent if not in so many words. He was next in line to succeed the current Marquis of Huntly, "the premier Marquis of Scotland and head of the Gordon clan." A life of exile in France with Margaret and Cicely would surely be a great disappointment to one who would inherit ten peerages, "no less than three earldoms, a viscount, a marquisate and five baronies." Lord Granville was the author of several books and known as a big-game hunter. He wrote largely of his sports experiences, and among his books was *Warned Off,* a title that "now suggests his present predicament forcibly."

He decided to forego his British future and moved to France, settling in Paris with Margaret and Cicely. According to her great-niece, Margaret never returned to England and died in 1920. "Mother and her parents [Mr. and Mrs. William Turner Humble, Margaret's brother] visited them in Paris when Ma was small. Margaret's daughter, Cicely, married a French doctor named Lefort. While working for the French Underground during World War II, Cicely was imprisoned by the Nazis and died in prison camp."[6]

THREE months after Fred Close's death on the Sioux City polo field, a new Close arrived in the world: Mary Paullin Close gave birth to a son, Herbert, on 29 September 1890. The baby was named after Mary's youngest brother, for whom William acted as guardian, and for William's half-brother, Herbert Close. William had been particularly paternal in matters of schooling and finances for Herbert Paullin, who had been barely thirteen when his father died. In 1885 Herbert graduated from Trinity College, Cambridge, but he died a few years thereafter.

Birth of a child to an unhappy marital union does not often bring about the expected mending of difficulties, and this was true for the William Closes. In 1891—the baby now one year old—a formal separation agreement was drawn up with ample financial provision for Mary and the infant. Two years later Mary took up residence in Brooklyn, New York, and proceeded to file for divorce on the only permissible legal grounds—adultery. Since the marriage had taken place in New York State and she was an American citizen, a severance of the bond there may have seemed a prudent legal step, but at no previous time had Mary resided in New York. Perhaps to further ensure the binding legality of the proceedings, William took out naturalization papers on

22 September 1892. The move seems to have been purely connected with the divorce action, and he did not become a United States citizen.

The initial hearing was held 18 July 1893 in the New York State Supreme Court. Mary was asked under oath if she had discussed with her husband the matters that "are the cause of this suit." When her answer was affirmative, she was asked to explain further.

"It occurred originally through his frequent absences from home, when he omitted always to mention where he was going and sometimes giving false answers or giving none."

Queried as to whether anything special had brought the situation to a head, Mary told of finding a letter "as if it had just carelessly fallen down....I spoke to him about it and asked him if it was with the woman who signed her name to the letter that he had been on these occasions of which I have spoken. He did not deny that it was and did not admit it at first."

"Did he subsequently admit it?"

"He subsequently admitted it."

Did she have any further conversations with her husband about this matter? Mary Close replied that if she went into detail she would "have to bring other evidence and other charges into the case."

Had she made any "requests of the defendant as to his changing his habits of life?"

"Yes, I did."

"In relation to spending his time with other people and at other places?"

"I did, frequently and decidedly."

"What reply did he make to you?"

"He said sometimes that he could not change, and sometimes that he would not change."

The prima facie evidence was a letter written by Mrs. Marie Howard, also known as Mimi Howard. Mary discovered the letter "In the autumn of 1891," or winter.

68 Carlisle Mansions

My dear Will:
    Will you come to the theatre with me tomorrow (the Gaiety, I should like). You could either dine here or we could dine out somewhere. Bring your bag. You can dress here, and I will put you up, of course. Wire me whether you are coming or not, but I hope you will, as I should so much like to see you.
                                                    Je v'embrasse
                                                        Mimi

"I wish to say that aside from any evidence that we have here, it is publicly known in London by all my husband's friends that he has been living with Mrs. Howard....No one knows her real name, but that is the name she goes by in

London, because she is well known among a certain set of men."

A deposition from Mimi Howard was obtained in London. In her testimony, entered into the record, she gave her age as "24 years and upwards, and my residence is No. 68 Carlisle Mansions, Victoria Street, London. I have no occupation." She admitted being acquainted with William B. Close and affirmatively identified the picture of him shown her. She gave her own description: "He is a tall man, with gray hair and gray moustache; has a florid complexion and wears glasses. His residence at present is 108 Victoria Street, London. He is a merchant by occupation.... I first met the defendant about three years ago, in London, and I do not recollect the circumstances of the meeting.... I saw the defendant very often during the year 1892. We were on terms of familiar intimacy."

When pressed to be specific, Mrs. Howard replied: "The defendant, during the year 1892, frequently stayed the greater part of the night with me at said 68 Carlisle Mansions. During the early part of 1892 he stayed with me as often as two or three nights a week." When questioned further she said: "The defendant and myself had carnal intercourse with each other during the period named and at the place named." When asked who paid the rent on her apartment, she replied that she did and refused to say whether or not she had ever received money from Close.

Now that the grounds for divorce because of adultery had been indisputably laid before the judge, the chief question involved custody of the child. William sought to keep Herbert, perhaps because of his intimate knowledge of Mary's psychological instability. He must have known that few judges ever separated mother and child, but he did not bring forward any clear reason for his request.

Mary was asked if she thought her husband a suitable person to have custody and education of Herbert. "I do not consider him so.... Because of the associates by whom he is surrounded and his present habits." In contrast, she saw herself as fully qualified and capable of rearing the boy properly. She was questioned regarding the boy's health. "He has been ill, but he is better now." Both William and Mary agreed that a referee should be appointed by the court. The subsequent report was at first refused by the judge because he suspected collusion. But upon reconsideration, he confirmed the referee's opinion. Mary was awarded custody of Herbert but no alimony, since the separation agreement had provided her ample financial security. William had to pay all court costs and lawyers' fees, although he strongly objected to this request from Mary.

Both parties no doubt desired the divorce and planned carefully how and where it should come about. Although Mary appeared in her testimony to be the wronged, put-upon spouse, she may by that time have been straying from marriage fidelity herself. In the opinion of Anne Eaden, who felt she had her Uncle William's confidence: "She left him to go to someone else. Long years after, when she was in trouble and difficulties Uncle Bill helped her, when she appealed to him. I believe he loved her to the end."[7]

If it was true that William was as much wronged as Mary claimed *she* was, such a construction could not have been placed on the issue in court. In order to achieve the desired end — a divorce — the conventional picture must emerge: a husband straying during his wife's pregnancy; her humiliation; more infidelities, culminating in a particular incident when she could stand it no longer. The court would be comfortable with this view of the Closes' troubles. The true circumstances surely were different from the official record of *Close vs. Close.*

William's family rallied to his support when they learned of the legal separation. His uncle, Sir William Cunliffe Brooks, wrote from Aboyne Castle, 17 September 1892: "Most deeply do we both sympathize with you — most keenly we feel for you. Of course it is beyond the power of anyone to help you — but you have our earnest and continued heartiest good wishes."

Again, on 23 November he wrote: "Alas! *dear* Willie, it is *so* sad — One can *only* give to you our heartfelt sympathy and love." William's brother John and cousin Jack Eaden also sent messages of reassurance. And pressing business matters helped him over this disruption in his private life.

The severe economic depression that began in the summer of 1890 caused a number of problems for Close Brothers, for "very few of the farmers have any money," as the railroad magnate James J. Hill reported to the president, "and the local banks are unable to aid them."[8] However, the firm was sufficiently clear of the mortgage business to weather the hard times, and the notes of obligation from cities were honored on schedule. James and Susan Close returned to England, where one son was born before Susan, still quite young, died in 1899.

FOR William the most exciting speculative venture involved the Alaska frontier. Close Brothers loaned money to the British Columbia Development Association with the provision that if they defaulted, their franchises to build a railroad from Skagway to the Yukon would revert to Close Brothers. In 1897 this happened, and plans for the railroad were drawn up — one of the most difficult rail lines ever laid. Workmen had to be slung on ropes from the mountains while they cut the grade. A total of 35,000 men worked on this project, 35 losing their lives. Crews were constantly changing because news of a gold rush somewhere caused massive leave takings. Close Brothers sank $7,143,373 into the White Pass and Yukon Railway merely to finish it, but once in operation, the line became profitable.[9] The bustling Alaskan scene proved to be rejuvenating for William, who was approaching fifty, overweight, and clearly looking middle-aged. Many years later his Alaskan acquaintances recalled the zest with which he participated in their parties, and especially his love of dancing.[10]

William's remarkable acumen in business enterprises continued until the end of his life. "He was always an enthusiast for the low temperature carbonization of coal," according to his (London) *Times* obituary, "and he took it up actively.... Though he has not lived to see the Smokeless City, up to the last he was convinced that it was not far off." The relatively clean air of London today would probably not surprise him. In 1922, the year before his death, he acquired the Shipley Collieries in Derbyshire and raised £800,000 ($4,000,000) among investors to proceed with his coal-processing plans. Another project of his last years concerned the use of "expanded metal as a reinforcement for concrete work and roads," the key architectural development responsible for the high-rise buildings throughout the world in the latter half of this century.

No life interest was more zealously followed than rowing; his fame as an oarsman made him welcome at trials of Cambridge crews—an "old boy" whose expert coaching advice was cherished. He was a familiar figure, almost a fixture, at annual rowing events. In one remarkable family photograph he is shown among May Week Cambridge revellers, a grey-haired man in conventional business clothes, in the midst of the party costumes worn by young university men and their girlfriends—a picture apparently taken at dawn, after a night of celebrating.

To follow rowing events as intimately as possible, William established his home near Henley-on-Thames; "Huntercombe Manor" became an integral part of subsequent Henley racing. The mansion contained eight small bedrooms in a row on the second floor, which were used by the Cambridge crews when they came to train or participate in Henley regattas. In later years the size of the place and the many bedrooms suggested a neatly ironic use, considering William's life-long involvement with the training of young men and his early tutorial role, when he viewed himself or his brothers as acting in loco parentis for the pups in Iowa. "Huntercombe Manor" has now become a Borstal, a home for delinquent boys and juvenile offenders.

"IF Uncle Bill had...had the children he longed for, all would have been well," Anne Eaden wrote in 1950—having forgotten, or never having known, that the child Herbert had once existed, his fate completely unknown to later Close family members. Perhaps what happened to Herbert was too painful for William to disclose. Given the "ill health" remark by Mary in her divorce testimony, Herbert may have died in childhood. Whatever happened to the boy, his immediate destiny was tied to his mother's. On 6 April 1895 Mary married Colonel Frederick Meyer Wardrop in London. He was the son of Henry Wardrop, Esq. of Blackfoulds, Lanarkshire, and he served as military attaché to the British embassy in Vienna. They left for Austria soon after the wedding. She remained in communication with William so that she might press him for needed extra funds. Her sister, Ada, who had always been part of the Close household, remained in England to keep a home for William.

"After his wife left him, his sister-in-law, who considered he had been shamefully treated, continued to live with him," Anne Eaden wrote. "There was *no cause* for scandal but naturally the world thought otherwise. Uncle Bill put himself in a position that was equivocal, to the sorrow of his family in particular." The presence of the unmarried sister, Ada Paullin, in his domestic circle was by then so familiar and right, William could hardly have given much thought to what wagging tongues might say. There does not seem much likelihood that Ada was one of his loves—he had plenty of others.

"To me, I always looked upon his life as a life that was ruined," said Anne Eaden. "He was a most kind uncle to me, kind to all the Closes, to *everyone*. As a result of his early education, like *all* his family, a splendid 'mixer' wherever he went and in any class." Perhaps indeed he would have preferred a conventional married life, but William found consolation in the company of young women, leading a life not untypical of wealthy, unattached Edwardian gentlemen. His final liaison is reported to have been with the actress Florence Desmond, much his junior. He died in her home on the Isle of Wight in 1923.

The last years of Mary's life are obscured by her removal to Vienna, a long way indeed from her girlhood home of Quincy on the Mississippi River. But one thing is certain: ill-health continued to plague her, in all the variations usually meant by that phrase. She committed suicide in September 1905.[11]

CHAPTER SEVENTEEN
In the Fullness of Time

N the June day in 1890 that Fred Close was killed playing polo in Sioux City, twenty-five miles away Lillias "Toogie" Cowan, the young sister of Walter and James, was a houseguest at the Sioux Valley Stud Farm and soon to end her visit. She had hand fed an orphaned foal, toured the shops of Akron, made a few acquaintances, and found the Iowa locale "very amusing, the people are so friendly and funny." Since women were supposedly specialists in love matters, one useful action Toogie attempted while in Iowa was to set up her bachelor brother James with some romantic possibilities, and to that end she became an intimate of a Mrs. Hall. In James's view, nothing but mischievous nuisance resulted. He reported to his sister months later: "I am not able to give you much news of your friend Mrs. Hall. The last time I saw her she tried to be very gracious in her bow, but it was not a success. She spread the report all over the country that I was about to marry a very busch [*sic*] young lady who I did not even know by sight. Having traced the report to Mrs. Hall, I told her husband one day that I had done so and requested him to see that his wife contradicted it. She now denies that she ever said anything about it, so I am not any more 'fought over' than I was before."[1]

During her June 1890 visit Lillias became better informed about the financial bind in which her brothers found themselves. They needed her as an ally to explain to their parents why salaried jobs in the near future would be necessary for them both, and why gentleman farming did not pay. Walter wrote his sister from Akron later: "The best thing we can do is to turn the farm over to Taylor and make a few dollars ourselves on the outside."[2]

Soon thereafter Walter accepted a job as hired hand on a large cattle ranch in Wyoming for $300 a year plus keep. Writing to his mother he justified this ignominious move by explaining that there was "not sufficient produce to come off the farm to support the two of us. . . ." James was angling to be taken on by a Texas stockman, and since Taylor was perfectly capable of running the farm "as well without either of us, I don't think I was wrong in accepting the offer. . . ." And James confided to his brother Henry: "I really think the wisest course is to sound the cease firing and not go to a cent more expense about it. Turn the thing as it stands over to Taylor, and I believe it will pay a small interest at any rate; and if we get a good offer for it, sell."[3]

Land all around them was going for less than what they were asking; the economic slump had worsened. Jim Taylor, though possessing little capital, finally bought a farm, but James feared Taylor was forced too deeply into debt. In any case, Taylor's leaving meant that James was stuck more surely than ever on the Iowa farm, while Walter in Wyoming reveled in his liberation. Walter's abilities proved so useful that by October he was earning $1,800 a year, and with his friend Joe he formed a speculative new company — Cowan and Jefferson Gold Mining Company, which alarmed the Cowan parents, who feared further plunging and no monetary returns. Walter quickly detailed the "claim" nature of the stakes involved — little real money risked.

The following spring the Cowans finally divested themselves of the Iowa farm, the sale accomplished 4 June 1891; a total of 302½ acres were exchanged for $15,300 — a little better than $50 an acre. The Cowans had to accept some of their payment in city real estate in Lincoln, Nebraska. Since one purchaser's signature was notarized by a Rawlins, Wyoming, notary public, Walter's connections there probably turned up a buyer. The issue now facing them was where to locate next?

In April 1892 they traveled to Vancouver, British Columbia, and decided the city was a "go ahead place," more life to it than the more sedate and long-settled Victoria, the provincial capital. James became a salaried office worker and described his new life to his sister in a June letter: "I am going off in the morning for a trip into the mountains to fish. Fortunately, Dominion Day falls on a Friday & so I am getting two clear days from the office with Sunday to back them and mean to utilise them to get all the fresh air and exercise I can cram into the time." He no longer owned a horse for recreational riding. "I had to find some means of early morning exercise and am walking about two miles for a swim every morning, going round in the first place to two houses to pull fellows out of bed to come with me. The weather is perfection now, very hot but a sort of heat that I rather enjoy, being always fresh & cool nights...." He luxuriated in the salubrious climate, after what he had been enduring so long in Iowa. But his new circumstances had their drawbacks, too: a set routine that bound his days. "Well, I think I must close now, as it is getting late and we had a pretty busy day in the office."[4]

After Richard Cowan's death some months later, in addition to their sorrow and shock the two brothers faced the need to re-examine their financial records. Were the remittances from their father gifts or chargeable to them as debts? There had to be a final accounting. They were anxious to assure their mother's reasonable financial security. Walter carefully tallied the pounds sterling sent to them that had been converted into dollars from 1883 through 1891, arriving at a grand figure of £6,450 ($32,250), of which £2,700 ($13,500) had been earmarked as loans, not gifts. To pay off their debt so that the estate could be settled, the brothers remitted the cash realized on their farm sale and relinquished their temporary investments in other property.

Since they had received only $15,300 for the farm, they ended far behind where they had started a decade ago.

The economic situation nationwide worsened, aggravated by the withdrawal of gold and silver by Europeans who had gambled on the rapid expansion of American business in land, railroads, and industries. Some American capitalists feared the effect of the 1890 Sherman Silver Purchase Act would drain the U.S. Treasury of gold, forcing the United States off the gold standard. Walter reported to his brother Henry about the panic in Denver, where twenty-five out of thirty banks closed or failed by midsummer 1893. Still, working for a living as they were now and hoarding their small amount of capital for the right new move, they were not in such dire straits as they might have been had they owned the Iowa farm.

In September Walter confided to his mother: "I am going to be married before very long. . . ." It was a romantic story that he unreeled fully, hoping to appeal to her sentiments. His fiancée was Julia Smith, whose engagement to Joe Jefferson had been broken nearly six years before. On one occasion her stagecoach going away from Rawlins stopped at the same station as Walter's coming in. To his astonishment she didn't appear to recognize him. He was deeply wounded and brooded over the incident for a year—until he met her at a dinner and asked her outright why she had "cut" him that day in the posthouse. Julia replied that if she'd spoken, she would surely have broken down and made a scene, so strongly were her feelings engaged at the sight of him. He told her of his love and they decided to become engaged at once. "She is what might be called refined and ladylike, with all the wit and sparkle of the average American girl, without verging on the coarse, as some of them do. She is very well posted in ordinary knowledge of things and is a good musician."[5]

Her social position, in American terms, was impeccable, for she was the daughter of a state supreme court justice in New Hampshire, one of eight children. "The fact of my marrying a teacher might be misunderstood and I think perhaps had better be kept to the family only." Young ladies of good standing often taught school in America, he explained. It was a highly respected position in any community, education being so important. "If outsiders want any information you may tell them that I am marrying the daughter of the American Judge of the Supreme Court, which to English ears will sound more imposing than a teacher in the Laramie Public School." Perhaps he suggested this to save his mother's social sensibilities; for himself, he surely knew that by marrying an American and earning a salaried, workman's income he had capitulated to a way of life not compatible with the gentleman's code.

James left his office job in Vancouver to become a mine surveyor in British Columbia, but he was almost destitute by the time he returned to Wyoming. Walter, now married, successfully managed a British-owned sheep and cattle ranch; he hired James as a foreman. During the next few years the brothers prospered, for sheep raising enjoyed quite a boom in the latter part of the decade. By 1899 the Cowans were able to pay off family debts and were enjoying a good rate of return on their various investments. However, a Cowan descendant reported that James in later years "often referred to his strong distaste for sheep; their smell and their stupidity revolted him!"⁶

A baby girl was born to Julia and Walter, and when the infant was old enough to travel they embarked for England, visiting Mrs. Cowan in London. Another daughter arrived before Walter, in 1900, suddenly took sick and died of peritonitis at the age of forty-one.

This blow ended James's ranching in the West, but he still did not become repatriated. He turned to mining engineering and prospected for gold at Cripple Creek, Colorado, during the great rush there. Afterwards, he set himself up as a civil engineer and lived in the handsome Broadmoor area of the "Li'l London" of the West, Colorado Springs. James married in England in 1902 or 1903 but returned to Colorado Springs, where his son was born in 1904. America, which James found uncongenial in most ways, was now claiming his own progeny. He had lived in the United States and struggled to earn a living for twenty years and was more qualified to call himself an American than many others from abroad. Finally he gave in, taking out naturalization papers and swearing his oath of allegiance, renouncing British citizenship.

After the shock of Walter's death and the subsequent important personal shifts that took place in his life, James might have imagined that the worst was over—that he was now more or less settled. But such was not to be the case. His wife died in London in 1906 while giving birth to a second son who was stillborn. James once again made the long trek to America and to Colorado Springs. He was accompanied by his sister, who had volunteered to run his household and care for his two-year-old son. Later, in the close-knit way of Victorian and Edwardian families, Walter's widow Julia and her daughters moved to Colorado Springs, and the two families joined by sorrow lived under the same roof.

In 1912 James returned to England and embarked upon a manufacturing business making egg cartons in the East End of London. These American containers had not yet been introduced in England. He teamed up with R. H. Bryant, a family member of England's leading match manufacturers, Bryant and May. They shipped special machinery from the United States to make the cartons, and the enterprise was an immediate success.

When World War I began, James happened to be in Colorado Springs. He'd been on the point of enrolling his son, Robert, in an English school for the fall term, American citizen though the boy was. James obtained a passport, stating commercial reasons for wanting to return to England. He and his son made the voyage successfully, and James joined the army as a second lieutenant at the age of fifty-one in 1915, believing himself to be the oldest volunteer thus accepted for service (though George Orwell's father and many others were even older enlistees). With this action James resumed his status as a British subject and never returned to the States.

During the war his horse experience in Wyoming served him well, for he was in charge of the Army Service Corps' horse-drawn wagons and saw action at Gallipoli. He remained healthy throughout, though he suffered an accident after the Alexandria evacuation—a horse bolted and fell on him, breaking his leg, shortening his leg permanently. Incapable of further military service, he was discharged and his partner, Bryant, went to war.

In succeeding years the egg-box factory evolved into carton making of all kinds; James was chairman of the board until his death in 1940 at age seventy-seven. Although often sharply critical of the United States and its citizens' customs, manners, and ways, his long stay made him familiar with American drive and commercial efficiency, which he found sadly lacking in England. What he'd learned in America gave him an edge over business competitors— an advantage he grudgingly had to admit, ironic though it was. James Cowan was one remittance man whose life tale encompassed almost every aspect of what young men of his age, class, and expectations experienced when they became colonials. Plus the happy ending: he came back home.

AN alternative ending might be just as happy: fulfill the original expectations of family and friends, stay on in Iowa, establish a family with sons and grandsons who would continue to live on the land—not as gentry in the British sense, but respectable, successful Iowa farmers. One such Close colonist was Malcolm Brodie, two of whose grandsons still farm in the region of the old colony. Malcolm was the grandson of the royal chaplain to George IV when he was prince regent, and on his mother's side, his great uncle, John Walter, "the Thunderer," was the proprietor of the *Times* of London. The Brodies were also related by marriage to Captain Reynolds Moreton, for his sister Eleanor had married Hugh Fife Ashley Brodie of Brodie Castle in County Nairn, Scotland.

Malcolm grew up in the genteel resort town, Eastbourne, on the south coast of England, studied law, then joined three brothers who operated a coffee plantation in the Nilgiris hills, Madras, India. He returned to England in 1882 and soon thereafter shipped out to the Close Colony with his brother, F. G. Brodie. "It was doubtful as to what the future would be," he wrote later. "People had not then forgotten the grasshoppers and money was scarce. West of the Broken Kettle Creek all the way to the [Big] Sioux River hardly a furrow had been turned."[7]

After serving an apprenticeship as a pup, Malcolm purchased a farm, but his brother decided to move farther West, eventually to Hawaii. Malcolm's place was about twelve miles west of Le Mars in the vicinity of the Farquhars' farm and an equal distance from the farms of Watson, Garnett, Sinclair, and the Cowan brothers. Two miles north lived a Scottish family from Nova Scotia named Ross, with six boys and six girls. Malcolm met Maggie Ross when she substituted for her ill sister, who worked for a family in the area; or, according to another family source, they met at the Presbyterian country church, both of them devoutly religious. They married 21 July 1885. Maggie proved to be an extremely able helpmeet, her Wisconsin farm background (the Rosses had emigrated from there by covered wagon) serving as proper training for the life she now shared with her Scottish-descended remittance man, who had been born and raised in a fashionable Sussex retirement town within sight of the sea. Maggie's grandfather, a piper in the Scottish Army at Skye, had eloped with the daughter of Lord MacKay, who strongly disapproved of the match, which caused the couple to emigrate to Canada.

Maggie accommodated herself to Malcolm's necessary trips home to visit relatives and to be measured for clothes by his tailor in Sackville Street, London. She did not make these journeys with him because she had the farm to manage, and her duties as mother were fully as demanding. Charles was born the year after the wedding, then six more sons.

Malcolm's parents came to Iowa for a visit in the summer of 1888, and his sisters were houseguests a year or so after that. Like Lillias Cowan, Malcolm's sisters had little grasp of what Iowa farm life entailed, nor did they perceive what hardships their presence imposed upon the Brodie household. Malcolm and Maggie gave up their bedroom for the comfort of the visitors. When numerous cotton and linen petticoats, summer dresses, and undergarments needed laundering and ironing, Maggie accomplished the task herself, secretly, without letting the Brodie sisters know how the laundry was managed. Finally the visit came to an end, and when Maggie returned to occupy the master bedroom, she discovered written on the bureau in the slight film that invariably covers Iowa farm furniture in summer—"Dusty!"[8]

In mid-1909 Malcolm Brodie was forty-eight and feeling his mortality. Something was wrong with his health; he didn't know quite what. Local doctors diagnosed gallstones. He had a persistent pain in his side, and his eyes bothered him. It had been ten years since he'd been home to England. He embarked on the voyage to consult family-recommended specialists, visit relatives, and enjoy a holiday—a needed relaxation after so many years of steady farm work. His oldest son, Charles, was twenty-three and able to manage the place with the help of younger brothers.

"O dear old England again! The hedges and the fields, the trees, the churches.... Such a beautiful green; we have nothing like it in the U.S.," he wrote in his diary. He was delighted by the warm family reception, "all my brothers and sisters very pleased to see me & all very kind."[9] During his two and a half months visit he would move from one family member to another—London and its suburbs, Sussex, and the Isle of Wight. At this stage of his life his years were rounded fully enough to be beyond career choices. There was only the question of judgment about how he had chosen to live, and the bittersweet nostalgia of sensing an entire world he'd once known intimately but now foreign to him. He'd gotten outside his own life and into another.

One of Malcolm's first acts upon his arrival in London was to stop at his tailors to order a suit. Next, he bought a good walking stick and some fashionable collars in the Burlington Arcade. "The English people certainly dress better and more extravagantly than they used to. This is a luxurious age." He felt so provincial in his Iowa clothes he could not bear to go to church the first Sunday.

In succeeding days he visited the Royal Academy gallery and the Tate museum, where he enjoyed in particular Rosa Bonheur's "original painting of the horse fair," and Westminster Abbey, where "The tombs of the Kings and mildewed banners looked very ancient." He consulted a doctor who prescribed no medicine but suggested a plaster to bind his side. He also had his eyes examined and discovered his glasses were one-third too strong—that explained the headaches! He felt somewhat relieved. "Dear old London: in spite of all people may say about the decadence of England, London is still the hub of the Universe and the swellest and most lively city in the world."

But he didn't yearn to remain in England and knew why his life had taken him thousands of miles away. One day he watched "About 1,500 or 2,000 boys playing on the heath—could not help but think of their future lot & wondered how many of them would find their way eventually to the Northwest." They would have to emigrate because there were few opportunities for them in England—his own motive. And although once during his visit, talking to a Pole, he agreed that Germany should be taught a lesson, he couldn't foresee that many of these games-playing boys, whose future he pondered, would end up part of the million dead young Englishmen in the Great War.

During his second week he had a tennis match with a stockbroker brother but discovered such activity was "too much of a strain at present." He suffered chills. After his long sojourn in United States, he had become so used to Iowa weather, he could not adapt to the unpredictable temperature changes in England. He was in and out of heavy underclothes and concluded: "This is a treacherous climate."

Sometimes old memories brought him to the brink of sadness. He walked to Bedford Square where relatives once resided. "I saw the house I slept in twenty-eight years ago, when I first left for the U.S." Monuments that merely glorified Great Britain were emotionally safer, and going down to Greenwich he reinforced his belief about Britain's importance in the world; after all, "Greenwich Observatory is where time is regulated." His own time had strangely slipped away: it was easier to contemplate "the old Kings who enjoyed themselves here hundreds of years ago."

Finally his new flannel suit was ready, and he was more secure about his appearance. Another suit, a blue serge, was in the works: "It seemed to fit nicely and looked very well. I think I shall like it." In between shopping excursions, especially to the American store in Selfridge's ("bought a blouse for somebody, probably Maggie"), he listened to choral music in Westminster

Abbey, "a nice quiet place, surrounded by the dust of many Kings and noblemen & great men & women of the past. Sat near the tomb of Sir Robert Peel."

Toward the end of June he traveled to Eastbourne, his birthplace, and walked by his "dear old home. . . . How I wished I could go in." During the day there was little to do except bicycle, sit on the Parade and listen to band music, and chat with the retired people on benches, some of whom remembered his parents, and one old lady "who said she remembers me in kilts." Sisters, brothers, and various relatives had Malcolm under their hospitable wings, though for two weeks he lived at a seaside rooming house. His family took him to Holy Trinity Church, "the church where we used to go when we were children. . . . Saw the same old windows & font where I was christened." These engulfing memories made letters from home that much more important and anchored his sense of well-being. On 11 July after a morning on the Parade watching the fleet, listening to band music, chatting, he returned to his lodgings and "still no more letters from home. Sent two photos of self to Maggie, also wrote her again. Went down on the Parade and came home by the electric bus." The next day: "Went up to the cemetery to see Dad's grave. Found it very easy . . . came back by the Gore road & went through St. Mary's church to see the old family vault, all the last generation gone. Very depressing." His grandfather had been vicar here from 1810 to 1828, but his grandmother "never entered the church again" after a subsequent vicar ordered major renovations.

Visiting a farm, he inspected four new milking machines run by a gasoline engine, "also machines for cooling milk," which caught his professional agricultural interest. "Saw a good deal of machinery, all much heavier than ours."

He received a letter from his eldest son, Charlie, on 21 July, then "two cards from the boys" plus two *Le Mars Sentinels*. A proper ballast was now in place, and he could pass the building "where I went to school thirty-six years ago" with equanimity. "Everything looked about the same."

Hours spent as a vacationer began to wear, however, in spite of golfing with his brother Stuart, playing tennis, cycling, visiting monuments, and long chats with relatives. He noted in his diary on 5 August: "Time getting very short now for Eastbourne, as I leave Monday for good and am not very likely to ever turn up here again." Meanwhile, his tailors in Sackville Street had measured him "for a great coat" and still other apparel.

Malcolm greatly missed his children, which he realized especially one fair day in early August when he decided to hire a rowboat. "As I was going out, a little boy about the size of Colin [his son] asked me if he might go out with me. He was a nice little chap & I took him in the boat and rowed him to Holywell. I thought his mother who was on the beach would be getting anxious, so I rowed him back & we then went out again to the pier & saw the Brighton boat come in. When it landed his father came down & was very profuse in his thanks & wanted to help pay the expense of the boat. I told him I wouldn't dream of such a thing." And that same day he found a "small boy crying in the road. I asked him what was the matter, and he said he didn't know where he was or how to get home. He had stolen a ride on a bus to Eastbourne & had been turned off, however. I got him to go & see if they would not take him back & gave him three pence. Tears all stopped & everybody happy." Especially Malcolm Brodie. He went through the woods to visit the Old Priory, which dated from 1100. After living so long in Iowa, a place with no recorded history to speak of, he could not get enough of these stretches into the past. "The ride was magnificent. . . . Old England cannot be beaten on such a summer day."

At lawn tennis and a garden party the following day he encountered an old acquaintance from his law-student days. He remembered how much the legal world had once interested him. "I am afraid the profession lost a coming star and shining light; however, it is all well, after all." He sensed old social skeins at this party when his hosts turned suddenly very sociable "when they knew I was a Brodie."

His visits to stately homes, parks, monuments, castles, churches, and ruins awakened class feelings once again. "Evidently in early days this was a swell place," he noted after one excursion with a relative, "as there are several very beautiful old places here belonging to the nobility of old but alas today are mostly inhabited by tradesmen, I believe. It is very sad to see the number of old families in England that have had to give up their land & their home. The cry now is down with the nobility, make the land-owners pay the taxes, etc. For another generation there will be great changes & few of the old families left to keep up the traditions of the past."

After a particularly extensive trip to the Cotswolds, rowing at Avon, a visit to Broadway, and inspecting old villages around the duke of Orleans' place, he became unwell: "All advised me to go to Birmingham to see a specialist. . . . Suffering some pain as of old. Very restless all night, rather feverish & had chills. O how I wish I was back home with Maggie again. I'll go, jolly soon." The Birmingham doctor was certain the difficulty wasn't gallstones. When a letter regarding the examination arrived on 19 August, Malcolm was cheered by the news that the physician "could find nothing organically wrong . . . said my complaint was mostly nervous, partly due to muscular rheumatism of the chest muscles. The best advice he could give me would be for me to return to my work & forget I had an inside at all. I must try & forget, forget. Psychology to the front. Forget, forget. Soon I will be home again. Soon, God willing, I shall see my dear Maggie again, and the children. Two weeks next Saturday the *Mauretania* leaves Liverpool." And he would be on board, eager to return to his real life in America—tired of these days on end, living at the fringes of a society where he no longer had a place.

The social high point of the trip was still ahead—a visit to the Isle of Wight, where he was to stay at Fernhill, which had belonged to his rich Uncle Fred. The house lay only three miles from Osborne, "Queen Victoria's favorite residence." Malcolm found Fernhill "a beautiful old place. . .water in the distance. . .such a large house & so unique. Met Aunt Ada." Soon they visited Osborne, presented a special card at the gate that allowed them to drive in. "I think the people thought we were some notables." That evening at Fernhill Malcolm and his cousin Gordon enjoyed tinkering in the observatory. "First we viewed some of the clusters & nebulae & one beautiful white and blue star through the large telescope that Uncle Fred had. . . .It cost £1,000 [$5,000]." On a subsequent day Malcolm helped Gordon in the workshop, which was fitted with "lathes, printing presses"; Gordon "was turning a brass fixing to go over a fountain pen. . . .He told me that the lathe and tools originally cost £2,000 [$10,000]." They also experimented on the printing press. "Uncle Fred must have been a very clever, mechanical genius."

On 25 August Malcolm and his Brodie relatives attended a lavish garden party given by Colonel C. V. C. Hobart and his wife at West Cliff Hall, Hythe, overlooking Southampton Water. Colonel Hobert was the commanding officer of the Isle of Wight, and the three hundred guests included "a large number of Island gentry," according to the press account. The occasion was a visit by H.R.H. Princess Henry of Battenberg, who would arrive in her yacht, *Sheila*. Guests boarded a steamer "especially engaged by Colonel Hobart to take his friends over to the Hobart place at Hythe," wrote Malcolm. It was a rainy, poor day for an outing. "After awhile, the Princess's band, which is on board, began to play. As we go down the Solent, flags flying & band playing, I think we are taken for people of importance." Carriages awaited them at the pier and the guests were transported to the "beautiful old house. . .gay with bunting. . .we were presented to Mrs. Hobart, a nice looking small woman whose great hobby is Shetland ponies." Her Royal Highness (Queen Victoria's daughter Beatrice) arrived in a dinghy from her yacht. Colonel Hobart escorted her past his troop of Boy Scouts lined up as guard of honor. The ponies paraded. The princess was fascinated by "these handsome little animals who trotted around with their miniature carriage in splendid style," wrote a reporter. Tea was served inside the house. Malcolm was impressed by "the armorial bearings & hawsers" he found displayed on the walls. "All of a sudden the National Anthem starts & the Princess arrives with her ladies in waiting. Everybody stands & bows."

Later there is music in the drawing room, and Malcolm reported: "I had the honor of sitting quite close to the Princess, who is decidedly a Lady. . . .Quite a distinguished company." After the princess left, Malcolm had a chance to speak to Colonel Hobart. Although this royal occasion would seem to be about as far from Iowa farm life as one could get, actually a connection was easily made. "I had met Lady Hobart and the Earl of Bucks in the West," Malcolm informed Colonel Hobart. Before he became the earl of Buckinghamshire in 1886 he was a Le Mars hog-dealer. To most American ears the subject of pigs would have seemed ludicrously inappropriate to mention at such a grand party, but Malcolm Brodie would know that hog breeding was a sound, aristocratic subject, upon which gentlemen might discourse with enthusiasm.

Malcolm found the Isle of Wight a fine place to get a strong sense of Victorian upper-class life, particularly as it was lived in previous decades. Later he visited Lord Tennyson's home and attached farm and noticed the harvesting in progress. "I was much amused...." So many men in the field doing not very much, and so little serviceable equipment. "So much for the English agricultural laborer." He expressed pride in his Americanness at that moment, but a few days later the old pull of England-of-yesterday took complete hold. He found the "ideal spot for an outing....How Maggie would have enjoyed it." He picked a bit of heather to take home to her, but this was not tribute enough to England's vegetation: "Such a beautiful day, the heather was simply gorgeous and so soft, I simply rolled in it." And even while he rolled in it, he wished Maggie were enjoying it with him. "I could not help but think of this when I was in the heather."

During his last days on the Isle of Wight, there were more elegant social occasions. The canon of Windsor Castle and his family came to call at Fernhill: "He is rector also of Whippingham, Queen Victoria's church....After tea I walked with Aunt Ada in the garden....She is a good sort. She gave me her and Uncle Fred's photos in nice frames and also promised to give me a back-gammon board to take home. Good-bye to Fernhill, dear old place." Just a few days later it would be good-by to England. Excitement over the prospect of returning to Iowa enfused his diary entries. He would soon be going to where he knew he now belonged, where his dearest ones were. The rest—all he had recently tasted and observed—was part of the past.

In touting the American West, John Walter of the *Times* of London had predicted that a man could retire by age fifty with a tidy fortune. Malcolm Brodie left farming in 1921, when he was fifty-nine, with $100,000 in cash and his farm sold to his renter on easy terms, holding the mortgage himself. Many retiring farmers in those years moved to the towns where they had always traded, attended church, and had their legal and medical needs provided. They often built small bungalows they expected would not be too difficult to keep up in their declining years. Malcolm and Maggie bought a fine Le Mars home, perhaps originally built by one of the Close colonists. Every afternoon, according to Brodie custom, tea was served, often with freshly baked tarts. Steak-and-kidney pie was another specialty Maggie frequently produced, which was enjoyed by any of the clan who happened by. I remember Malcolm Brodie (who died in 1947) as a somewhat shrunken, distinguished-looking old man in a black suit—grandfather of a close high school friend. He did not look much like a farmer.

A FEW blocks away lived a different sort of relic from the Close Colony, George Hotham, who never retired from any occupation in life that one could give a name to. He didn't have to work, having an income from abroad, and he didn't particularly want to. Such a phenomenon seemed most peculiar to local inhabitants — an able-bodied man without any occupation whatever and who never had had one. But look where such leisure got him — mostly in and out of saloons. The Lord God surely meant everyone to work at something.

In the heyday of money-from-England, George Hotham was believed to be receiving an income of thirty dollars a day, chiefly from British railway stocks, but he was notoriously tight with his funds. He often walked into the lobby of the local hotel, where the stack of daily newspapers had been put out for the guests to take free of charge, and calmly folded the paper and walked off with it. He died at age eighty-six in 1948.

The virus of inactivity and living off an inheritance from England infected the next generation as well. George Hotham, Junior, was a replica of the old man and "never did a day's work in his life." According to local hearsay, "on the first of the month when that check came" (probably mixing today's Social Security payment days into the tale), the son of the original remittance man would make the rounds of the bars in Le Mars, taking one gentlemanly drink in each but becoming fairly unsteady by the time he got home to his mother.

Young George spent money more freely than his father had. Whereas his high school friends might be saving to buy a bicycle, George put down cash for a snazzy red Buick convertible and often sported a girl on each arm. He loved to dance, and double-dating with George became a sought-after opportunity. Since *he* provided the elegant transportation, he often claimed to have left his money at home and someone else would have to cover his expenses for the evening — a rich man's defense against constantly being taken advantage of by friends, but regarded as a strategy of his stinginess. On one of these double dates, the two girls sneaked his wallet out of his pocket before it was time to pay the bill. When the check was presented, George professed to be without funds, but the girls hauled out his billfold and began to peel off banknotes.

George in later years became a town character, recognized, patronized, almost cherished for his peculiarity; everyone knew him by sight, and he could usually be found whiling away the breakfast hours in the Pantry Cafe. After his mother's death in 1958, George's health began to fail; for years he lived alone in a seedy downtown rooming house.

In June 1980 I found George Hotham in a Le Mars nursing home. He was thoroughly dried out, his face wizened in a remarkably distinguished fashion, his speech not as local in inflection as I expected, considering he had lived here all his life. When he learned I wished information about his family, he began coming closer behind his remote eyes until almost a joyful release broke from him — especially upon realizing that I knew something of him and his people already. "My uncle was an Admiral in the British Navy. Nobody believes it, but he was. A ship was named after him — a warship, in World War II." I nodded and reviewed a little Hotham family history. When his uncle Admiral Charles Hotham was appointed junior lord of the English Admiralty in 1888, Editor Dacres of the *Globe* wrote about the shake-up in the high command of the navy, "and we know whereof we speak."[10] All of George's uncles were officers in the army or navy. "One was in Aden," he said, "which he called The Cinderheap because it was so hot. Another in India. My father was the only one who came to America." And why did he emigrate, I asked? "People *were,* at the time." His father, born in 1862, made the move when he was twenty-one or twenty-two, but he never experienced the life of a pup. "He bought a farm because land was so cheap, but he didn't work it."

What *did* he do?

The grey-blue eyes turned blank and distant. "He owned a few buildings in town, which he looked after and rented out."

I asked why he'd stayed on, when so many others left.

"He was married — my mother — she was from here." Louisa Neumeister, a German farm girl. "There were a few who stayed, 'Deacon' Colpoys for one. The two of them would go out walking together. Take along things to make tea somewhere."

He told me a little about the ancestral Hotham family seat near Scarborough on the northeast coast of England. No, he'd never seen it — even a picture — and he didn't know who owned it now, but his father had visited home thirteen times while *his* mother was alive. "After she died, he never went back."

Did the Hothams ever come here to visit your father?

No, they sailed to ports in South America and Asia, but Le Mars was too far inland, too much trouble to make a trip. His father's sister, who lived in Scotland, used to write, but not for a long time. "She's probably dead." He paused. "Would have to be, by now."

"My father went to Oxford University. People don't believe that, either. And he studied at Heidelburg." But it was unknown what particular field or subjects especially interested him.

The mystery to me, I said, was what he *did* with himself, hanging around this small town — considering his cosmopolitan background.

"He got used to it — it was home to him."

Perhaps to George's family in England he was the only son who failed to live up to their expectations of useful service. The mystery of what he had accomplished by his removal to Iowa could always be wrapped in the blanket phrase, "Went West." He had emigrated to a remote place, like any other colonial, and made it his home. And stayed. It only seemed odd as a career to natives of this Iowa town, who had lost the knowledge of what pressures had been brought to bear upon the sons of Victorian upper-class households, sending them to the ends of the earth.

In Le Mars the Hothams lived next door to another permanent English settler from the heyday of the colony, Frederick Veal, the lumberyard man. "You heard about what happened in that family?" George asked, coming alive with the glee of tale telling. Veal had a grandson, also named Fred, who lived in Palm Springs, California. "He was playing around with women, but his wife caught him at it. She killed him with a shotgun and then turned it on herself, after cleaning up his blood."

Hotham scrutinized my reaction closely to see if I had been properly shocked by this abrupt tale of violence. I couldn't decide if the story had been intended in any way other than as a grisly incident bearing upon the subject before us — what happened to those English and their descendants — or if the sardonic, almost satisfied look in his eye meant he was informing me of something I ought to know about bloodlines petering out in strange, far-flung places. I said good-by shortly thereafter to one of the last living connections to the remittance men, with an uncanny sense that a generation had been leapt over and a specimen himself sat before me: out of time and out of place and lost in the West.

CHAPTER EIGHTEEN

The Vanished Colony

ESTERDAY a wilderness, today an empire," wrote a Le Mars editor in 1882, three years after Close Brothers arrived, but it did not turn out to be part of the British empire. The House of Lords and House of Commons saloons changed identities. The Albion House was torn down in 1910, and a newer hostelry, the Union Hotel, was named in keeping with life in the United States. British yeoman labor helped build it—men like "Gunner," who had served on a British warship, and Frank Gibbons, "who is the leading hand of hod-carriers."

> *Gunner:* I say, Frank, how heavy is that hod of bricks?
> *Frank:* Oh, not so bleeding heavey, it's about 86 pounds at the bottom story and about a bloody 'undred at the top.
> *Gunner:* Well, I think I could carry one up.

"At this stage," according to the reporter, "Gibbons placed the hod of brick on the Hon. Mr. Gunner's shoulders. He started up the ladder to the first story, but he sloped the article like he would shoulder a Martin Henry rifle, and the consequence was the 36 pounds of brick was precipitated to the cellar. The cigars are on Gunner."

Working-class Englishmen adjusted with relative ease to the rural Midwest, since they spoke more or less the same language as the American locals and saw an opportunity of greatly improving their prospects. The presence in the same area of Britons from the upper classes and gentry often meant the likelihood of employment and plenty of money for various commercial enterprises. And no doubt much to their surprise, they discovered that in America their social standing as farmers was no different from that of the British gentlemen immigrants in farming.

John Hope in *Blackwood's,* recalling his experience as an Iowa pup, remarked that "in the States the farming community is considered in every respect to be the lowest grade in the social scale. The small 'store-keeper' (tradesman), his 'clerks' (counter-jumpers), the saloon-keeper, and even the artisans of all kinds, whether paper-hangers, painters, or what not, are all looked upon by the community at large as occupying a much better position in the world than the farmer. Why? For this reason, that the business man in town requires not only a fair education, but also a fair amount of capital, before he can start his store; the artisan likewise requires education (i.e., his apprenticeship), in order that he may become a skilled workman; whereas the farmer requires no literary or scientific education, as his work is merely unskilled labor, and his capital is, as a rule, only nominal."[1]

Hope admitted that farming required some intelligence, but the best schooling for it would be to be raised, oneself, on a farm. A primitive sort of house, rudimentary machinery, and a few animals could suffice at the start. Land was cheap and remained relatively inexpensive until fairly recently, which meant that a man with modest capital could set himself up as a farmer without difficulty, if he was up to the hard manual labor.

The farmers' lower social standing as a group also came about because many immigrants went directly into agriculture. Their peculiar foreign ways, odd clothes, and incomprehensible speech set them apart and the popular notion of farmer-as-clod was further enhanced. The drudgery demanded of many farm wives and small children also weakened the esteem of townspeople for farmers. "Such is the class which English parents deem the appropriate one for their sons to join," said Hope scornfully.

In America, "young men are distinctly urban in their inclinations," commented another observer in *Macmillan's* (1890). "They hate the country and farming life." A young man "would a good deal sooner measure tape or sell shoes across a counter than work on a farm, though he owned it himself." Invariably he opted for the noise of cities, the crowded streets; he hated the solitude and silence found on a farm. In town he took on "an air of social superiority, as such things are judged in the limited sphere of a small town, over the farming folk from whom he has sprung."[2]

A young, educated English gentleman, in contrast, was often genuinely fond of country life and would cheerfully do field work, while he would disdain easier tasks such as using a tape measure or selling sugar. W. Hyndman Wann, the Belfast-born husband of Carrie Wygant—William Close's former Denison, Iowa, girlfriend—was not physically suited to rugged farm life, yet he persisted in spite of weak lungs and poor eyesight. He and Carrie moved to the Close Colony in 1879 and farmed twenty miles from Le Mars, where their two children were born. The pure air of the prairie did not work the health cure anticipated, and he and Carrie finally gave up Iowa for the dry, warm air of southern California, where he died of consumption in 1884.

In the years since the heyday of the Close Colony, the typical American's love of machinery and labor-saving devices had resulted in a workable equation for setting the social hierarchy: the less physical work a man did, the higher he rated. Soft white hands, skin not reddened by the sun, bodies plump in business suits, necks tight in white collars and ties—these signified a man who was somebody! Nature's hard regime diminished a man's importance, and the farther he seemed to remove himself from forces of this elemental kind, the greater his social standing. And his wife would stop baking wholesome bread in favor of cottony white "baker's bread" soon available in waxed paper, shipped from metropolises, because it seemed more "genteel."

While the Close Colony lasted, the British were untouched by the low social standing of farmers. Walter and James Cowan seemed unaware of it, or they would have been struck by the irony. But as the colony faded, the British who stayed were increasingly exposed to prevailing social attitudes; certainly their children were part of this American world. Perhaps they came to realize the import of an early British writer's comment on the West: "Land there has no prestige, no attraction of the kind it has in this country." Furthermore, "the rural 'buck' beyond the Atlantic would far sooner sell ribbons or saucepans across the counter than work upon his father's farm or even upon a good one of his own."[3]

The best route to becoming a gentleman in America would be to go into business. No one lost status by work of any kind, as John Hope found out: "There is no such thing as the idle gentleman." Many Close Colonists, including Captain Moreton, formed companies that produced goods or provided services in order to make money. As early as 1881 the *Field* correspondent noted that "no caste is lost by pursuance of any occupation; a little badinage or chaff, perhaps, leads off the new enterprise, but soon...the auctioneer, the butcher, and the livery-stable keeper" resumed their equal status with the sons of earls and various lords who were their friends.[4]

The ease with which these British gentlemen colonists went mercantile and "Yankee" was naturally applauded in the local press. Rugby Colony had collapsed because the sons of the gentry played too many games, drank and lounged about the Tabard Inn; but the British in Iowa continued to flourish because "they have acquired a taste for business." In Le Mars, prominent colonists sat on the boards of half a dozen companies at once, young men like Thomas Aldersey of the Germania Brewing Company, whose grandfather was the canon of Chester. "We have room enough in the all-absorbing West.... They will find ample scope for their energies on these undeveloped prairies, but they must know that the price of success is—attention to business."[5]

In subsequent years, the occupation of farming has increasingly required business acumen, scientific knowledge, and technical skills. The farmer must be able to handle an enterprise worth hundreds of thousands of dollars. Before the severe farm depression of the 1980s set in, the fertile tracts of the old Close Colony sold for as high as $3,000 per acre. Investors from abroad during the period of booming land prices in the 1970s eagerly purchased Iowa soil, and the state responded with laws preventing absentee ownership by foreign nationals. However, certain midwestern banks and investment companies managed to set up syndicates to get around the legal obstacles. "Leviathan squatters" and foreign money pressures once again agitated the U.S. Congress, as it had in 1884. In this respect the past had become present.

Farmland was sought for its capacity to produce wealth in the form of food and fiber in an increasingly overcrowded world—and as a tangible hedge against inflation and unstable currencies. While land prices were soaring, Iowa ranked near the top in the number of millionaires per population. Those farmers who were large operators were accorded the kind of social respect the profession had enjoyed in the early years of the republic, when landowning farmers were assured the highest place in the Jeffersonian scheme of things. Holding title to productive land meant having a tangible piece of the future— which was what the gentlemen immigrants to Iowa had always assumed. How- ever, their attempt to transplant a social heirarchy from Great Britain was doomed to fail. Americans could never be counted on to recognize agricultural entrepreneurs as true aristocrats, and even the concept, based as it was on class notions, did not pertain. "In every city there is a standard of money, according to its size," concluded Maurice Low shortly after the turn of the century in his study of the basis of social standing in the United States.[6] The British who came out to the Close Colony and stayed on soon learned that the only way to become an American gentleman was to see to it that one became rich enough.

Those who could turn to commercial activities without feeling ensnared in a tawdry shopkeeper's world soon earned their way into the money-based aris- tocracy of the new world. A large bankroll was certification enough as to who counted and who didn't. Famous family surnames from Great Britain meant little to anyone.

Captain Moreton's Dromore Farm continued to be worked—the years of crops and livestock rolled on—but its name was forgotten. The custom of naming farms never took hold in the Midwest. The Moreton place (as it was known) remained a conspicuous establishment on the ridge west of Le Mars, but its reason for being, the busy life that it once contained, was largely lost to local residents. For fifty years a series of renters farmed the land, which had been divided into ordinary 160-acre parcels. The central homestead had exces- sively large buildings and orchards for the modest farm it now was, and when Karl Ahrendson bought it for fifty dollars an acre in 1939 at the bottom of the Depression, drastic measures had to be taken. The 180-foot major barn was partially falling down, and he demolished it, saving the lumber, which I saw stacked in a neat pile when I visited the site in 1953.

Ahrendson planted a new grove for a windbreak because he decided most of the land directly around the buildings could never be farmed, being too cluttered with pipes, bricks, and foundation stones; he figured he might as well have a good stand of trees. "Pipes everywhere. You dig down and you come up with pipes. They even run under the road—I don't know to where." A second barn was still usable with its solidly built partitions for livestock, beautifully laid out brick floor, and drainage troughs. At first Ahrendson had numerous accidents with his livestock—they fell into sudden cave-ins where the coal-mine digging had taken place, or into partially closed-over wells.

Ahrendson plugged these excavations as well as he could. "Neighbors came and threw their junk down the holes. None of 'em any trouble now, but look—look at that ground. See the foundation outline there where them stones are? Can never use this land here for anything but pasture. It's too full of junk." He had discovered, also, a layer of gravel under the entire yard and figured it had been put down for the polo ponies.[7]

"You should've seen this place when I got it." Cockleburrs everywhere, all over the fields, in the barns, and even in the house. The sheds were collapsing; the house was a wreck. The famous orchard, ten acres of apple, pear, cherry, and other fruit trees, was now largely dead and he had to clear the area. The great drouth of the 1930s was as responsible for the dead trees as tenant neglect. By 1953 Ahrendson had at last begun to till the old orchard area. Most of the original walnut trees in the grove had died; he grubbed them out but saved the lumber for his father, a fine craftsman, who made furniture for the family.

The Moreton residence had been remodeled into a much smaller house. "What could we do with a thing that size?" Ahrendson asked. "Oh, some people...when they heard what I was up to—come and took pictures, but what the hell? Junk is all right for some folks, but it sure gets in the way."

Ahrendson had pulled off the rear of the house and turned it around; it became his chicken house. Then he cut off half the front of the house and used the lumber to repair the rest of the structure. The slats on his corncrib were floorboards from that part of the house. The long hallway upstairs had been shortened, the walnut staircase removed, and small, steep stairs installed. The newel post "was too pretty to throw away," and so Mrs. Ahrendson used it as a stand for her potted ivy and ferns. Spokes from the banister served as legs for a small end table and other furniture subsequently created. The downstairs sitting room, now one large square room, retained its original windows, nuisance though they were, since storm windows had to be custom built—they were no ordinary dimensions. A front sitting room, possibly the original library and first meeting place of the Prairie Club, was still intact in 1953 but closed off. Through the center of the house ran a huge chimney, so big "it'll never get clogged up." Ahrendson had noticed a date scratched in the brick but couldn't remember it, except that "it was an awful long time ago."

Upstairs the small eight-by-twelve bedrooms with one window each, which Mrs. Ahrendson showed me, were much as they were when Lord Hobart, Lord St. Vincent's sons, and other genteel boarders lived here. I opened a wall cupboard and Mrs. Ahrendson pointed out the lack of a horizontal bar for hanging clothes—only the wooden pegs at the back. "That's the English way," she said.

As we emerged into the hallway, I noticed a ceiling trapdoor to space under the roof. "Anything up there?"

"Nothing now. When we insulated the house awhile back, our kids found some cowboy boots—like they wore then, and little suitcases. Weren't anything much. You know, under the hot roof all these years—what it does to leather. But I suppose they were real good leather once. Like briefcases—sort of small—more'n suitcases."

"Could I see them?"

"Oh, we threw 'em down the coal mine holes! Had to fill up those holes with anything we could lay hands on."

I glanced again at the ceiling.

"Nothing up there now."

AS the decades passed, remnants of the Close Colony occasionally turned up: bone china sets, polo mallets, a silver tea service—or living artifacts like Richard Latham, Linotype operator at the *Le Mars Sentinel.* He was a tall, gaunt, extremely shy old man when I knew him in 1943, with a clipped, terse manner of speaking, which seemed unfriendly at first. As editor of the high school newspaper, I worked with Latham each week when the paper was put to bed; but we spoke very little. He had been born in the north of England and had tried cattle wrangling out West before arriving in Le Mars during the waning days of the colony. We all knew he was one of those remittance men; it was generally thought that having a small income from overseas had been bad for him. He drank too much, had never "made much of himself." Why Dick Latham happened to be left in Le Mars and what fate had befallen the British community were facts lost in the mists of misinformation and unconcern, for it was not the past that interested midwestern Americans then, only the promising future. Whatever memories Dick Latham had of the fairgrounds, the annual Derbys, polo, he never communicated them to me. His report on the colony was destined to be lost along with so much of America's pioneering past—deliberately discarded in the rush to be modern, to make over the old and forget yesterday. The specialness of the Close Colony was the very aspect that made it a target to be obliterated and all participants assimilated. The one thing every immigrant seemed to have experienced was the crushing out of his cultural uniqueness by the pressure to be the same as everyone else. "You're in America now, *talk* American, *be* American. Forget the old country—you'll be better off, the sooner you do." Under this dictum the gentleman-settler and lower-class immigrant finally became joined—and shared a pioneering experience that lay outside status.

NOTES

INTRODUCTION

1. *Macmillan's* 44:68.
2. William B. Close, *Farming in North-Western Iowa, United States of America: A Pamphlet for Emigrants and a Guide to North-Western Iowa* (Manchester: A. Ireland, 1880), 2.
3. Thomas Hardy, *Tess of the D'Urbervilles* (New York: Harper, 1921), 130.
4. Jacob Van Der Zee, *The British in Iowa* (Iowa City: State Historical Society of Iowa, 1922), 75.
5. William B. Close to James Close, Autumn, 1879, Close Papers. All Close family personal and business letters courtesy of James Close.
6. Close, *Farming in North-Western Iowa,* 17.
7. Turner, *The Frontier in American History* (New York: Henry Holt, 1921), 4.
8. Bigelow, *Harper's New Monthly Magazine* 62:764.
9. *Le Mars Sentinel,* 7 Apr. 1881; 11 Apr. 1884.
10. 27 Mar., 3 June 1884, *Congressional Record,* 48th Cong., 2359, 4794.
11. Van Der Zee, *British in Iowa,* 108.
12. James P. Reed, "The Role of an English Land Company in the Settlement of Northwestern Iowa and Southwestern Minnesota" (Master's thesis, Univ. of Nebraska at Omaha, 1974), 166.
13. Mrs. E. W. Harriman to author, 18 Oct. 1953.
14. *Le Mars Sentinel,* 6 Oct. 1881.
15. Arthur O'Shaughnessy, "Ode" in *Familiar Quotations,* 14th ed., ed. John Bartlett (Boston: Little, Brown, 1968), 807.

CHAPTER 1: *Athlete into Immigrant*

1. *New York Times,* 21 July 1876.
2. James Close to Thomas Close, ca. 1862, Close Papers, courtesy of Roger Close-Brooks; *Manchester School Register,* 68; James Close, "Own Life," manuscript, courtesy of Jonathan Close-Brooks.
3. William B. Close, "The Prairie Journal," manuscript, courtesy of Susanne Knowles and James Close.
4. *New York Times,* 23 July, 24 July, 28 July 1876.
5. Bruce Haley, *The Healthy Body and Victorian Culture* (Cambridge and London: Harvard Univ. Press, 1978), 20.
6. Jacob Van Der Zee, *The British in Iowa* (Iowa City: State Historical Society of Iowa, 1922), 58.
7. *Pall Mall Gazette* quoted in *New York Times,* 27 Aug. 1876.
8. Anne Eaden to James Close, 14 Nov. 1950, Close Papers.
9. William B. Close, *Farming in North-Western Iowa, United States of America: A Pamphlet for Emigrants and a Guide to North-Western Iowa* (Manchester: A. Ireland, 1880), 15.

10. Anthony Trollope, *North America* (New York: Alfred A. Knopf, 1961), 400.

11. James R. Paullin, "The Paullin Family of Southern New Jersey," manuscript, 1934, courtesy of James R. Paullin.

12. James P. Reed, "The Role of an English Land Company in the Settlement of Northwestern Iowa and Southwestern Minnesota" (Master's thesis, Univ. of Nebraska at Omaha, 1974), 40–41; ibid., 35.

13. *History of the Counties Woodbury and Plymouth, Iowa* (Chicago: A. Warren, 1890–1891), 432.

14. Reed, "The Role of an English Land Company," 40.

15. Trollope, *North America,* 155.

16. Van Der Zee, *British in Iowa,* 258.

CHAPTER 2: *The Prairie Lords*

1. Dan Elbert Clark, *The West in American History* (New York: T. Y. Crowell, 1937).

2. Anne Close's "Commonplace Book," manuscript, courtesy of Susanne Knowles.

3. Mrs. W. H. McHenry to author, 15 July 1980.

CHAPTER 3: *The Prospect Before Them*

1. Thomas Close to William Close, 27 Jan. 1878, Close Papers, courtesy of Roger Close-Brooks.

2. Mark Girouard, *The Return to Camelot* (New Haven: Yale Univ. Press, 1981).

CHAPTER 4: *Going Out to Iowa*

1. Arthur Larson, "Le Mars: The Story of a Prairie Town" (Le Mars, 1969), 6.

2. William B. Close, *Farming in North-Western Iowa, United States of America: A Pamphlet for Emigrants and a Guide to North-Western Iowa* (Manchester: A. Ireland, 1880), 2.

3. C. Addison Hickman, "Barlow Hall," *Palimpsest* 22 (1941).

4. *Sioux City Journal,* 14 Nov. 1943.

5. *Le Mars Sentinel,* 14 July 1881.

6. James P. Reed, "The Role of an English Land Company in the Settlement of Northwestern Iowa and Southwestern Minnesota" (Master's thesis, Univ. of Nebraska at Omaha, 1974), 49–50, 54.

7. *Iowa Liberal,* 9 July 1879.

8. E. Maxtone Graham, *The Maxtones of Cultoquhey* (Edinburgh and London: Moray Press, 1935), 195–96.

9. Cowan Papers, microfilm, London School of Economics Library.

10. Graham, *Maxtones of Cultoquhey.*

CHAPTER 5: *Landed Gentry in the Making*

1. *Macmillan's,* vol. 58.

2. Bruce Haley, *The Healthy Body and Victorian Culture* (Cambridge and London: Harvard Univ. Press, 1978), 127–28.

3. Anne Close's "Commonplace Book," manuscript, courtesy of Susanne Knowles.

4. Christable S. Orwin and Edith H. Whetham, *History of British Agriculture, 1846–1914* (London: Archon Books, 1964), 240–43.

5. William Close to James Close, Fall, 1879, Close Papers, courtesy of Roger Close-Brooks.

6. *Iowa Liberal*, 24 Dec. 1879.

7. *Field*, 15 Oct. 1881.

8. *Iowa Liberal*, 12 May 1880.

9. *Le Mars Globe-Post*, 14 Jan. 1943.

10. William Silag, "City, Town, and Countryside: Northwest Iowa and the Ecology of Urbanization, 1854–1900" (Ph.D. diss., Univ. of Iowa, 1979), 111.

11. *Iowa Liberal*, 11 Mar. 1881.

12. *Sioux City Journal*, 5 Dec. 1972.

13. *Le Mars Sentinel*, 10 Apr. 1881.

14. Ibid., 22 Dec., 21 Apr. 1881.

15. *Iowa Liberal*, 14 Aug. 1882; *Le Mars Sentinel*, 22 Apr. 1884.

16. *Field*, 15 Oct. 1881.

17. *Le Mars Sentinel*, 18 May 1882.

CHAPTER 6: *Some Difficulties Surmounted*

1. Myrtle Case Tierney to author, 24 Aug. 1964.

2. Franklin Humble to author, 23 Feb. 1979.

3. Jacob Van Der Zee, *The British in Iowa* (Iowa City: State Historical Society of Iowa, 1922), 228.

4. *Le Mars Sentinel*, 20 Jan. 1881.

5. *Times* (London), 7 Oct. 1907.

6. Anne Eaden to James Close, 14 Nov. 1950, Close Papers.

CHAPTER 7: *Gentlemanly Activities*

1. *Manchester Courier* quoted in *Le Mars Sentinel*, 27 Jan. 1881.

2. Jacob Van Der Zee, *The British in Iowa* (Iowa City: State Historical Society of Iowa, 1922), 143.

3. See *Alumni Cantabrigienses.*

4. *Iowa Liberal*, 19 May 1880.

5. Ibid., 2 June 1880.

6. Ibid.

7. Ibid., 9 June 1880.

8. *Sioux City Journal*, 16 June 1880; Van Der Zee, *British in Iowa*, 287.

9. *Sioux City Journal*, 16 June 1880.

10. *St. Paul Pioneer Press* quoted in *Iowa Liberal*, 31 Mar. 1880.

11. Van Der Zee, *British in Iowa*, 213.

12. *Le Mars Sentinel*, 3 Feb. 1881.

13. Anthony Trollope, *North America* (New York: Alfred A. Knopf, 1961), 152.

14. *Sioux City Journal*, 30 Oct. 1881.

15. Walter Cowan to Mother, 24 May 1883, Cowan Papers, microfilm, London School of Economics Library.

16. *History of the Counties Woodbury and Plymouth, Iowa* (Chicago: A. Warren, 1890–1891); *Le Mars Sentinel*, 9 June 1881.

17. *Le Mars Sentinel*, 14 Feb. 1881.

18. Heacock memoir, courtesy of E. V. Heacock.

19. *Iowa Liberal*, 24 July 1882; *Le Mars Sentinel*, 16 Mar. 1882.

20. T. J. Maxwell interview with author, 1953.

21. *Le Mars Sentinel*, 8 Dec. 1881.

22. Bruce Haley, *The Healthy Body and Victorian Culture* (Cambridge and London: Harvard Univ. Press, 1978), 133.

23. Robert Louis Stevenson, *Across the Plains* (New York: Charles Scribner's, 1905), 45.

24. *Le Mars Sentinel*, 12 May 1880.

25. *Iowa Liberal*, 19 May 1880.

26. Poultney Bigelow, *Harper's New Monthly Magazine*, Apr. 1881.

CHAPTER 8: *The Faces of Success*

1. *London Times*, 31 Aug., 28 Sept. 1880.

2. W. H. Russell, *Hesperothen: Notes from the West* (London: Sampson Low, Marston, Searle and Rivington, 1882), 195.

3. *New York Times*, 6 Oct. 1880, 1 Mar. 1881.

4. Ibid., 1 Mar. 1881.

5. *New York Times*, 6 Oct. 1880; *Field*, 15 Oct. 1881.

6. *New York Times*, 6 Oct. 1880.

7. *Le Mars Sentinel*, 7 Apr. 1881.

8. James P. Reed, "The Role of the English Land Company in the Settlement of Northwestern Iowa and Southwestern Minnesota" (Master's thesis, Univ. of Nebraska at Omaha, 1974), 122.

9. *Macmillan's*, vol. 44.

10. William Silag, "City, Town, and Countryside: Northwest Iowa and the Ecology of Urbanization, 1854–1900" (Ph.D. diss., Univ. of Iowa, 1979), 162.

11. *Times* (London), 27 Sept. 1923.

CHAPTER 9: *The Colony Portrayed*

1. *Le Mars Sentinel*, 2 Feb. 1882.

2. *Iowa Liberal*, 14 July 1880.

3. William Close, *Farming in North-Western Iowa, United States of America: A Pamphlet for Emigrants and a Guide to North-Western Iowa* (Manchester: A. Ireland, 1880).

4. *Le Mars Sentinel*, 21 Apr. 1881.

5. *Field*, 15 Oct. 1881; *Le Mars Sentinel*, 19 May 1881.

6. Keith Caldwell to author, 25 Nov. 1956.

7. *Le Mars Globe*, 1 Mar. 1888.

8. Ibid., 8 Feb., 31 Mar. 1888.

9. Katherine Dickman, interview with author, 1953.

10. *Le Mars Sentinel*, 18 Apr. 1884; Jacob Van Der Zee, *The British in Iowa* (Iowa City: State Historical Society of Iowa, 1922), 176; *New York Times*, 13 Nov. 1895; *Le Mars Sentinel*, 5 June, 26 June, 1885, 2 Mar. 1886, 2 May 1885, 6 June 1884.

11. Edward Walford, *The County Families of the United Kingdom* (Chatto and Windus, 1920), 212.

12. *New York Times,* 22 May 1980.
13. *Le Mars Sentinel,* 26 May 1881.
14. *Iowa Liberal,* 8 July 1882.
15. *Le Mars Sentinel,* 2 May 1881.
16. Ibid., 11 Nov. 1881.
17. *Iowa Liberal,* 26 July, 24 Aug. 1882; *Le Mars Sentinel,* 7 Dec. 1882, 28 June 1883.
18. Ibid., 3 Feb., 18 Aug. 1881, 2 Aug. 1883.
19. Ibid., 29 Feb., 19 Apr. 1884; Van Der Zee, *British in Iowa,* 177, 229, 276.
20. Philip H_____ to William Close, 5 Oct. 1880, Close Papers, courtesy of Roger Close-Brooks.
21. T. G. Mellersh, "The English Colony in Iowa," (Cheltenham: T. Hailing, Oxford Printing Works, 1881), pamphlet.
22. Mark Girouard, *Life in the English Country House* (New Haven: Yale Univ. Press, 1978), 276.
23. A. James Mammerton, *Emigrant Gentlewomen: Genteel Poverty and Female Emigration, 1830–1914* (London and Totowa, N.J.: Croom Helm, Rowman and Littlefield, 1979), 45.
24. James Cowan to Father, 24 Nov. 1883, Cowan Papers, microfilm, London School of Economics Library.
25. Ibid., 10 Aug. 1884, Cowan Papers.
26. *Macmillan's,* Feb. 1882, 312.
27. Robert G. Athearn, *Westward the Briton* (New York: Charles Scribner's, 1953), 85.
28. Malcolm Brodie diary manuscript, courtesy of Gordon and Malcolm Brodie.

CHAPTER 10: *How the Game Was Played*

1. Philip Magnus, *King Edward the Seventh* (London: Penguin, 1979), 91.
2. Giles St. Aubyn, *Edward VII: Prince and King* (New York: Atheneum, 1979), 126.
3. Ibid., 154.
4. W. H. Russell, *Hesperothen: Notes from the West* (London: Sampson Low, Marston, Searle and Rivington, 1882), 195.
5. Ibid., 199.
6. James P. Reed, "The Role of the English Land Company in the Settlement of Northwestern Iowa and Southwestern Minnesota" (Master's thesis, Univ. of Nebraska at Omaha, 1974), 114, 116–17, 120–21.
7. William Close to Jacob Van Der Zee, 10 Jan. 1923, courtesy of Robert Van Der Zee.
8. Jacob Van Der Zee, *The British in Iowa* (Iowa City: State Historical Society of Iowa, 1922), 198.
9. *St. Paul Pioneer Press* quoted in *Le Mars Sentinel,* 21 Apr. 1881.
10. Ibid., 14 Apr. 1881.
11. Ibid., 18 Aug. 1881.
12. *Sibley Gazette* quoted in *Le Mars Sentinel,* 28 July, 1881.
13. Ibid., 23 June 1881.
14. Van Der Zee, *British in Iowa,* 194–96.
15. E. F. Benson, *As We Were* (London, Toronto, New York: Longmans, Green, 1930), 252.

16. *Sioux City Journal,* 1 July 1881; *Iowa Liberal,* 6 July, 1881; Van Der Zee, *British in Iowa,* 198.

17. Arthur Larson, *Le Mars: The Story of a Prairie Town* (Le Mars: Le Mars Daily Sentinel, 1969), 27.

18. *Le Mars Sentinel,* 7 July 1881; Walter Cowan to Mother, Mar. 1884, Cowan Papers, microfilm, London School of Economics Library.

19. James Cowan to Mother, 6 Oct. 1883, Cowan Papers.

20. *Le Mars Sentinel,* 28 July, 1881.

21. *Sioux City Journal,* 9 July 1881.

22. *Le Mars Sentinel,* 22 Sept. 1881.

23. *Sioux City Journal,* 5 Oct. 1881; *History of Western Iowa* (Sioux City: Western Publishing, 1882), 395; *Iowa Liberal,* 24 July 1882.

24. *Le Mars Sentinel,* 17 Aug. 1882.

25. Ibid., 18 Aug. 1881; Van Der Zee, *British in Iowa,* 234; *Le Mars Sentinel,* 2 Feb. 1882.

26. Ibid., 25 Aug. 1882.

27. John Durant and Otto Bettmann, *Pictorial History of American Sports* (New York: A. S. Barnes, 1965), 75.

28. Ibid., 118.

29. *St. Louis Republic* quoted in *Le Mars Globe,* 24 Oct. 1893.

30. *Le Mars Sentinel,* 19 Jan. 1886; Van Der Zee, *British in Iowa,* 188.

31. *Le Mars Sentinel,* 12 Oct. 1882; Van Der Zee, *British in Iowa,* 143.

32. *Le Mars Sentinel,* 7 Dec. 1882.

33. *Alton Review,* 18 Jan. 1884; *Le Mars Sentinel,* 29 Mar. 1883.

34. Ibid., 22 Dec. 1881.

35. *History of the Counties Woodbury and Plymouth, Iowa* (Chicago: A. Warren, 1890-1891), 752.

36. Edward Walford, *The County Families of the United Kingdom* (London: Chatto and Windus, 1920), 209.

37. *Iowa Liberal,* 2 June, 16 July 1880; *Le Mars Sentinel,* 28 Apr. 1881, 16 Feb. 1882, 31 May 1881, 12 Oct. 1881, 18 Mar. 1884.

38. *Le Mars Sentinel,* 8 Feb. 1883.

39. *Alton Review,* 1888.

40. *Le Mars Sentinel,* 13 July 1882, 10 Mar. 1881, 10 Nov. 1977, 2 June 1881.

41. Ibid., 11 Aug. 1881.

42. James Cowan to Mother, 22 July 1883, Cowan Papers, microfilm, London School of Economics Library.

CHAPTER 11: *Colony Concepts, Personal Destinies*

1. *Le Mars Sentinel,* 22 Dec. 1881, 5 Jan., 28 Jan. 1882.

2. *Macmillan's* 43:312.

3. *Le Mars Sentinel,* 12 May 1884.

4. Ibid., 13 Apr. 1882.

5. *Chicago Tribune* quoted in *Le Mars Sentinel,* 9 Feb. 1882.

6. Ibid., 23 Mar. 1883.

7. Thomas Hughes, *Tom Brown's Schooldays* (New York: Macmillan, 1881), 133.

8. *Le Mars Sentinel,* 21 Apr. 1881.

9. Ibid., 30 Mar. 1882.

10. Ibid., 29 June 1882.

11. Ibid., 13 July 1882.

12. William Close, "The Prairie Journal," manuscript, courtesy of Susanne Knowles and James Close.

13. *Sioux City Journal,* 6 Oct., 5 Oct. 1881.

14. *Le Mars Sentinel,* 15 Dec. 1881.

15. William Silag, "City, Town, and Countryside: Northwest Iowa and the Ecology of Urbanization, 1854–1900" (Ph.D. diss., Univ. of Iowa, 1979), 135.

16. *Le Mars Sentinel,* 11 May 1888.

17. Ibid., 6 Apr., 20 July, 26 Jan., 9 Feb. 1882.

18. Ibid., 6 July 1882.

19. Ibid., 12 Oct. 1882, 2 Oct. 1885; information from Mauer family, Le Mars, to author, June 1982.

20. *Le Mars Globe,* 3 Aug. 1887.

21. *Le Mars Sentinel,* 9 Mar., 18 May, 31 May 1882.

22. Mary Close testimony, archives, New York State Supreme Court, New York, N.Y.

23. *Le Mars Sentinel,* 2 Mar. 1882.

24. James P. Reed, "The Role of the English Land Company in the Settlement of Northwestern Iowa and Southwestern Minnesota" (Master's thesis, Univ. of Nebraska at Omaha, 1974), 135; *Iowa Liberal,* 2 June 1882; *Le Mars Sentinel,* 11 May 1882.

25. Reed, "Role of the English Land Company," 38; Jacob Van Der Zee, *The British in Iowa* (Iowa City: State Historical Society of Iowa, 1922), 104.

26. Reed, "Role of English Land Company," 136.

27. Ibid., 140.

CHAPTER 12: *Two Colonials*

1. Brian P. Birch, "An English Approach to the American Frontier," *Journal of Historical Geography* 7 (1981):397–406.

2. Ibid.

3. Walter Cowan to Mother, 10 Apr. 1883, Cowan Papers, London School of Economics Library.

4. *Blackwood's* 135:766.

5. Ibid., 135:766.

6. Jacob Van Der Zee, *The British in Iowa* (Iowa City: State Historical Society of Iowa, 1922), 178–86.

7. *Le Mars Sentinel,* 16 July 1886.

8. Plymouth County plat records, Le Mars, Iowa.

9. *Blackwood's* 135:762–69, 404–20.

10. *Le Mars Sentinel,* 20 July, 25 Aug., 20 July 1881.

CHAPTER 13: *Getting On with It*

1. Walter Cowan to Father, 27 July 1884, Cowan Papers, London School of Economics Library.

2. James Cowan to Father, 10 Aug. 1884, Cowan Papers.

3. James Cowan to Lillias Cowan, 8 Sept. 1884, collection of J. O. C. Willson.

4. Walter Cowan to Mother, 12 Oct. 1884, Cowan Papers; *Blackwood's* 135:768.

5. Walter Cowan to Mother, 23 Jan. 1885, Cowan Papers.

6. Walter Cowan to Mother, 23 May 1885, Cowan Papers.

7. James Cowan to Mother, 3 Aug. 1885, Cowan Papers.

8. *Le Mars Sentinel,* 19 June, 16 June, 1885.

9. James Cowan to Henry Cowan, 14 Aug. 1885, Cowan Papers.

10. Walter Cowan to Mother, 27 July 1884, Cowan Papers.

11. Walter Cowan to Mother, 13 Sept. 1885, Cowan Papers.

12. James Cowan to Mother, 30 Sept. 1885, Cowan Papers.

13. Walter Cowan to Father, 28 Oct., 21 Nov. 1885, Cowan Papers.

14. Walter Cowan to Lillias Cowan, 2 Dec. 1885, Cowan Papers.

15. Walter Cowan to Father, 28 Oct. 1885, Cowan Papers.

16. James Cowan to Father, 20 Jan. 1886, Cowan Papers.

17. Ibid.

18. Walter Cowan to Father, 21 Nov. 1885, Cowan Papers; James Cowan to Lillias Cowan, 18 Mar. 1886, collection of J. O. C. Willson.

19. James Cowan to Father, 20 Jan. 1886, Cowan Papers.

20. James Cowan to Mother, 18 Feb. 1886, Cowan Papers.

21. James Cowan to Lillias Cowan, 18 Mar. 1886, collection of J. O. C. Willson.

22. *Le Mars Sentinel,* 14 Aug. 1975.

CHAPTER 14:   *The State of the Colony*

1. *Alton Review,* 31 Aug. 1883.

2. *Le Mars Sentinel,* 21 Sept. 1882, 11 Oct. 1883; Centennial Book Committee, *Kingsley, Iowa* (Odebolt, Iowa: Miller Printing and Publishing, 1983).

3. *Le Mars Sentinel,* 2 Aug. 1883; *History of Woodbury and Plymouth Counties, Iowa* (Chicago: A. Warren, 1890–1891), 500.

4. *Le Mars Sentinel,* 19 Apr. 1883, 26 Jan. 1882.

5. James P. Reed, "The Role of the English Land Company in the Settlement of Northwestern Iowa and Southwestern Minnesota" (Master's thesis, Univ. of Nebraska at Omaha, 1974), 155.

6. *Le Mars Sentinel,* 5 Apr. 1884.

7. Ibid., 25 Feb. 1884.

8. *Pipestone Star,* 2 July 1883; Reed, "Role of English Land Company," 158–60.

9. Jacob Van Der Zee, *The British in Iowa* (Iowa City: State Historical Society of Iowa, 1922), 118.

10. Maud and Delos Lovelace, *Gentlemen from England* (New York: Macmillan, 1937).

11. *Pipestone Star,* 10 Feb. 1885.

12. Lovelace, *Gentlemen from England,* 347.

13. Van Der Zee, *British in Iowa,* 117.

14. George Potter in *National Review,* Apr. 1883.

15. *Times* (London), 15 Aug. 1883.

16. *Blackwood's* 135:762.

17. Hugh Davies-Cooke to Parents, Apr. 1883, Davies-Cooke Papers, courtesy of Rupert Davies-Cook.

18. *Macmillan's* 62 (July 1890).

19. *Le Mars Sentinel,* 9 June 1885.

20. Ibid., 30 June 1885, 21 Dec. 1886.

21. "The Colourful History of Close Brothers" (London: Shell House, 1978); R. W. P. King to author, 19 Jan. 1978.

22. *Le Mars Sentinel,* 26 June 1887.
23. Van Der Zee, *British in Iowa,* 207.
24. *Le Mars Globe,* 12 Nov. 1887.
25. *Le Mars Sentinel,* 31 May, 16 Feb., 23 Feb. 1882.
26. Ibid., 27 July, 24 Aug. 1882.
27. *Iowa Liberal,* 14 Aug. 1882.
28. *Le Mars Sentinel,* 19 Oct. 1882, 8 Feb. 1883.
29. Ibid., 26 July 1883.
30. Van Der Zee, *British in Iowa,* 219.
31. *Le Mars Sentinel,* 19 Jan. 1887.
32. *Le Mars Globe,* 10 Aug. 1887.
33. Ibid., 6 Nov. 1887.
34. Ibid., 30 Nov. 1887.
35. Ibid., 21 Dec. 1887.
36. Van Der Zee, *British in Iowa,* 281.

CHAPTER 15: *A Bit of a Struggle*

1. James Cowan to Father, 13 Apr. 1886, Cowan Papers, London School of Economics Library.
2. James Cowan to Mother, 15 June 1886, Cowan Papers.
3. Walter Cowan to Family, 4 Jan. 1887, collection of J. O. C. Willson.
4. Walter Cowan to Mother, 4 July 1886, Cowan Papers.
5. James Cowan to Herbert Cowan, 28 Jan. 1888, Cowan Papers; James Cowan to Lillias Cowan, 16 Oct. 1888, collection of J. O. C. Willson.
6. James Cowan to Father, 7 June 1888, Cowan Papers.
7. Walter Cowan to Mother, 21 July 1888, Cowan Papers.
8. James Cowan to Mother, 20 Sept. 1888, Cowan Papers.
9. Walter Cowan to Mother, 19 Nov. 1888, Cowan Papers.
10. Walter Cowan to Mother, 24 Dec. 1888, Cowan Papers.
11. James Cowan to Father, 15 Jan. 1889, Cowan Papers; James Cowan to Henry Cowan, 27 Jan. 1889, Cowan Papers.
12. James Cowan to Lillias Cowan, 23 June 1889, collection of J. O. C. Willson; James Cowan to Henry Cowan, 23 June 1889, Cowan Papers.
13. James Cowan to Henry Cowan, 10 Dec. 1889, Cowan Papers.
14. James Cowan to Mother, 29 Jan. 1890, Cowan Papers.

CHAPTER 16: *Dramatic Endings*

1. *Lyon County Reporter,* 29 June 1888.
2. Frederick Close to Grace Close, 12 Feb. 1890, courtesy of Susanne Knowles.
3. T. J. Maxwell, interview with author, 1953.
4. *Sioux City Journal,* 19 June 1890.
5. Hearst syndicate, 23 Feb. 1903.
6. Cynthia Brants to author, 11 Feb. 1979.
7. Anne Eaden to James Close, 14 Nov. 1950, courtesy of James Close.
8. Ray Ginger, *Age of Excess* (New York: Macmillan, 1965), 160.
9. R. Minton, White Pass and Yukon Railroad, Vancouver, B.C., interview with author, 1980.

10. "The Colourful History of Close Brothers" (London: Shell House, 1978).
11. Close family Bible entry, courtesy of Roger Close-Brooks.

CHAPTER 17: *In the Fullness of Time*

1. James Cowan to Lillias Cowan, 16 Nov. 1890, collection of J. O. C. Willson.
2. Walter Cowan to Lillias Cowan, 1 July 1890, collection of J. O. C. Willson.
3. Walter Cowan to Mother, 11 July 1890, Cowan Papers, London School of Economics Library; James Cowan to Henry Cowan, 29 July 1890, Cowan Papers.
4. James Cowan to Lillias Cowan, 30 June 1892, collection of J. O. C. Willson.
5. Walter Cowan to Mother, 24 Sept. 1893, Cowan Papers.
6. Preface to Cowan Papers, London School of Economics Library.
7. *The Illustrated Historical Atlas of Plymouth County, Iowa* (n.p. 1907).
8. Mrs. Malcolm Brodie, interview with author, 1980.
9. Malcolm Brodie Diary, 1909, courtesy of Gordon and Malcolm Brodie.
10. *Le Mars Globe,* 18 Apr. 1881.

CHAPTER 18: *The Vanished Colony*

1. *Blackwood's* 135:767.
2. *Macmillan's* (July 1890), 193–98.
3. *Macmillan's* 58:37.
4. *Le Mars Sentinel,* 8 Mar. 1883.
5. *Le Mars Globe,* 20 Aug. 1887.
6. A. Maurice Low, *America at Home* (London: George Newnes, 1908), 18.
7. Karl Ahrendson, interview with author, 1953.

INDEX

ABOUT THE AUTHOR

CURTIS HARNACK, a native Iowan, was raised on a farm near Le Mars, the site of the Close Colony portrayed in *Gentlemen on the Prairie.* A graduate of Grinnell College and a Roberts Fellow at Columbia University, he has taught at Grinnell, the University of Iowa, and Sarah Lawrence College, where he cofounded the American Studies program. He has received a Guggenheim Award in Creative Writing as well as the Blackhawk and Johnston Brigham awards. His works of fiction and nonfiction include: *The Work of an Ancient Hand* (1960), *Love and Be Silent* (1962), *Persian Lions, Persian Lambs* (1965, reprinted 1981), *We Have All Gone Away* (1973, reprinted 1981), *Under My Wings Everything Prospers* (1977), *Limits of the Land* (1979), as well as numerous essays and poems. He is currently executive director of Yaddo, an arts organization in Saratoga Springs, New York.